Michele Esposito

Michele Esposito

Jeremy Dibble

Field Day Music 3

Series Editors: Séamas de Barra and Patrick Zuk

Field Day Publications
Dublin, 2010

Copyright © by Jeremy Dibble 2010

ISBN 978-0-946755-47-9

Published by Field Day Publications in association with the Keough-Naughton Institute for Irish Studies at the University of Notre Dame.

Field Day Publications
Newman House
86 St. Stephen's Green
Dublin 2
Ireland

www.fielddaybooks.com

Set in 10.5pt/14pt Quadraat
Designed and typeset by Red Dog Design Consultants
Printed on Munken Lynx

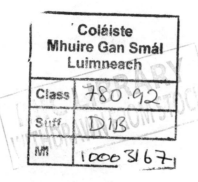

Contents

Field Day Music

This series of monographs was conceived to provide a scholarly and readable account of the careers and creative achievements of some of the most significant figures in Irish composition. Each volume will provide the reader with some idea of the nature and extent of a composer's work and the context in which it was produced. The monographs are aimed at the general reader as well as at the specialist and will appear in pairs, one devoted to an historical figure and the other to a living composer. Forthcoming volumes will survey the careers of Ina Boyle, Seóirse Bodley and James Wilson, and it is envisaged that every major figure will be covered in due course.

Séamas de Barra and Patrick Zuk

Acknowledgements

Many people have assisted me in various ways since I started to carry out research on Michele Esposito.

I am grateful to the librarians and archivists at the following institutions: the Biblioteca Nazionale Braidense, Milan; the Boole Library, University College, Cork; the Conservatorio S. Pietro a Majella, Naples; the Conservatorio di Musica Giuseppe Verdi, Milan; the Cork City Library; the Hallé Orchestra Archive, Manchester; the London Symphony Orchestra Archive; the National Library of Ireland; the Music Department of the British Library; the Library of Trinity College Dublin; the Palace Green Library, University of Durham; the Library of the Royal Irish Academy of Music.

I would like to thank Garret Cahill, Walter Clark, Francesca Calciolari, Federico Federici, David Greer, Peter Horton, Max Paddison, Richard Pine, Philip Shields and Nicholas Temperley for their generous assistance. A special word of thanks is due to Antonio Caroccia and Folco Perrino for sending me copies of their publications, and to Michael Gorman, who kindly permitted me to consult a copy of the Aiello monograph in his possession which had been annotated by Mario Esposito.

The Arts and Humanities Research Council (AHRC) of Great Britain provided significant financial support for this undertaking, as the present study of Esposito forms part of a wider research project on Irish music between 1890 and 1990 in which I am engaged together with my Durham colleague Patrick Zuk. In this connection, I would to express my deep appreciation of the contribution of Alasdair Jamieson, our AHRC-funded Postdoctoral Research Assistant, who helped to a considerable extent with archival work in addition to typesetting some of the musical examples. The Arts Faculty at the University of Durham provided supplementary funds to cover the cost of travel. I would also like to express my gratitude to the Bogliasco Foundation, which granted me a residential fellowship at the Liguria Study Centre for the Arts and Humanities near Genoa in September—October

2007. In these idyllic surroundings, free from distractions and interruptions, I was able to make considerable progress with the early chapters.

I would like to offer my heartfelt thanks to my editors Séamas de Barra and Patrick Zuk for their work in bringing the book into a final form, as well as for their assistance with translations (especially from Irish and Russian) and advice on various points of detail. I would also like to thank Seamus Deane of Field Day Publications for recognizing the importance of this series on Irish composers, Ciarán Deane of Field Day for copy-editing the text and compiling the index, and Katherine Brownridge and Stuart Bradfield at Red Dog for their excellent graphic design work

My wife Alison, as always, was an unfailing source of encouragement and loving support. Finally, I would like to pay special thanks to my colleague at the University of Durham, Lucia Gri, with whom I studied Italian for the purposes of writing this book. It is no exaggeration to say that it would not have been possible to write it without her, and I am deeply grateful not only for her skilful teaching, but also because she afforded me an opportunity to deepen my understanding of Esposito's Italian milieu and cultural heritage.

Jeremy Dibble
Durham 2010

Abbreviations

GB-BEq	Library of Queen's University, Belfast (Hamilton Harty Archive)
I-Baf	Library of the Accademia Filarmonica, Bologna
I-Nc	Naples, Conservatorio di Musica S Pietro a Majella, Biblioteca
I-Mb	Biblioteca Nazionale Braidense, Milan (Archivio Casa Ricordi)
IRL-Da	Library of the Royal Irish Academy of Music, Dublin
IRL-Dna	The National Archive, Dublin
DOS	Dublin Orchestral Society
DCMU	Dublin Chamber Music Union
ISM	Incorporated Society of Musicians
RIAM	Royal Irish Academy of Music
RCM	Royal College of Music, London
RDS	Royal Dublin Society

Michele Esposito *c.* 1923
Courtesy of
Royal Irish Academy
of Music, Dublin.

Introduction

In the context of Irish cultural studies the career of Michele Esposito is of no small interest, as he is a figure of seminal importance in the history of Irish music. Born in 1855, Esposito studied piano and composition at the Naples Conservatory, where he was a close contemporary of Giuseppe Martucci. Like Martucci, his remarkable musical gifts were apparent at an early age and by his early twenties he had earned a notable reputation as a pianist and conductor. He also made his mark as a composer, aligning himself with the progressive coterie of Italian musicians who, under Liszt's influence, chose to cultivate instrumental music based on Austro-German models rather than opera. In 1878, finding that Naples offered limited scope for his talent, Esposito moved to Paris on the advice of Anton Rubinstein, hoping to forge a reputation there. His public appearances as a pianist were well received, but the lucky break which might have launched him on an international career somehow eluded him. After four years of eking out a precarious living, he accepted a teaching post at a private music school in Dublin, the Royal Irish Academy of Music (RIAM), in order to provide adequately for his own family. Paris's loss was Dublin's gain: in the event, Esposito remained in the Irish capital for forty-six years, quickly establishing himself as a leading figure in the country's musical life.

For complex reasons bound up with Ireland's colonial past, musical culture in Ireland had remained rather undeveloped in comparison with other European countries. Dublin had no symphony orchestra, opera house or ballet company. Concert life was fairly restricted and educational opportunities, particularly for advanced students, were almost entirely lacking. With remarkable energy and determination, Esposito promptly set about transforming these circumstances and greatly enriched Irish musical culture in the process. At the RIAM, he proved himself to be a dedicated and exacting teacher of piano, setting new standards of artistic accomplishment and technical excellence. He was tirelessly active as a performer, appearing in recital with some of the most eminent instrumentalists of the period. His appearances as a solo recitalist and in programmes of chamber music were a constant fixture in the city's calendars of musical events, and over several decades he introduced an enormous repertoire of unfamiliar works to Dublin audiences. He went on to found Ireland's first professional symphony orchestra, the Dublin Orchestral Society, which was run on a cooperative basis and presented annual seasons of concerts between 1899 and 1914. In later life, his scholarly interests came increasingly to the fore: Esposito became a prolific editor, producing a pioneering anthology of early Italian keyboard works, an edition of the Beethoven piano sonatas and a great deal else besides.

He also continued to compose to the extent that his heavy professional schedule allowed. His output is not very voluminous, but it includes orchestral music, substantial chamber works, two operas, songs and much music for the piano. This corpus of work is uneven, but at its best, Esposito's music is imaginative and skilfully wrought. In his lifetime, his compositions attracted distinguished advocates of the calibre of Hamilton Harty and Vittorio Gui, which testifies to the high regard in which they were held. Some of the chamber and orchestral works — particularly the *Neapolitan Suite*, the violin and cello sonatas, the string quartets — are of notable distinction and would amply reward the attention of enterprising performers. For the most part, they are couched in the idioms of late Romanticism, although some of Esposito's later music reflects modernist influences such as that of Debussy. Listeners familiar with late nineteenth-century Italian instrumental music will immediately recognize its kinship to the music of Sgambati, Martucci and other figures. From an Irish perspective, a few of Esposito's scores are of particular interest: his *Irish Symphony* and the *Irish Suite* are notable early attempts to use Irish folk tunes as a basis for serious symphonic works; while his operas and the cantata *Deirdre* engage with a new kind of subject matter, principally drawing on Gaelic mythology and folklore as well as contemporary rural life, which came to be favoured by many Irish writers during the Literary Revival. These works are amongst the most interesting attempts by composers at the period to forge a distinctively 'Irish' mode of musical utterance.

As will be apparent from the foregoing account, a survey of Esposito's career as composer, performer and scholar is consequently richly interesting on many levels, and sheds a fascinating light on both Irish and Italian musical life in the late nineteenth and early twentieth centuries. In trying to reconstruct this career, however, the researcher is beset with practical difficulties of a kind that complicate his task considerably. Although information about Esposito's professional activities is reasonably abundant, there is a striking paucity of materials providing information about his personal life and the earlier phases of his career. As is explained in the Epilogue, virtually all of Esposito's personal papers have disappeared without trace, and only a handful of his letters are known to be extant. For information about many aspects of his life, particularly his childhood and early adulthood, one is almost wholly reliant on a small commemorative monograph in Italian that was published in Esposito's birthplace of Castellammare di Stabia in 1956,

Al musicista Michele Esposito nel prima centenario della nascita, a title which might be loosely translated as 'In commemoration of the musician Michele Esposito on the centenary of his birth'. A few remarks should be made about this book here, as its authorship has been disputed in several publications and it has been the subject of various misunderstandings.

This monograph was the brainchild of Giuseppe Lauro Aiello, a local historian who both contributed to it and edited it. It comprises four sections, the first of which is a tribute by the distinguished Italian conductor Vittorio Gui, who befriended Esposito at the end of his life and came to know him fairly well. The second section is an extended biographical sketch of the composer's career by Aiello himself. The third section is a catalogue of Esposito's compositions, which is unattributed, but may well have been compiled by the author of the fourth section, Otello Calbi, a composer and member of staff at the Naples Conservatoire, who contributed a concluding essay on Esposito's music.

In 1995, John Bowyer Bell published an article in the periodical *Éire-Ireland* in which he asserted that the biographical section of this book had in fact been written by the composer's son Mario Esposito, adducing as evidence the fact that when Mario presented a copy to his Irish relative Morgan Dockrell in 1968 he crossed out Aiello's name on the title page and replaced it with his own.[1] The matter does not appear to be quite that simple, however, and there is persuasive evidence on purely stylistic grounds to cast a doubt on Mario's claim to authorship. If one examines his published writings on medieval Hiberno-Latin literature — a subject on which Mario was a leading authority — it is immediately evident that he was a man of remarkable intelligence and erudition. As one might expect from a scholar with a disciplined and critical cast of mind, these publications are models of clarity, lucidly expressed and meticulously referenced. The biographical chapter in the Aiello book, on the other hand, is anything but scholarly. It is couched in bombastic, effusive language redolent of the worst excesses of nineteenth-century biography and presents a mawkishly idealized, wholly two-dimensional view of its subject. It contains glaring misprints and other errors. It is poorly structured, chaotic in its presentation of information and frustratingly imprecise about facts and dates. Documents are regularly quoted without indications of their source, and sometimes even without indications of when they were written or by whom. In short, it is a thoroughly amateurish production — exactly the kind of thing one might expect from an amateur local historian, which Aiello was.

To be fair to Bell, Mario makes similar claims about the book in a letter to the Belgian historian Hubert Silvestre, a fellow medievalist, which contains the following passage:

---

[1]   J. Bowyer Bell, 'Waiting for Mario: the Espositos, Joyce and Beckett', *Eire-Ireland* 30, 2 (1995), 11, 20. This assertion is also repeated in Richard Pine and Charles Acton, eds., *To Talent Alone: The Royal Irish Academy of Music 1848–1998* (Dublin, 1998), 561–62, 77n

Je tiens à vous faire remarquer que je suis moi-même l'auteur de presque tout ce livre, mais il m'a semblé préférable de ne pas mettre mon nom sur le titre. Mon langage a été souvent altéré et des additions d'authenticité douteuse ont été faites. *Les épreuves ne me furent pas soumises ...*

[I am anxious to make you aware that I wrote virtually all this book myself, but it seemed to me preferable that my name should not appear on the title page. My language has been often altered and additions of questionable authenticity have been made. *The proofs were not shown to me ...*][2]

One the face of it, these remarks might seem to leave little room for doubt about his authorship, but they are still difficult to reconcile with the actual nature of the book. Moreover, Mario's claim to have written 'virtually all' of it is almost certainly an exaggeration: Otello Calbi undoubtedly existed and there seems no reason to doubt that he contributed the concluding essay on the music.

A plausible explanation for this conundrum is not too hard to find if one turns to consider Aiello's prefatory remarks in which he describes how the book came to be written. In 1955, it came to his attention that plans were afoot in Dublin to commemorate the centenary of Esposito's birth. Feeling it would be a great pity if this event passed unmarked in the composer's native town, he conceived the idea of producing a commemorative publication. He goes on to explain in his rather stilted and self-consciously 'literary' prose, of which the following is a representative sample:

La raccolta degli elementi necessari per fare opera degna, si presentava però irta di difficoltà. Dove trovare le notizie, i dati, i documenti, e almeno una fotografia di Michele Esposito? Un primo, ma ben luminoso fascio di luce ci venne dal Maestro Vittorio Gui, che si risultava essere stato amico di Michele Esposito. Interpellato, con un semplice biglietto, il Maestro Gui rispose con una lettera che è lo specchio di quanta possa un animo nobile quando è spinto dal sentimento ... . Fu in seguito possibile metterci in rapporti epistolari con i congiunti del Maestro Esposito e propriamente col figlio Mario, residente a Firenze ... . Giunsero, così, musica, notizie, fotografie: un'autentica scoperta, una documentazione emozionante, una vera rivelazione! Preziose informazioni ci pervennero anche da Dublino. ... Il Maestro Gui, col suo consiglio, alimentava un fuoco che ormai non poteva più spegnersi.

2   Letter from Mario Esposito to Hubert Silvestre, 28 July 1958, quoted in Hubert Silvestre, 'Mario Esposito. Brève evocation de sa vie et de son oeuvre', in Mario Esposito, *Studies in Hiberno-Latin Literature*, ed. Michael M. Gorman (Aldershot, 2006), 1–13, 4. Emphasis in the original.

Assembling the necessary materials to produce a work worthy [of its subject] seemed fraught with difficulties. Where could I find the information, the dates, the documents and at least a photograph of Michele Esposito? A first, but brightly luminous ray of light reached us from Maestro Vittorio Gui, who, it transpired, had been a friend of Michele Esposito. Consulted by means of a brief note, Maestro Gui responded with a letter revealing what a noble heart is capable of when moved by emotion … . As a result, it was possible to enter into correspondence with Maestro Esposito's relatives and in particular with his son Mario who resided in Florence … . In this way, I obtained music, information and photographs — a real discovery, exciting documentation, a true revelation! Valuable information also reached me from Dublin. … Maestro Gui, with his advice, nourished a fire which henceforth could never be extinguished.[3]

From this, it seems clear that Mario supplied information by letter and is thus the 'author' of the biographical chapter in the sense that Aiello had drawn extensively on his contributions, but not in any literal sense. In the absence of the original documentation, the factual accuracy of Aiello's essay must remain open to question: as Mario informed Silvestre, he was never shown the proofs and had no opportunity to correct various errors that had crept in.[4] As a result, although the monograph contains a great deal of useful information, it cannot be considered altogether reliable.

Fortunately, documentation about Esposito's career becomes much more abundant after he moved to Ireland in 1882, and it has proved possible to piece together a fairly detailed — and, one hopes, more or less accurate — account of his professional activities from articles in contemporary newspapers and periodicals, as well as various works of reference. I would like to acknowledge my particular indebtedness to the standard history of the Royal Irish Academy of Music edited jointly by Richard Pine and Charles Acton, To Talent Alone: The Royal Irish Academy of Music 1848–1998, which contains a great deal of useful information not readily available elsewhere.

In addition to the difficulties inherent in giving a satisfactory account of Esposito's life, it is also impossible, as matters stand, to offer a comprehensive evaluation of his creative achievement. Some of his most important compositions — including two piano concertos, several major orchestral works, a string quartet, a piano quintet and two piano quartets — were not published in his lifetime and the manuscripts seem to have disappeared along with his personal papers, together with the full orchestral scores of his

---

3   Giuseppe Lauro Aiello, ed., Al musicista Michele Esposito nel prima centenario della nascita (Castellammare di Stabia, 1956), 14–15; hereafter Al musicista. The spelling of Gui's name has been standardized from the variant form 'Guy'.

4   Mario sent Hubert Silvestre a copy of the Aiello monograph which is annotated in his own hand: see Michael M. Gorman, 'Mario Esposito (1887–1975) and the Study of the Latin Literature of Medieval Ireland', in Esposito, Studies in Hiberno-Latin Literature, 312, 46n. I would like to express my sincere thanks to Dr Gorman for making a copy of this document for me. Unfortunately, the annotations provide little new information of significance and mostly indicate typographical errors in the text.

two operas and the cantata *Deirdre*. (Fortunately the vocal scores of these have survived, as they were published). In the cases of the works that have been lost, the researcher is entirely reliant on newspaper reviews or published programme notes for an idea of what they might have been like. Should these scores ever come to light, they could well add considerably to Esposito's stature as a composer. Only one commercial recording of music by Esposito is currently available — a selection of his piano works performed by the Irish pianist Miceal O'Rourke which was issued on the Chandos label, recorded in 1997.[5] It is to be hoped that the present study might help to revive interest in this unjustly neglected figure and stimulate further performances of his work.

5   *Esposito: Works for Piano*, CHAN 9675

Michele Esposito, Pianist and Composer (1926)
Sarah Cecilia Harrison (1863–1941)
Collection, National Gallery of Ireland
Photo © National Gallery of Ireland

Per Lucia senza cui
questo libro non sarebbe stato scritto mai

1 Neapolitan Origins and Early Maturity, 1855–78

The town of Castellammare di Stabia is situated at the inner edge of the Sorrentinian peninsula in the Gulf of Naples, not far from Mount Vesuvius. The Romans knew it as Stabiae — a popular resort, frequented by the wealthy and famous for its panoramic views of the bay. But like nearby Pompeii and Herculaneum, it was buried when Vesuvius erupted cataclysmically in A.D. 79. Although the town was destroyed, the area soon attracted new settlers as the soil of the region had been made very fertile by the volcanic residue and proved ideally suited to growing fruit and vines. The modern town took the first part of its name, Castellammare, from the thirteenth-century castle built by Emperor Frederick II that overlooks it from the hill above. By the mid nineteenth century, it had a population of about 22,000. Many of its inhabitants were employed by naval shipyards, of which there were a considerable number in the region. The town was a busy commercial centre and much railway traffic passing between Naples and Rome halted there. It offered little by way of cultural life, however; for such diversions Naples, some twenty miles further up the coast, was the capital of the region, enjoying a notable reputation as a lively centre for theatre and opera. The upper and middle classes who patronized such fashionable entertainments were scarcely visible on the uninviting streets of Castellammare, preferring their retreats in the surrounding hillsides. Industrialists from the increasingly prosperous north of Italy and wealthy aristocrats holidayed in imposing villas and *palazzi* at nearby Quisisana, where even the king and other members of the royal family came to bathe in the town's famous *terme* (thermal springs) and partake of the mineral waters, which, some believed, offered cures for everyday ailments and an occasional miracle remedy for serious illnesses.

Such was the place where Michele Esposito was born at 10 pm on 29 September 1855. The birth was registered the following day, and on 1 October he was baptized in the cathedral.[1] His father, Domenico Esposito, a 28-year-old mariner, was from the lower middle classes. Domenico's wife, Rosa D'Angelo, an illiterate yet intelligent woman of peasant stock, was five years younger than him. Michele was the fourth of seventeen children, and the first of three sons. The family home was evidently a very modest one, being situated in the Strada della Marina, an area of the town which has since been reconstructed extensively. The boy's father, although not wealthy, was an upstanding member of society. He was employed by Baron Giovanni Barracco, an important Neapolitan dignitary with connections to the royal court. An enormously successful merchant, the baron was keenly interested in politics. He and other members of his family were fervent supporters of Italian unification and supplied funds to Garibaldi for the liberation of the Kingdom of Naples and the Two Sicilies in 1860. Thereafter, he became a prominent deputy in the newly formed Parliament of the Nation from 1861 and was later made a Senator.

Domenico Esposito was recalled as 'an energetic, serious [and] severe man', who, although somewhat volatile, 'regained his composure just as easily, given the fundamental goodness of his character'.[2] He also had a reputation for honesty. He was often engaged in important commercial activities for Barracco, travelling between Castellammare, Naples and other parts of Italy with substantial sums of money. Although he must have handled millions of lire, he never appropriated a penny for himself, being zealous for his family's good name.[3] We may assume that Domenico, like his anti-Bourbon employer, was in favour of Italian unification. When the Bourbon kingdom fell in 1860, he was in Naples among the crowds to greet the victorious Garibaldi. As Michele Esposito's son, Mario, recalled many years later, his father 'always liked to tell of his first memory of childhood which was being carried as a baby to see the triumphal entry of Garibaldi into Naples on 7 September 1860, and how they had to wait for several hours on a roof in the baking heat'.[4] After Naples was incorporated into the larger kingdom of Italy, the city rapidly became more cosmopolitan in outlook.

Michele was evidently a precocious child with a quick intelligence. At an early age he asked to be given music lessons and declared his desire to become a musician. His father secretly opposed the idea, as he hoped his son would go into business. The boy's first instruction in music consequently came about in a rather unusual manner. The new political regime set up a communal band in Castellammare and some of the local young

1   The surname 'Esposito' is very common in Naples and the surrounding area. Prior to unification in 1860, it was a name given to children who were given up for adoption by their parents. Derived from the Latin *expositus*, the past participle of *exponere*, it literally means 'placed outside'. It remains today a name associated with the Neapolitan region.
2   Aiello, *Al musicista*, 18
3   Aiello, *Al musicista*, 18
4   Aiello, *Al musicista*, 61

men, principally labourers and fishermen, volunteered to take part, although some were unable to read music or play a note on any instrument. Accordingly, it was decided that they would study after hours with a teacher at the local elementary school. When he heard about these classes, Michele expressed a wish to attend even though he was too young to do so. With the encouragement of this mother — she gave him some extra food to bring with him, so that he would not miss out on anything by having to return home to eat — he contrived to eavesdrop on the lessons, and while these proceeded in an upper room of the school, he hid outside on the stairs, often numb with cold, listening attentively to what the music master was saying. After some months, the teacher discovered that his class seemed to have learned very little:

> 'Tell me this', he asked the class one day, 'what is the value of a semibreve?' Silence. 'And a minim?' Silence. 'Have you have learned absolutely nothing, for heaven's sake? I repeat: how many beats are there in a semibreve?' The silence was broken by a small voice coming from the top of the stairs, saying 'There are four beats in a semibreve.' The surprised teacher looked up, saw the child … and said: 'Come down here, boy! Who are you? The son of the concierge, perhaps?' He replied: 'No, I am the son of Domenico Esposito!' 'And where have you learned these things?' 'From you!' 'And when?' 'When you are giving the lessons, I listen from the stairs!'[5]

The teacher, at first dumbfounded, realized the young boy's innate ability and asked his father if he might continue to teach him. When he promised to furnish the boy with an instrument for the band as well as a uniform, Domenico finally relented.

Michele made rapid progress and was soon given a solo on his cornet in a concert which the new band gave in a local theatre. Domenico, wishing to surprise his wife, brought her to the event and she beamed with pride as her son played his piece and subsequently acknowledged the applause. Unfortunately, the occasion was spoiled by a fracas between Michele and another member of the band who slapped him on the back to congratulate him, causing him accidentally to split his lip on his instrument. Domenico rushed into the fray, gave his son a thrashing and returned the instrument to the teacher. This incident threatened to put an end to his music lessons. But yielding to entreaties from the boy and his mother, Domenico bought his son a small piano. The boy's interest in music steadily intensified, and Domenico was impressed, in spite of himself, by his son's evident dedication. He eventually agreed to approach Francesco Simonetti at the Real Collegio di Musica in Naples, the most important music school in the region, with a view to enrolling Michele as a student there. Simonetti agreed to teach the nine year-old privately in order to prepare him to compete for a scholarship. Michele evidently made rapid progress and was considered ready for the competition in just over a year. Thirty-two candidates vied for only two bursaries, which covered the winners' tuition fees in music and other subjects for eight years, in addition to providing them with full maintenance during this period. Michele was fortunate in being awarded one of the bursaries: given the size of his family, it was highly unlikely that his father could have afforded to spend so much money on his training. The Collegio's director, the eminent composer Saverio Mercadante, who by this stage had gone blind and was in poor health, appears to have been deeply impressed by the boy's talent: he asked for Michele to be placed next to him and 'caressing his little hands', asked him 'From whereabouts are you?' The boy replied: 'From Castellammare di Stabia!', whereupon the old Maestro exclaimed: 'Long live Castellammare, for giving us another Palumbo' — a reference to a former pupil of the Collegio, Constantino Palumbo, who had since embarked on a brilliant career as a pianist.[6]

By the time Michele enrolled there, the Real Collegio (which in 1889 was renamed the Conservatorio S. Pietro a Majella, after the monastery to which it relocated in 1826) had come to be regarded as one of the leading music schools of its kind in the country. It had come into being when various local music schools merged during the period of French occupation between 1806 and 1815. By all accounts, it had been somewhat moribund in the earlier decades of the century, but had been revitalized to a remarkable extent under Mercadante's able leadership after he was appointed director in 1840. Mercadante is a figure of considerable importance in the history of Italian music at this period. A prolific composer, he had, like many of his contemporaries, largely devoted himself to writing for the operatic stage in his earlier career, but in later life he was increasingly drawn to composing instrumental music — which up to this point had been largely neglected by composers and audiences alike, and even regarded as something alien to the Italian temperament. As one nineteenth-century commentator observed:

> Twenty years ago, pure instrumental music was a thing unknown in Rome. ... [A] few maestri cultivated the German classics. ... The pianists played nothing but opera-music in poor arrangements ... . Tullio Ramacciotti, an excellent violinist, a highly educated and progressive-minded artist, was the first to venture upon the unpopular mission of inviting the public to attend quartet-soirées — with slight success; some few foreigners came to them; Roman society, even the liberally educated, felt a holy horror when anybody so much as mentioned classical instrumental music... . It was a thankless apostolate.[7]

During his period of tenure, Mercadante trained quite a number of musicians who would remain at the forefront of Italian musical life for the rest of the century. His composition students included Mariani and Serrao, both of whom made their debuts with operas

6   Aiello, Al musicista, 25
7   Oscar Sonneck, Suum Cuique: Essays in Music (New York, 1900), 255

that were deeply indebted to his style. A musician with extensive practical experience of performing, Mercadante also took great pains to raise the standards of instrumental playing. He enlarged the repertory of the student orchestra by introducing the music of Beethoven, Weber, Auber and Offenbach, constructing novel and unusual programmes. His task was facilitated to some extent by a series of extensive reforms of national musical institutions that got underway in the 1850s, which not only overhauled the curriculum, but also introduced a number of important administrative measures, one of which was to require new teaching posts to be awarded on a competitive basis. Mercadante was also successful in attracting to the staff a number of highly gifted executants — particularly pianists — and by the 1860s the Collegio had come to be regarded as a major centre for pianistic training. This was a highly significant development. During the first half of the nineteenth century, public piano recitals (and, indeed, performances of chamber music generally) were rare in Italy, but the piano had nonetheless grown steadily in popularity as a domestic instrument. The Italian tours of renowned international pianists such as Henri Herz and Theodor Doehler were undoubtedly important in this regard. However, the regular visits of Franz Liszt to Rome from 1861 onwards, and the decision of Sigismond Thalberg to settle in Posillipo near Naples, did even more to heighten the prestige of the keyboard virtuoso in Italy, as both men were regarded as two of the greatest performing artists of their era.

The young Esposito had clearly entered the institution at a propitious stage in its development. He was also to prove fortunate in his first piano teacher, Benjamino Cesi, whose rise to prominence as a pedagogue had been made possible by the recent reforms. A one-time pupil of the Roman pianist Luigi Albanesi, Cesi had gained a teaching position in the Real Collegio in 1863 at the age of only eighteen, having competed against other well-established figures such as Simonetti and Palumbo. In 1866, by royal decree, he was given the position of *secondo maestro*. Moreover, his talent had been recognized by Thalberg, who took him on as his only pupil and promoted a concert in 1865 to enable him display his talents to the Neapolitan public. His playing was acclaimed and the event effectively launched Cesi's career as a leading figure in Italian musical life and as one the country's major exponents of the piano.

Cesi's importance in the wider context of Naples's musical life cannot be underestimated. As a pupil of Thalberg, he enthusiastically assimilated his teacher's techniques and theories of piano-playing, which not only aimed to develop brilliance of fingerwork, but also placed great emphasis on the cultivation of a singing tone that strove to emulate the human voice. Thalberg's important treatise *L'art du chant appliqué au piano* [The Art of Song Applied to the Piano] provided detailed guidance on how to achieve this 'singing style' and the projection of tone. He advocated a firm, measured touch, the cultivation of steady tempi, and the intensive study of contrapuntal music to develop discipline and clarity of execution. Between 1853 and 1863, Thalberg published a series of twenty-five transcriptions of vocal works by other composers which illustrated all of these facets of his performance style. His pedagogical approach was enthusiastically adopted by Cesi, whose own output of compositions — operatic fantasias, nocturnes and studies (some of which aimed to develop proficiency in playing polyphony) — were followed later by his substantial *Metodo teorico pratico per lo studio del pianoforte* [Practical Theoretical Method for the Study of the Pianoforte], which he brought out between 1893 and 1904. Here, technique was imparted with a carefully considered view of the canon of the classic repertoire, a stance which was further affirmed by the ten volumes of his *Repertorio del pianista: Pezzi scelti di autori antichi* [Pianistic Repertoire: Selected Pieces from Old Masters] and the twenty-one volumes of *Pezzi scelti di autori classici* [Selected Pieces by Classical Masters]. Moreover, Cesi did much to arouse interest in early music through his activities as a performer and teacher. He was a passionate exponent of the harpsichord music of J. S. Bach and J. P. Rameau, and he greatly admired the keyboard sonatas of Domenico Scarlatti, a composer whose work was being rediscovered around this time. His own recital programmes were notable for their enterprise: he gave the first performances in Naples of such demanding repertoire as Beethoven's *Hammerklavier* Sonata. Cesi's activities also brought a more international dimension to Neapolitan musical life. He founded a journal, the *Archivio Musicale*, which not only reported on local musical activities, but also contained coverage of important international figures. Much space was devoted in the first issues to Wagner, for example, and in particular to the premiere of *Parsifal* at Bayreuth. The journal also featured articles by internationally renowned correspondents such as Emil Naumann, Ludwig Nohl and Arthur Pougin, which offered a broader purview of European musical developments beyond the confines of Italy. Cesi's charismatic personality attracted a circle of enthusiastic disciples who constituted a distinctive Neapolitan school of pianists, to which Michele Esposito would himself belong in time.

Like most students at the Real Collegio, Michele boarded — although day students were also accepted. Pupils were admitted up to fifteen years of age and usually left when they were about twenty-two. The students' timetable was onerous. Music lessons took place on Mondays, Wednesdays and Fridays. They were suspended during the whole of October and during the periods of Christmas and New Year, the last three days of the Carnival (usually the last week of February), Easter and Pentecost. During the October holiday, pupils worked on tasks set by their teachers, which represented the culmination of their studies for that academic year. In addition to their musical training, students were expected to study writing, arithmetic, Latin, Italian, history and other subjects. Discipline was strict and students had to wear a uniform. They rose before 6.30 am, washed and tidied their rooms before attending daily Mass at 7.15. Classes began at 7.45 and finished at 11.30. After lunch at midday, the boys were permitted a short period of recreation before lessons resumed at 1.30. At 4.30, they were permitted to take an hour's break, until 5.30, when the younger boys attended further lessons under the direction of the senior students, who were known as *maestrini*.[8] Dinner was served at 9 pm following a second visit to church. After this the boys were free for a further hour's relaxation before bed.[9]

On entering the Collegio, Esposito was assigned to Cesi for piano lessons, although part of his pianistic studies (most probably in the area of duet-playing and chamber music) were overseen by Luigi Caracciolo. He went to Paolo Serrao for training in composition and may have taken lessons in harmony and counterpoint with Carlo Conti.[10] With the latter's death in 1869, this responsibility probably also fell to Serrao. Esposito was an exceptionally disciplined student and his assiduous practising of technical exercises seems to have been a source of much irritation to the local residents and shopkeepers. Indeed, he often practised late into the night and even when the other students were taking their afternoon recreational outings.[11] He made rapid progress and at the age of fourteen was himself nominated a *maestrino*. Two years later he was promoted to the privileged position of *primo alunno* [senior prefect] — an indication that he was considered the most distinguished student of the Collegio at that time.

Esposito's contemporaries included several individuals who would, in their various ways, make their mark in the musical profession. Paolo Tosti, who entered the Collegio in 1858 and later became famous as a singer and composer of popular songs — especially in England — was studying the violin and composition. Luigi Denza, best known today for his celebrated song *Finiculì finiculà*, was also from Castellammare and had enrolled around 1862 to study composition with Serrao. He also taught theory to the younger students. Other notable contemporaries included Luigi Caracciolo, an able pianist, who entered the Collegio in 1864 at the unusually advanced age of 17 and, as already has been mentioned, acted as Cesi's assistant. Caracciolo was to play a vital role in bringing about Esposito's eventual move to Ireland. Florestano Rossomandi, known later for his eight volumes of *Guida per lo studio tecnico del pianoforte* [Guide to the Technical Study of the Pianoforte], became a student in or around 1867; Leopoldo Mugnone, known later as an opera conductor, enrolled some time around 1868; and Ruggero Leoncavallo, most famous for his one-act opera *Pagliacci*, registered as a student in 1866.

But without doubt Esposito's closest friend at the Collegio was Giuseppe Martucci. A brilliant pianist, Martucci had started at the Collegio in 1867 as a day-boy largely because this was less onerous financially for his father. Martucci's father, Gaetano, himself a musician, was very ambitious for his son. The boy came to the attention of Cesi, who persuaded Martucci's father to allow him to become a boarder in 1868, after

---

8   The title *maestrino* was bestowed on a student who was seen to possess special abilities and who had successfully completed an advanced stage in the curriculum. A *maestrino* was also expected to assist with teaching younger pupils, enforcing discipline, directing public performances of the choir and orchestra, and other tasks.

9   The foregoing account of the daily routine for students at the Real Collegio is based on Folco Perrino, *Giuseppe Martucci: Gli anni giovanili 1856–1879* (Novara, 1992), 28

10 Perrino, *Giuseppe Martucci: Gli anni giovanili*, 28

11 Aiello, *Al musicista*, 26–27

which the friendship between him and Esposito grew more intimate. In 1872, however, Martucci's father, still in difficult financial circumstances, withdrew his son with a view to launching him immediately on a career as a virtuoso pianist. The abrupt end of their friendship was upsetting for Esposito, but the five years of their association had been highly beneficial nonetheless. As two of the most promising students, they developed a healthy sense of rivalry, one always trying to outshine the other. For some years, in order to facilitate additional practice, the two boys shared a piano, which was partly paid for by prize money — five gold Napoleons — won by Esposito in a competition sponsored by Prince Umberto, son of Victor Emanuel II.[12]

In addition to his pianistic studies, Esposito obtained a thorough grounding in elementary music theory — initially under Conti and then with Serrao, who not only had a considerable reputation as a pedagogue but also as a composer of opera. On completion of these basic courses, he was able to progress to the so-called Scuola d'armonia [School of Harmony] and to embark on the study of harmony and counterpoint, which required the composition of canons, two-part and three-part inventions and fughettas and culminated in the writing of fugues for string quartet and settings of movements from the Mass for various combinations of voices.[13] When Mercadante died in 1870, Serrao temporarily took over the role of Director of the Collegio. His national standing is indicated by the fact that he was appointed the following year to a committee chaired by Verdi to consider national reforms to the study of music. The thoroughness of his teaching is evident from a short manuscript compilation of his course notes entitled Corso di contrappunto [Counterpoint Course], which the young Esposito assembled in 1875.[14]

At sixteen, Michele had begun to undertake more demanding assignments. Besides monitoring the progress of the day-boys (which was one of the duties of a primo alunno), Serrao also entrusted him with conducting the student orchestra. Esposito later acknowledged that this experience was of immense value in acquiring a fundamental knowledge of how to write for the medium, especially as orchestration was not taught as a separate subject in the Collegio's curriculum.[15]

It was only upon completion of this rigorous preliminary training that students proceeded to study original composition. Several of Esposito's juvenilia survive, the first being a short song Canzonetta per gli Asili infantili [Little Song for the Orphanage], which was dedicated to Raffaele de Novellis, the author of the text. The manuscript is dated August 1871 and also bears the annotation Michele Esposito Anni 16 Pianista da due anni alla Scuola d'Armonia a Contrappunto [Michele Esposito, 16 years old, pianist for two years in the School of Harmony and Counterpoint], which reveals that the young man had already

12 Aiello, Al musicista, 27
13 See Perrino, Giuseppe Martucci: Gli anni giovanili, 40–41, for the programme of composition exercises undertaken by Martucci.
14 Aiello, Al musicista, 82–83
15 'Signor Michele Esposito', Weekly Irish Times, 8 September 1900

completed two years of compositional training. A simple *ninna nanna* or lullaby, this song may be undistinguished melodically but amply demonstrates the young composer's competence in the manipulation of standard harmonic resources and the handling of the through-composed structure.

Two years later, in September 1873, he submitted a single-movement *Sinfonia* in F minor in part requirement for his diploma. This may have been publicly performed by the college orchestra, as it is described as being '*scritta per gli esperimenti pubblici dell'anno 73*' [written for the public performances in [18]73]. A slow introduction was added in September 1874. While this overture-like work is clearly an apprentice piece, it nonetheless demonstrates an impressive level of technical accomplishment. It is scored for an orchestra of double woodwind, horns, trumpets, trombones, ophicleide, timpani and strings. The rhythmical energy of the principal *Allegro* clearly recalls Mendelssohn, as does the lyrical second subject which is first heard on clarinet and bassoon. The work is in sonata form and follows standard classical procedures in its use of the relative major A flat for the second subject. The reference to the first-subject material at the close of the exposition is perhaps indebted to Mozart's use of this device in the movement of the G minor Symphony K. 550, a work that Esposito is likely to have known. The development section features a severe fugato, demonstrating his recently acquired contrapuntal skills, while the recapitulation is distinguished by an imaginatively re-orchestrated version of the second subject.[16]

Esposito's elevation to *primo alunno* appears also to have been prompted by a piano work he composed in honour of Vincenzo Bellini, which impressed the professors so much that the Collegio printed it for use as an entrance test piece for new candidates.[17] Two further works written around this time reflect the prevalent fashion for fantasias on operatic themes. Both employed melodies from operas by Lauro Rossi, who had succeeded Mercadante as director of the Collegio in 1870. The *Fantasia per pianoforte* on themes from *Benvenuto Cellini* was first performed by Esposito as part of a concert given in honour of Rossi himself and was published by Cattrau of Naples as the composer's Op. 1 in 1874. This piece effectively marked Esposito's successful attainment of the Collegio's diploma. The second work, dated 22 July 1874, is an orchestral fantasia based on Rossi's opera *La Contessa di Mons*, which had been premiered in Turin the previous January. Later in the same year, Esposito went on to win the *premio d'uscito* or 'graduation prize', which entitled him to a grant of funding for a further three years, allowing him to continue his studies and to launch his professional career.[18] He was not quite twenty years of age.

During these years, Esposito assisted Serrao and Cesi with teaching and other responsibilities. He was already acquiring a reputation as a musician of promise: he

---

16 The catalogue of works in Aiello's monograph also refers to a Symphony Op. 24 which Esposito apparently composed in Naples in 1874: see Aiello, *Al musicista*, 72. This was never published and, like all of Esposito's unpublished works, is missing.

17 Aiello, *Al musicista*, 27

18 Alessandro Longo, 'Michele Esposito', *L'Arte pianistica*, 1, 2 (1914), 1

earned the nickname of *Maestrino di Castellammare* and potential students from good Neapolitan families requested to study with him.[19] Serrao also entrusted him with some deputy conducting work. Esposito's first appearance in this capacity occurred when Serrao was unable to direct the first act of an opera one evening and asked his protégé to take his place in the orchestra pit:

> The youthful leader got on remarkably well, but he says he will never forget the look of surprise upon the face of the *prima donna* of the evening when she came upon the stage, and, glancing down at the orchestra, noted the change of conductors. However, everything proceeded with great *éclat* and absolutely without a hitch, and at the fall of the curtain a well-known voice from the back of the theatre called out 'Bravo' in stentorian tones. It was Serrao, who had been in the audience for some time, a genuinely delighted witness of the ability and success of his pupil on his first public appearance in the role of conductor.[20]

Esposito's professional standing received an unexpected fillip in 1874 when the legendary Anton Rubinstein visited Naples.[21] The Russian composer and pianist was then at the height of his career and was generally regarded as being one of the greatest virtuosi of his age, with a reputation that rivalled even that of Liszt. Having resigned as Director of the St Petersburg Conservatoire in 1867, he toured Europe extensively before undertaking marathon tours of the United States, where he gave some 215 concerts with the renowned violinist Henryk Wieniawski in 1872–73. Although he professed increasing repugnance for the career of a touring virtuoso, and repeatedly declared his intention of giving it up in order to concentrate on composition, Rubinstein undertook further tours in Europe after his protracted sojourn in America, one of which brought him back to Naples. The city had changed considerably since his previous visit, having become much more international in outlook. Although the appetites of Neapolitan audiences for opera remained undiminished, there were now more opportunities to hear instrumental music and chamber music. A *Società Filarmonica* had been founded in 1867 and expanded rapidly after the resounding success of its initial concerts. Its first orchestral concert was given on 25 August 1868 and, the following year, a mixed orchestra of professionals and amateurs accompanied the young Palumbo who had just returned from a tour abroad. From the 1870s onwards, instrumental music was cultivated more intensively. And not only had the musical fare on offer in Naples become varied and interesting, but the city could now boast a distinguished school of local pianists. Rubinstein, who was

19 Aiello, *Al musicista*, 29

20 'Signor Michele Esposito' *Weekly Irish Times*, 8 September 1900

21 The article on Esposito in the *Weekly Irish Times* of 8 September 1900 gives the date of Rubinstein's visit as 1873; Alessandro Longo, in the article in *L'Arte pianistica* cited above, gives the year as 1874 and Aiello, more specifically, as January 1874: see *Al musicista*, 29.

known for his generous support of young talent, made it his business to keep abreast of the latest developments at the Real Collegio. He heard Esposito perform Beethoven's *Moonlight* Sonata at a student matinée concert and subsequently conduct a performance of Mozart's late G minor Symphony. The Russian was clearly impressed and personally invited Esposito to attend one of his own forthcoming recitals in the city. Afterwards, he made a point of singling out the eighteen-year-old, who had come backstage with his friends to join the throng of admirers wishing to see the great man. He had been standing shyly near the door, whereupon 'Rubinstein, with kindly enthusiasm, rushed forward, and bringing the lad into the midst of the group of his favoured intimates, introduced him frankly and genially as a coming pianist of most promising talent.'[22] As a further mark of his esteem, Rubinstein effected an introduction to Pietro Clausetti, the manager of the Naples branch of Ricordi, the distinguished Italian music publisher — a contact that eventually led to the inclusion of two of Esposito's early piano works, *Pensiero malinconico* [Melancholy Thought], Op. 2, and *Romanza*, Op. 6, in Ricordi's rapidly expanding catalogue of keyboard music in 1877.[23]

Rubinstein evidently believed that it was imperative for the young man to leave Naples if he were to realize his gifts to the full. Before his departure from the city, he offered him some advice: 'You are young now and Naples's sky is far too beautiful to allow you to work … you must go away… !'[24] This remark can be interpreted in several ways. First of all, it would seem to suggest that Neapolitan musical life struck Rubinstein as still being rather parochial, recent developments notwithstanding. Although Esposito had come into contact with several fine pianists — Cesi, Palumbo, Martucci and others — Rubinstein probably thought that he needed to experience life in a larger and more challenging arena. And as far as composition was concerned, the city was undoubtedly a backwater in comparison with major cultural centres such as Berlin, Vienna or Paris. For the time being, however, Esposito was simply not in a position to take such a momentous step, tempting though it must have been. A seemingly insurmountable difficulty was presented by the fact that the young man was now the principal breadwinner for his sizeable family, as his father had gone blind and been forced to give up work. His parents and younger siblings were thus completely dependent on his income from teaching or performing, which was supplemented for the time being by his government grant. The young man was obliged to work very hard, his days being filled with an arduous round of lessons, rehearsals and concerts. For a time, he travelled back and forth every day between Naples and the family home in Castellammare, but found this so fatiguing as to be completely impractical. He

---

22 'Signor Michele Esposito', *Weekly Irish Times*, 8 September 1900

23 Esposito subsequently managed to negotiate more advantageous terms with the firm of Lucca, Ricordi's principal Italian rival, which published all of his piano works and songs between 1877 and 1879. He did not place works with Ricordi again until 1882, as shall be detailed in Chapter 2.

24 Aiello, *Al musicista*, 29

eventually managed to persuade his parents — though with much difficulty — to move the entire family to Naples.[25]

In spite of his heavy responsibilities, life in Naples was not without its compensations, however. He came to increasing prominence as a composer and a performer through his appearances with the so-called *Circolo Cesi* or 'Cesi Circle', a group of musicians — mostly pianists — which was closely associated with Cesi and which organized regular concerts from about 1876 onwards. The circle's activities elicited favourable comment in the press, notably from Michele Ruta, a senior professor at the Collegio and a musician of progressive views who made much valuable propaganda on behalf of instrumental music.[26] The *Circolo Cesi* provided Esposito with opportunities not only to make public appearances alongside notable musicians such as Palumbo and Cesi himself, but also to perform his own works.

Esposito's creative development continued apace during these years. Between 1873 and 1878, he was steadily productive of new compositions, writing a considerable quantity of short piano pieces, three substantial chamber works and some songs. In most cases, it is not possible to establish dates of composition with certainty, as the manuscripts have not come to light and must be presumed lost. The only thing that we can be reasonably sure of is the order in which they were composed, as Esposito appears to have assigned them opus numbers as he completed them. Apart from the *Pensiero malinconico* and *Romanza*, which, as has been previously mentioned, were published by Ricordi, all of these pieces, with the exception of the chamber music, were brought out by the firm of Lucca, Ricordi's principal Italian rival, with whom the young composer may have succeeded in negotiating more advantageous terms. The chamber works from this period — a piano trio and two piano quartets — remained unpublished and, unfortunately, the scores of all of them appear to have vanished without trace.

Esposito's early piano pieces can be divided into two categories. The first consists of impressive display pieces, which he no doubt conceived as vehicles for his own pianistic abilities. These compositions bear an obvious relationship to similar works written by earlier generations of Romantic pianist-composers such as Liszt, Thalberg and others, which were designed for a similar purpose. The pieces in the second category are far less technically demanding and are more in the nature of salon pieces — for which there was a considerable demand at the period, leading publishers to issue them in large quantities. As one might expect, the style of these early piano works is to a certain extent derivative, revealing the influences of composers such as Mendelssohn, Chopin and Schumann. In the finest of them, however, a distinctive musical personality is clearly in evidence.

25 Aiello, *Al musicista*, 30
26 In 1877, he published *Storia critica delle condizioni della musica in Italia e del Conservatorio di S Pietro a Majella di Napoli* [Critical History of the State of Music in Italy and of the S Pietro a Majella Conservatoire in Naples]. He had been a vocal critic of what he perceived to be musical atrophy in the Collegio and, with others such as Bonamici, sought to draw more attention to instrumental and symphonic music, especially through his journal *La musica*, which he founded in 1855.

The *Pensiero malinconico*, Op. 2, is an elegant sonata-type structure in F minor. It opens with an introduction featuring striking successions of rising fourths, which culminate on the dominant chord in preparation for the meditative main theme in the tonic. A contrasting thematic idea in D flat of a distinctly operatic cast is introduced in the tenor register — a favourite texture of Esposito's which is employed in several of the piano works from this period. In the development section, this melody forms the basis for a quasi-operatic duet between the hands prior to an excursion to the tonally remote region of C flat, whereupon the principal theme returns in F minor. The second theme is restated in the expected tonic major but in a more elaborate form, being transferred to the right hand on its repetition. A series of progressions at the close recalls Liszt in its oscillations between the tonic chord and that of the flat submediant, and is perhaps intended as a reference to the D flat major in which the second theme originally appeared.

Ex. 1: *Scherzo*, Op. 3, opening

The gossamer textures and *moto perpetuo* character of the *Scherzo*, Op. 3, in G minor, are clearly reminiscent of Mendelssohn's keyboard miniatures in a similar vein. It opens in a hushed *pianissimo* with delicate *staccati* and fleet double-thirds (Ex. 1), a style of writing that may also have been inspired by some of Cesi's technical exercises. A contrasting lyrical theme in the relative major is initially presented in a tenor register (Ex. 2) and is notable for its subtly irregular phrase structure. This idea is restated in a decorated fashion after a brief modulatory episode that moves through D minor and F major before returning to B flat. The music rises to a strenuous climax on the dominant, which heralds a reprise of the opening material. The restatement, to begin with, is largely literal, but becomes increasingly developmental and triggers an unexpected tonal divergence by way of the Neapolitan to G flat major before deftly returning to the dominant of G. The ample textures at this point may owe something to Chopin in their exploitation of the full compass of the instrument and the concluding bars develop the second theme into an impressive peroration, culminating in a *prestissimo* coda based on the first idea.

Ex. 2: *Scherzo*, Op. 3, central section

The *Allegro* in B minor, Op. 4, is also scherzo-like in character and has a similar formal organization to its predecessor. It opens with a chorale melody (Ex. 3), which betrays no hint of the drama to which it subsequently gives rise. The more expansive and lyrical second theme offers an effective contrast in mood. Somewhat unusually, this is presented in the tonic major, but Esposito is careful to compensate for this rather static tonal organization by approaching B major obliquely, making it the unexpected outcome of the dominant of C sharp (Ex. 4). These two opposing themes are subsequently restated in a more virtuosic guise. The first is presented in a texture reminiscent of an étude, to which *strepitoso* triplet figurations in octaves provide a restless undercurrent. The restatement of the second theme rises to an ardent climax, but its affirmative mood is dispelled by a return to the agitated movement of the previous paragraph, leaving the piece to conclude in tragic and stormy mood.

Ex. 3: *Allegro* in B minor, Op. 4, opening

Ex. 4: *Allegro* in B minor, Op. 4, second theme

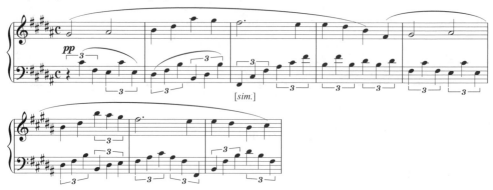

The *Allegretto* in D, Op. 5, is also straightforward in design, though quite different in character from the preceding works. This charming miniature is a serenade with a light, guitar-like accompaniment. The lyrical second theme has the flavour of a Neapolitan popular song and is first heard in a rich tenor register, with the right hand supplying a virtuosic accompaniment of *pianissimo* double thirds and octaves. On its subsequent appearance in the tonic, this melody is cleverly combined with the first theme. The *Romanza* in B flat, Op. 6, may perhaps have been inspired by Sgambati's *Romanza* from his *Fliegende Blätter*, Op. 12, or possibly the *Tre romanze* published by Martucci as his Op. 27 in 1875–76. This miniature has a simple three-part structure. The opening section features a long-breathed melody in six-eight time sounded against arpeggiated figurations in the left hand, while the middle section again deploys a quasi-vocal tenor melody of an indubitably popular cast. This piece is perhaps somewhat less successful than the preceding works, the reprise of the opening material striking the listener as perhaps a little too overblown for the context.

The *Album*, Op. 7, is a set of miniatures clearly tailored to the capacities of amateur pianists. They bear a strong resemblance to similar pieces written by Sgambati and Martucci, some of which were intended for pedagogical use. This fact notwithstanding, they are written with considerable imagination and skill. A mood of childlike simplicity predominates in the opening *Augurio* [Greeting], into which a hint of sentimentality occasionally intrudes (Ex. 5). The subsequent *Malinconico* and *Duetto* clearly owe something to Schumann's *Kinderscenen*. The fourth piece, *Visione*, is more individual: the ethereal texture of the opening idea (Ex. 6) is striking, as is the manner in which Esposito allows a contrasting chorale-like idea in the major mode (Ex. 7) to be influenced by the fluctuating 3/4 and 4/4 metres of the initial material. The coda's enigmatic and inconclusive termination on the dominant of C sharp minor links the movement to the ensuing *Allegro appassionato*, which brings the entire set to a tempestuous conclusion in that key.

Ex. 5: *Augurio*, from *Album*, Op. 7

Ex. 6: *Visione*, from *Album*, Op. 7, opening

Ex. 7: *Visione*, from *Album*, Op. 7, subsidiary theme

The *Fantasia*, Op. 8, is conspicuously indebted to German models: its pianistic rhetoric clearly evinces the influence of Schumann, as does Esposito's employment of an extended multi-sectional form recalling works such as the *Humoresque*. Unfortunately, the piece suffers from serious shortcomings — particularly rhythmic and textural monotony — and does not merit detailed consideration here, despite some imaginative touches. The element of fantasy in the *Momento di Fantasia*, Op. 10, on the other hand, is more evident in the imaginative elaborations of its melodic material as it proceeds, rather than in its basic structure, which is an uncomplicated sonata design. This work also features an expansive Neapolitan-style 'tenor' melody, which is enveloped in delicate figuration akin to that employed in Chopin's Étude in A flat, Op. 25/1, on being repeated, with a 'soprano' voice added in counterpoint (Ex. 8). In the recapitulation, this material makes a triumphant return in F sharp major, in a sonorous piano texture more redolent of Liszt (Ex. 9). Esposito clearly thought highly of this piece, as he programmed it frequently in his own recitals. A similar formal scheme underlies the *Capriccio*, Op. 11, but, as its title would suggest, this structure is dramatized by unpredictable changes of mood. The transition between the lyrical first and second subject, for example, is effected by a boisterous *scherzando* passage, while in the recapitulation, this juncture is handled differently: the first subject is accompanied by a persistent countermelody which eventually yields to groups of limpid quadruplets that form a counterpoint to the restatement of the second subject in B major. A *Presto* coda reverts to the *scherzando* mood, featuring octave passagework derived from the opening melody.

Ex. 8: Momento di Fantasia, Op. 10

Ex. 9: *Momento di Fantasia*, Op. 10, subsidiary theme

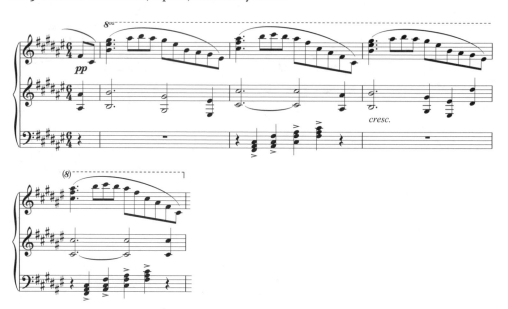

The four *Notturni*, Op. 13, and the *Valzer*, Op. 14, are musically undistinguished and need not detain us here. A further miniature, published as *Alla memoria di Vincenzo Bellini*, Op. 16, is of greater interest on account of the circumstances leading to its composition. Although Bellini came from Sicily, he had developed close ties with Naples in the course of his career: he studied at the Conservatorio di San Sebastiano and his first opera, *Adelson e Salvani*, was produced in the city in 1825. After the composer's death, one of his close friends, the Neapolitan archivist and bibliophile Francesco Florimo, set about organizing the erection of a monument in his memory. The realization of this plan took many years and the monument was eventually unveiled in 1886, not far from the Conservatorio di S Pietro di Majella, as the Real Collegio was eventually renamed. Florimo co-opted a number of prominent local musicians to assist him with the project, including Ruta, Serrao and Rossi. The idea was mooted of commissioning a series of short piano pieces from various eminent composers, which could be sold to generate funds. The list of composers who agreed to participate was an impressive testament to the high esteem in which Bellini's music was held internationally. Tchaikovsky contributed a *Danse russe*, Liszt a *Recueillement*, Rubinstein a *Romance* and Herz a *Minuetto nello stile antico* for four hands. Needless to say, many significant Italian composers also contributed, including Palumbo, Serrao, Martucci, Sgambati and others. These pieces initially appeared in the *Album pianistico Bellini*, which was published in monthly instalments in 1878 by the Associazione Musicale Industriale di Napoli, an organization that had been founded the previous year by a group of musicians that included Rossi, Serrao and Cesi. Only nineteen pieces appeared in this publication, however, and the project seems to have run into difficulties.[27] The commission responsible for erecting the Bellini monument eventually offered the entire collection to the firm of Ricordi, which published it in 1884 under the title *Alla memoria di Vincenzo Bellini*. Pieces by thirty-six composers appeared in this volume. Esposito's name did not initially feature in the list of contributors whose work was sent to Ricordi, but he was evidently approached to write something when a projected contribution by Miguel de Follij did not materialize.[28] The pieces in the collection vary widely in style, but unsurprisingly, many are elegiac in tone, Esposito's included. His contribution is a melancholy nocturne in C sharp minor, prefaced with the following lines from Ugo Foscolo's *Dei sepolcri* [Of Graves] of 1807:

> *Ahi! sugli estinti*
> *non sorge fiore, ove non sia d'umane*
> *lodi onorato e d'amoroso pianto …*

> [Alas! Over the dead
> no flower can spring up if it is not honoured
> with human praises and loving tears …]

This quotation, associated with sentiments of national identity and cultural nationalism, would have been familiar to many Italians, and Esposito's allusion to it undoubtedly reflected his sense of Bellini's iconic status not only as a patriotic Italian, but also as a great creative artist whose career had been tragically cut short by his early death.[29] His nocturne features his favoured device of a tenor-register melody in the outer sections, which combines in the more Chopinesque central section as a duet with a soprano melody as if in tribute to the operatic style of his illustrious predecessor.

In comparison with the preceding opuses, the *Due pezzi* [Two Pieces] of Op. 19 are of much greater interest. The *Andante tranquillo* in B major at times suggests a stylistic kinship with the music of Fauré, particularly in passages such as Ex. 10, with its dialogue between the punctuating bass figure (derived from the constituent intervals of the syncopated chords in the inner voices) and the answering strands of melody in the right hand. The *Lento* in A flat is quite bold in its harmonic explorations: its opening dissonance of E flat and F flat not only generates much of the prevailing harmony and some significant melodic shapes (Ex. 11), but also gives rise to a series of striking semitonal shifts in the bass — features which

27 See Antonio Caroccia, 'Florimo e L'Album Pianistico Bellini', in Graziella Seminara and Anna Tedesco, eds., *Vincenzo Bellini nel secondo centenario della nascita: atti del convegno internazionale, Catania, 8–11 novembre 2001* (Florence, 2004), 57–76, 58.

28 Caroccia, 'Florimo e L'Album Pianistico Bellini', 63, 70

29 See John Hamilton, 'The Revival of the Ode' in Michael Ferber, ed., *A Companion to European Romanticism* (Oxford, 2005), 353–54.

are even more fully accentuated in the reprise and especially in the closing progressions (Ex. 12). Such harmonic experimentation is quite rare in Esposito's output, as is the evident concern to achieve such a remarkable degree of motivic consistency, although regrettably, the strength of these paragraphs is vitiated by the more conventional central trio.

Ex. 10: *Andante tranquillo* from *Due pezzi*, Op. 19/1, opening

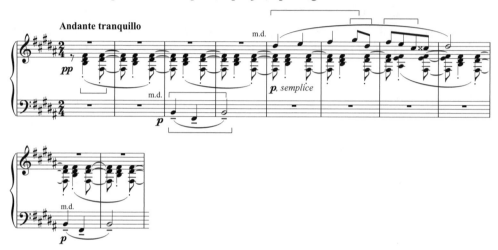

Ex. 11: *Lento* from *Due pezzi*, Op. 19/2, opening

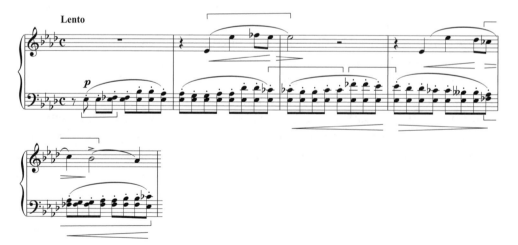

Ex. 12: *Lento* from *Due pezzi*, Op. 19/2, conclusion

Esposito's only other published work of this period was the set of songs *Canti di Lorenzo Stecchetti*, Op. 15, which he dedicated to the Neapolitan singer and teacher, Ester Trifari-Paganini. 'Lorenzo Stecchetti' was a fictional persona invented by the poet Olindo Guerrini (1845–1916), whose collection of poems *Postuma* [Posthumous] appeared in 1877. These purported to be the work of Guerrini's cousin, Lorenzo Stecchetti, a *poète maudit* in the Romantic mould of Byron and Heine, who had supposedly died of consumption at the age of thirty. The collection provoked a scandalized response when it appeared in print on account of its frank treatment of erotic themes and the overtly blasphemous sentiments expressed in some of the verse. Nonetheless, *Postuma* sold extremely well and became widely popular, so much so that its publisher was compelled to reprint the volume several times to meet public demand. The poems, which are generally short, concise and couched in straightforward language reminiscent of folk poetry, dwell on themes of lost love and world-weariness.[30] They proved highly amenable to musical treatment and were much set by contemporary Italian composers, including Tosti, Denza, Leoncavallo, Sgambati and even the young Toscanini, amongst others.

Esposito's three songs must have been amongst the first settings of these poems to appear in print — they were brought out by Lucca in 1879. The text of the opening song, *Spes, ultima dea* [Hope, the last goddess] consists of two verses of an aphoristic brevity which encapsulate the lover's hopeless predicament:

> *Perché questo languor, questo sconforto?*
> *È morto amore!*
>
> *Perché dunque sperare se amore è morto?*
> *Chi non spera, muore.*
>
> [Why this languor, this dejection?
> Love is dead!

---

30 Benedetto Croce, *La letteratura della nuova Italia, Saggi critici*, vol. 2 (Bari, 1942), 138.

Why then hope when love is dead?
He who does not hope, dies.]

Esposito's setting is deft and economical. The vocal part is initially marked *parlando*, but becomes more expansive and animated in anticipation of the reply to the opening rhetorical question. A sense of weariness is conveyed by a stark diminished seventh on G sharp and a striking move directly to the tonic, D minor (Ex. 13), which omits an intervening dominant chord. This material accompanies the insistent opening of the second verse, and also features in the last ten bars, in which the music moves to D major and the reluctant F natural is finally drawn upwards to F sharp, creating the sense of hope alluded to in the poem's title (Ex. 14).

Ex. 13: *Spes, ultima dea, from Canti di Lorenzo Stecchetti, Op. 15/1, opening*

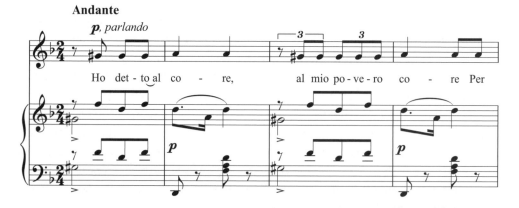

The second song *Scritto sopra un sasso* [Inscribed on a stone] is rather less memorable. This is a lament in F minor in which the poet observes lovers dallying in a wood and a mountain spring, but, in his hopeless isolation, begs them to take pity on him, as he has not known love. In the third of these lyrics, *Fior di siepe* [Flower of the hedgerow], the poetic persona compares his own hopeless passion to a flower which, if denied sunlight, withers and dies unheeded. Esposito divides Guerrini's stanza of seven lines into two unequal portions, setting these as separate sections. The straightforward tonal organization of the first section (G major — B minor — D major) is varied in the second (G minor — B flat — D minor — G major), in keeping with the darkening mood of the text. An introductory phrase in the piano returns at the conclusion to provide a telling comment on the closing vocal phrase *Povero amore!* [Poor love!] (Ex. 15).[31]

---

31 'Fior di siepe' received a performance many years later at a concert given by Esposito's Dublin Chamber Music Union (DCMU) on 29 March 1900.

Ex. 14: *Spes, ultima dea,* from *Canti di Lorenzo Stecchetti,* Op. 15/1, conclusion

Ex. 15: *Fior di seppe,* from *Canti di Lorenzo Stecchetti,* Op. 15/3

It is greatly to be regretted that Esposito's most ambitious works from this period have all been lost. According to the work-list given in Aiello's monograph, the Piano Trio, Op. 9, received its premiere in Naples in 1878.[32] The Piano Quartet, Op. 12, was completed in November 1876. One of the contributors to Aiello's book, Otello Calbi, who evidently had a chance to examine the score, describes it as a 'solid composition, memorable for its impetuous introduction leading to a cantabile theme which is subjected to contrapuntal elaboration; a technically taxing, headlong Scherzo; and an *Adagio cantabile* with a theme like a popular song, preceding a finale which is predominantly relaxed in mood [*leggermente drammatico*]'.[33] The work was first performed in Naples in January 1877 at a concert promoted by Cesi, and subsequently in Turin. It evidently met with an enthusiastic reception, to judge from a letter sent by the critic Federigo Polidoro to Ruta, which was printed in the latter's journal *La musica*:

> In the second concert ... the quartet of M. Michele Esposito was performed. You are, like me, an admirer of this highly accomplished young pianist. If you had heard this work, you would have been captivated, as I have been, by the composer. And truly, my dear friend, more expert composers would be happy and proud if they had written something like it. Our friend *Lelio* of the *Corriere del mattino* says in his review (and I am of exactly the same opinion):
>
> 'It has been said that the Italians do not know how to write quartets. To which I reply: they know now, and are writing them, and here is an example of one of them. It has majestic, imposing, *melodious* themes; there is a marvellous sense of interplay between the instruments; it evinces a loftiness of soul and feeling; it reveals the author's innermost imaginings; and then — and then, it has something that makes you leap out of your seat and fills your soul with I know not what — something which makes you want to run and embrace the performers and the composer, and also the person standing close to him last night — Maestro Cesi, proud and pleased with the work of his beloved student.'
>
> It is precisely thus. It is one of those enlightened compositions, such as can only be written by a mind nurtured by profound study, like that of Esposito.[34]

---

32 Aiello, *Al musicista*, 71

33 Aiello, *Al musicista*, 92. The copy of the work seen by Otello Calbi does not appear to be the original MS: he mentions that it bears the signature of a copyist by the name of Cotrufo, who dated it 22 February 1879 — by which time Esposito had moved to Paris. Perhaps this copy was prepared for another prospective performance.

34 'Circolo Cesi', *La musica*, 20 January 1877

To judge from this review, the young composer demonstrated an impressive competence in handling the difficult medium of the piano quartet. The quality of the work's lyrical invention clearly made an impression on the critics, as did the arresting quality of its rhetorical gestures. It is naturally impossible to make a meaningful appraisal of the piece without seeing the score, but to judge from the style of Esposito's early piano works, one can reasonably conjecture that it was probably modelled on the piano quartets of Mendelssohn and Schumann, or possibly those of Brahms.

Esposito's interest in chamber music clearly demonstrates his alignment with the progressive tendency in Italian music which sought to redress the previous neglect of non-operatic music by native composers. Of contemporary figures, Giovanni Sgambati (1841–1914) was particularly significant in this respect. A student and subsequently a close friend of Franz Liszt (with whom he had studied in Rome), Sgambati developed an international reputation as a pianist and conductor by the mid-1870s. He was also highly respected as a composer, and interestingly, first came to prominence in this capacity with two piano quintets, Op. 4 and Op. 5. Esposito's contemporary Giuseppe Martucci went on to make a creative contribution of even greater importance to the national repertory of instrumental music. Two of his most important early works, the Violin Sonata, Op. 22, and the Piano Quintet, Op. 45, were completed in 1874 and 1878, respectively, more or less contemporaneously with Esposito's Piano Trio and Piano Quartet.

The Piano Quartet undoubtedly marked a watershed in Esposito's development as a composer. From this point onwards, his reputation grew steadily. In a further article in March 1877, Polidoro returned to the subject of Cesi's remarkable circle of disciples. He singled out for special mention Esposito's abilities as a composer and executant, emphasizing Cesi's role in the formation of his artistic personality. Polidoro concluded by congratulating Cesi on his achievement and on the recent success of two concerts of solo and duo works that he and Esposito had recently given in Turin.[35] Esposito made an appearance there with the leader of the Turin Quartet Augusto Ferni and other local professional players in a performance of his Piano Quartet.

By June 1878, Esposito, encouraged by the success of his first major chamber composition, had completed a Second Piano Quartet, Op. 17, which was included in a concert given that month in Naples. The review in La musica was once again highly favourable:

> Cesi and his disciples continue to give new and splendid proofs of their abilities and are now also distinguishing themselves as composers of chamber music: this was demonstrated by a concert given by Michele Esposito, in which a quartet by the same worthy young maestro stood out. This composition evinces a technical assurance and stylistic maturity which assure his fame and will cause his name to be entered in the rolls of the great composers. The entire concert was a resounding success

35 'Concerti', La musica, 17 March 1877, 4

and all of the pianist's compositions — with their rich harmonies, bright melodies, formal elegance and pervasive poetic impulse — received preferential applause. There is no need to discuss the quality of the pianist's performance, because it is superfluous by now to describe the intrinsic excellence of the Cesi School, of which Michele Esposito is certainly the foremost ornament. Cesi must be proud of having the opportunity of bringing about an improvement in the standard of compositions for the piano, as he has already done with the standard of performance.[36]

This concert provided Esposito with a notable opportunity to display his talents as a pianist. The remainder of the challenging programme included Beethoven's *Appassionata* Sonata, extracts from Schumann's *Humoresque*, a Chopin nocturne, Liszt's *Valse d'après Schubert* and Tausig's arrangement of a Schubert *Marche militaire*. In addition, he played his contribution to the album written *Alla memoria di Vincenzo Bellini*, Op. 16; his *Scherzo*, Op. 3; one of his nocturnes from Op. 13; the *Allegro* in B minor, Op. 4; and the *Allegretto* in D, Op. 5.[37]

Like its predecessor, the Second Piano Quartet was never published and the score has disappeared. One's sense of loss is rendered all the more acute by a glowing review of the work published by Polidoro on the occasion of its second performance in September 1878:

> This time we prefer to dwell on a composition which has deservedly received general praise — the Quartet of the young Michele Esposito, one of Cesi's most outstanding pupils.

> A notable feature of Esposito's quartet is the rigorous connection of the musical ideas. Equally noteworthy and deserving of praise is its manifestation of a new sensibility which is an infallible means of recognising the true artists of our time — namely, a striving to achieve independent artistic mastery. Esposito has studied the works of the classical masters and has been able to adduce therefrom the secret of their mastery — but he does not compose old-fashioned music as a consequence. On the other hand, his music does not evince any of those eccentric characteristics which in certain circles, heaven help us, some strive to pass off as originality, but which are actually proof positive of incompetence or conceited sterility. ... His aim is not to be crudely up-to-date: he possesses that higher impulse which is only given to great men and true artists, which enables him to respect the eternal principles and healthy traditions of the past, yet approach the future without an attitude of effrontery or self-indulgence.

36 'Concerto Michele Esposito', *La musica*, 21 June 1878, 3
37 'Concerto Michele Esposito', *La musica*, 21 June 1878, 3

We cannot commend this young pianist-composer highly enough for his attitudes and for the notable composition in which he made them manifest; he has not only composed a fine quartet, but he has produced a work of much significance from the point of view of art and all the questions of progress that are attendant on it.[38]

In November of the same year, Cesi and Ruta put on two concerts of a more ambitious nature, this time of orchestral works. The anonymous reviewer writing for *La musica* (who was probably Polidoro) opined that the second of these 'could never be equalled' in the quality of its interpretation and performance. Once again, a work of Esposito's featured in the programme and drew special praise: 'The piece which one listened to in the most devout silence — of which one did not want to miss a note — the piece which crowned the triumph of the country's art … was the *Adagio and primo tempo* for piano [and orchestra] of Esposito', performed by Rossomandi and conducted by Cesi.[39] The composition in question was his newly composed Piano Concerto, Op. 18. The score of this is also lost, but it seems to have been in two movements, an *Adagio* and *Allegro*.[40] It was received with 'clamorous acclamation' by the large audience, but the composer was not there to hear the applause, for in October he had finally decided to take Rubinstein's advice and move to Paris.

38 'Circolo Cesi', *La musica*, 16 September 1878, 4
39 'Secondo Gran Concerto', *La musica*, 11 November 1878, 3
40 Aiello, *Al musicista*, 72

2 A Parisian Interlude, 1878–82

It is not entirely clear why Esposito decided to move to Paris at this juncture. One wonders whether he had become increasingly dissatisfied with the limited scope that Naples offered for the development of his talents, as Rubinstein had foreseen, and was anxious to try his luck in the wider musical world of the French capital. He almost certainly would have been aware of the burgeoning career of Martucci, which had developed rapidly after a four-month visit there in 1878.[1] Esposito's friend not only had the opportunity to hear considerable amounts of new French music and sample the atmosphere of Paris's vibrant concert life, but also to make the acquaintance of prominent figures such as Saint-Saëns, Gounod and Massenet. Despite a measure of local acclaim, Esposito's career seemed set to remain parochial by comparison. There may also have been financial considerations. Working conditions in Italy were far from ideal: talented young musicians often found it difficult to make a decent living, leading some to seek a better life abroad. Several of Esposito's associates had already taken this step, Tosti and Caracciolo amongst them. Esposito resolved to follow the same course. Naples, the city that had nurtured his talent, would be impoverished by his departure, as it would by Denza's emigration in 1879, Cesi's removal to St Petersburg in 1886 and Martucci's decision in the same year to take up an appointment at the Liceo Musicale in Bologna.

Esposito may also have taken this decision at the prompting of the woman who would shortly become his wife, a young Russian girl by the name of Natalia Klebnikoff, who, according to Aiello, had become one of his students several years previously.[2] Natalia, who

---

1   Perrino, *Giuseppe Martucci: Gli anni giovanili*, 133–49
2   Aiello, *Al musicista*, 30. Kees van Hoek states that Esposito met the Klebnikoffs at Rubinstein's lodgings, but does not specify whether this occurred in Paris or Naples: see Kees van Hoek, 'Michele Esposito: Maestro of Dublin', *The Irish Monthly*, 71 (1943), 223–30, 224. This article contains errors and statements uncorroborated by other sources.

was two years younger than him, was the only daughter of Peter Klebnikoff, a lecturer in physics and chemistry at the University of St Petersburg who had reputedly been banished from Russia. It is not known what brought the Klebnikoffs to Italy — it may have been their contact with Rubinstein — but they were able to settle in a villa in Portici, owned by a brother of Luigi Caracciolo.[3] Neither do we know a great deal about Natalia herself, beyond the fact that she was a highly intelligent and cultured young woman, who was well-known amongst the sizeable and wealthy expatriate Russian community in Naples. The relationship between herself and Esposito quickly became more intimate. In 1878, the young couple declared their intention to marry and move to Paris. This plan may have been made more feasible by the fact that Natalia had a private income and seems to have been well-connected socially, particularly with the Russian émigré community in the French capital.[4] In September she travelled there to arrange for her fiancé to give a concert. She made an appointment to meet the directors of the Pleyel piano manufactory and evidently achieved her aim, as she subsequently arranged for posters to be put up advertising Michele's forthcoming appearance. She then telegraphed to inform him that everything had been organized and that he should join her at once.[5]

By all accounts, Esposito's parents were understandably distraught at the prospect of being abandoned and left without any means of support. The young man eventually managed to reassure them that he intended to find more profitable work in Paris which would place him in a better position to provide for them. Before his departure in October 1878, there was a highly emotional leave-taking: Esposito's mother was beside herself with grief, and her son knelt at her feet seeking to convince her that all would be well. According to Aiello, he implored her to trust him, telling her: 'I may fail to put bread in my mouth but not in yours. I will never abandon you and I will always think first of you rather than myself.' This promise was strictly honoured and Esposito continued to send a monthly remittance to his family.[6] It would, however, be thirty-one years before he returned to Italy and saw his mother again.

On his arrival in Paris, he was met by Natalia and her father. According to Aiello, the couple encountered what he describes as 'procedural difficulties' when organizing their marriage in France on account of Natalia's Russian Orthodox faith. It was consequently arranged for the young couple to go to London in January 1879 and get married there. They remained in London for some weeks before returning to Paris.[7] Natalia was evidently pregnant before the marriage took place: the couple's first child Bianca was born on 13 July.[8]

3 Aiello, *Al musicista*, 30
4 Aiello, *Al musicista*, 35
5 Aiello, *Al musicista*, 31
6 Aiello, *Al musicista*, 31
7 Aiello, *Al musicista*, 35
8 Richard Pine and Charles Action suggest that Michele and Natalia eloped to London, but Aiello makes no mention of this: see Pine and Acton, *To Talent Alone*, 195.

Esposito would remain in Paris for four years, but unfortunately our knowledge of his activities during this period is exceedingly scant. Aiello indicates that he gave a number of concerts shortly after arriving in the city which brought him to attention in artistic circles, but is rather vague as to the details, saying only that they were warmly received and elicited complimentary notices. As a result of these successes, he received invitations to appear in various salons held by Russian émigrés or by wealthy families such as the Rothschilds, on which occasions the quality of his playing and his charming personal manner appear to have made an invariably favourable impression. Natalia's social connections may presumably have helped considerably to open doors to him, besides which he had arrived in the city armed with impressive testimonials from his professors at the Real Collegio.[9] He presumably hoped that these appearances would assist in the growth of his reputation as a performer and cause him to be sought after as a teacher by wealthy private pupils. He subsequently took part in concerts at the Salle Pleyel and the Salle Herz, two of the most popular venues for chamber music in Paris. His performances were, by all accounts, enthusiastically received, and the fact that the firm of Pleyel subsequently put one of their pianos at his disposal suggests that he was held in considerable regard. A review of one of these events on 28 May 1879 at the Salle Pleyel in the La revue et gazette musicale de Paris suggests that Esposito might often have appeared in a subsidiary capacity, as a supporting artist to more eminent expatriate Italian musicians, of whom there were a considerable number in the French capital. On this particular occasion, Felice Lebano, Professor of Harp at the Naples Conservatoire and the well-known cellist Giuseppe Magrini received top billing. Esposito and the violinist Sighicelli joined Magrini in a performance of Mendelssohn's Piano Trio in C minor, which elicited a brief, but appreciative notice.[10]

In spite of these signs of growing recognition, it quickly became evident that establishing himself in the fiercely competitive musical world of Paris was not going to prove easy. When Michele and Natalia Esposito arrived in the French capital in late 1878, the city was still recovering after the traumatic events of 1870–71 — the humiliating defeat suffered in the Franco-Prussian War, the collapse of the Second Empire, invasion and the period of the Commune. Nonetheless, it had re-emerged as a vibrant cultural and intellectual centre, in which some of the greatest creative minds in Europe were to be found. This sense of national renewal undoubtedly engendered an atmosphere of excitement and dynamism, but also tended to give rise to attitudes of chauvinism and cultural exclusivity. As far as music was concerned, Parisian audiences often proved stubbornly unreceptive to works by foreign composers: the contributors to Cesi's musical journal, Archivio musicale, ruefully noted that their interest in the music of even great Italian figures such as Verdi, Rossini, Bellini or Donizetti seemed to diminish year on year.[11] This chauvinistic tendency

9   John. F. Larchet, 'Michele Esposito', in Pine and Acton, To Talent Alone, 429
10   'Concerts et auditions musicales', La revue et gazette musicale de Paris, 46, 23 (1879), 190
11   'Parigi 4 gennaio', Archivio musicale 1, 1 (1882), 26

became if anything more pronounced after the Franco-Prussian War: in its immediate aftermath, a number of prominent French composers founded the Société Nationale de Musique in February 1871, which aimed to promote what were deemed to be authentically French styles of musical composition. In practice, views on this subject were highly polarized, particularly when it came to questions such as the extent to which French composers should allow themselves to be receptive to foreign influences, and especially to the music of Richard Wagner. Feelings on these subjects tended to run very high, and an outsider such as Esposito had to tread very cautiously, lest he alienate prominent native musicians who might potentially be of assistance to him. Esposito was evidently highly sympathetic to Wagner's music — Aiello mentions that he transcribed extracts from the German composer's operas during his time in Paris— and one conjectures that he would probably have been keenly interested in the music of contemporary composers such as César Franck, on whom the influence of Wagner is very evident.

The young Italian quickly discovered that it was often prudent to refrain from discussing his musical tastes openly. Not long after his arrival in Paris, he arranged to meet Camille Saint-Saëns who by this time enjoyed a pre-eminent position in French musical life as a composer, piano virtuoso and teacher (he had also been one of the principal instigators of the Société Nationale de Musique). The composer John F. Larchet, one of Esposito's Irish students, recounted the story of their first encounter:

> Musical Europe was then in turmoil about the music and personality of Richard Wagner and bitterly divided into Wagnerites and anti-Wagnerites. When Esposito called on Saint-Saëns with a letter of introduction of the Naples Conservatoire he was received rather coldly and was left standing while the letter was being read. Saint-Saëns then addressed him with the question, 'Are you a Wagnerite?' 'No,' was the reply. Thereupon Saint-Saëns said, 'Very good, sit down,' and shaking Esposito warmly by the hand, struck up a pleasant conversation.[12]

Esposito subsequently remained on cordial terms with the older man and received invitations to his house as a guest. He also became acquainted with other eminent French composers such as Massenet and Gounod, whom he met at soirées given by the wealthy expatriate Italian artist Giuseppe de Nittis. Many years later, Esposito recalled that Gounod had complimented him on his piano-playing:

> One of my pupils at Naples [Esposito recalled] ... was a daughter of the famous [singer] Madame Marchesi and sister of Blanche Marchesi. We met again in Paris. On the occasion of the début there of Blanche Marchesi, Gounod was present. Earlier in the evening I had played Beethoven's Sonata Appassionata. After Blanche

Marchesi had sung two songs composed by Gounod, she was anxious to obtain the maestro's verdict upon her interpretation of his music. He said: 'Those songs of mine, Mademoiselle, are not to be sung, but *said*, just as our friend Esposito in his playing made the piano speak.[13]

Through de Nittis, Esposito also met the conductor Camille Chevillard and the composer André Messager, for whom he played some of his Wagner transcriptions, as they shared his enthusiasm for the German composer's work.[14]

De Nittis, who had made a name for himself on both sides of the English Channel, enjoyed patronage of a kind that his younger associate could only dream about, having built up a wealthy clientele that included prominent financiers. He and his wife were socially ambitious, and their Saturday night soirées became a popular meeting place for many eminent figures in the Parisian artistic world. Their guests regularly included such luminaries as Edgar Degas and Édouard Manet, Alexandre Dumas *fils*, Alphonse Daudet, José María de Herédia, Émile Zola and the brothers Goncourt. Esposito was a frequent visitor to their home and would often practise the fine Érard piano in the studio while the artist was at work.[15] He also performed regularly at his soirées when de Nittis was in Paris, playing chamber music with eminent Parisian musicians.[16] Apart from the social contacts he made through de Nittis, Esposito is also known to have associated with an informal fraternity of expatriate Italian creative artists which adopted the whimsical name of *Circolo della polenta* or 'Polenta Circle'. For this convivial group he composed a *Valzer della polenta* in 1881, a simple melodic essay in a popular Neapolitan idiom, which was subsequently published by Ricordi.

Esposito's four-year sojourn in Paris was not especially productive from a compositional point of view and he seems to have completed only a handful of works. He is known to have written three sets of songs, two of them in French, but frustratingly, these have all been lost — the *Trois mélodies*, Op. 20, of 1880–81 (settings of Gautier and Hugo); the *Trois chansons*, Op. 27, of the same year (to poems by Émile Blémont); and three further settings of 'Lorenzo Stecchetti', which constituted the composer's Op. 25. Also lost is a set of two pieces for viola and piano, listed as *Due pezzi*, Op. 22, in the work-list given in Aiello.

Unlike these works, the piano pieces were published and copies of them have fortunately survived. The *Sei canzoni* [Six Songs], Op. 23, are similar in nature to the *Due pezzi*, Op. 19. Esposito's stylistic indebtedness to early Romantic composers such as Schumann is still evident in these pieces, although their harmonic language displays some points of contact with that of Fauré. The *Tre pezzi caratteristici* [Three Characteristic Pieces] of Op.

13 F. G. Edwards, 'Michele Esposito', *Musical Times*, 44, 729 (1903), 706
14 Aiello, *Al musicista*, 37
15 'Signor Michele Esposito', *Weekly Irish Times*, 8 September 1900
16 Aiello, *Al musicista*, 36. Until 1882, de Nittis spent several months each year in London where he completed views of the capital for his major patron, Kaye Knowles, including the famous *Piccadilly*.

26 were published by Ricordi in 1882. These are more overtly virtuosic in style, leading one to suppose that Esposito probably wrote them for inclusion in his Paris recitals. The composer clearly thought highly enough of the first of the set, the *Berceuse*, to produce a version of it for small orchestra many years later in 1924. Much of the charm of this piece derives from the piquant added-sixth harmonies accompanying the principal melodic idea (Ex. 16), and the decidedly modern-sounding parallel fourths and fifths that accompany its repeat (a feature which looks forward to Debussy's early *Arabesques* for piano). *Serenata*, the second piece, is more exotic in character, partaking of the stylized Hispanicism of Bizet and Lalo; while *Papillon* contrasts a texture of semiquavers nimbly alternating between the hands in the outer sections (which are in E major) with a more lyrical central paragraph in the surprising tonal area of the Neapolitan (F major). Though little known today, this delightful miniature, full of humour and zest, deserves a place in the repertoire as much as Grieg's celebrated piece of the same title, Op. 43/1.

Ex. 16: *Berceuse*, from Tre *pezzi caratteristici*, Op. 26/1

By far the most substantial work that Esposito wrote in Paris was the Sonata for Violin and Piano in G major, Op. 32, which was completed in 1881 but only published over a decade later by the London firm of Stanley Lucas, Weber, Pitt and Hatzfeld Ltd. in 1892. It was dedicated to Guido Papini, an expatriate Italian violinist prominent in Parisian musical circles.[17] The sonata comprises three movements. The first of these, *Moderato*, is predominantly pastoral in character and proceeds in a flowing six-eight, with limpid

<hr />

17 For details of Papini's career, see Anthony Hughes, 'The Society and Music' in James Meenan and Desmond Clarke, eds., The *Royal Dublin Society 1731–1981* (Dublin, 1981), 266; and B. Henderson, 'Guido Papini', The *Strad*, 17 (1906–07), 234–35.

textures that recall the restrained elegance of Saint-Saëns's chamber music. The graceful first subject, which is shown in Ex. 17, with its gentle syncopations, is announced first on the violin, before being restated in dialogue between the two instruments. At the end of this paragraph, it rises to an ardent culmination that diverts unexpectedly from the dominant of the relative minor, E minor, to the remote region of A flat, thereby effecting a seamless transition to the second subject, which is stated in the subdominant. Esposito's management of this somewhat unorthodox procedure is notably skilful, and his subtle handling of phrase structure and the distribution of harmonic tensions within the second subject paragraph lends it a sense of buoyant expansiveness. The development section also explores darker subdominant regions of C minor, F minor and A flat before working up to a strenuous climax that effectively prepares for a radiant return of the first subject at the opening of the recapitulation. Esposito maintains interest in his recapitulation by restating his first subject in the piano, giving a counter-melody to the violin. The second subject also returns in the tonic, though, in response to its more turbulent character, a sense of tonal equilibrium is restored by the tranquil coda in which a curtailed reference to the first subject is stated over twenty-one bars of tonic harmony.

Ex. 17: Sonata for Violin and Piano in G major, Op. 32, I, first subject

Ex. 18: Sonata for Violin and Piano in G major, Op. 32, II, opening

The charming middle movement is in E major and has a straightforward ternary structure. The elegant main theme, to which piquant chromatic inflexions and pervasive

syncopations lend a rather quirky character, unfolds in a broad paragraph of twenty-two bars over a simple chordal accompaniment in the piano (its opening bars are shown in Ex. 18). The more animated central section features a new idea in triplets, which quickly rises to a sonorous climax with ornate sextuplet figurations in the piano and persistent cross-rhythms between the two instruments. This leads to a climactic reprise of the opening idea in the subdominant, which subsides in intensity for its continuation in the tonic, the semiquaver figuration of the preceding section now transformed into delicate arabesques in the piano. The music rises once more to a brief climax, but this too quickly subsides, leaving the movement to die away in a serene coda. The energetic *Allegro vivace* that concludes the work is in sonata form and makes play with two effectively contrasted themes — a vigorous idea in the tonic minor accompanied by impetuous semiquaver figurations (Ex. 19) and a lyrical contrasting theme, which commences in B flat but is highly tonally labile. Interestingly, the first subject is reworked and disguised at the opening of the recapitulation — perhaps because it features so extensively in the development. The movement is much more overtly virtuosic than the preceding ones, featuring brilliant passage work. It concludes with an exciting climactic recapitulation of the opening theme, which culminates in a headlong *Presto*. The level of technical finish and sheer quality of invention manifest in this score cause one to regret the loss of the earlier chamber music all the more keenly: it is a highly attractive piece which would amply repay the attention of performers, being superbly conceived for the medium and gratefully written for both instruments.

Ex. 19: Sonata for Violin and Piano in G major, Op. 32, III, first subject

The other notable event of 1881 for Esposito was the renewal of his acquaintance with Rubinstein when the latter paid a visit to Paris that year. Aiello recounts that the Russian pianist was gratified to hear of his young colleague's recent successes and that the relationship between the two men became more intimate.[18] But in spite of the various contacts he had made in the musical world and his successful public appearances, he obviously found it difficult to make a living. Esposito and his wife lived a considerable distance from the city centre — presumably because it was cheaper to rent lodgings in the suburbs. We know next to nothing about the state of their finances, but it seems likely that they lived very modestly. To judge from one suggestive anecdote, they were unable to afford luxuries like a cab if they missed the last train home at night. One evening, Esposito was invited to a musical soirée given by Saint-Saëns. The night wore on, and

> Esposito, finding that the hour was late and that he had only a few minutes to catch the last train to convey him home, went up to the distinguished host to pay his compliments and make his adieux. 'No, no,' said Saint-Saëns, gripping his guest's hands, 'you must not go away yet: wait and hear my piano quintet.' This request was in the nature of a command. Esposito stayed; but on that bitterly cold mid-

18 Aiello, *Al musicista*, 36. Van Hoek claims that Esposito took lessons with Rubinstein in Paris, though there is no mention of this in other sources: see Van Hoek, 'Michele Esposito', 224.

winter's night he had to tramp all the way home along several miles of deserted, frozen roads in the small hours of the morning.[19]

Further unpleasantness awaited him when he eventually arrived home: as he subsequently related to a colleague at the Royal Irish Academy of Music in Dublin, he discovered that he had forgotten his key. When he knocked on the door, his wife refused to open it and threw the key out into the snow in a fury. Unable to find it, Esposito was forced to spend the night in the underground station.[20] While Natalia's overreaction may simply have been a result of her fiery temperament, it is also possible that financial worries and other anxieties may have placed their marriage under a certain amount of strain — particularly if she had been used to a life of greater affluence, as seems to have been the case. And Esposito had a responsibility to provide not only for his wife and daughter, but also for his large family back in Naples.

While his concert and salon appearances had been received favourably, it is unlikely they provided much of an income. We do not know how successful Esposito was in earning money as a teacher: It has been suggested that he worked at the Conservatoire Nationale de Musique, but there seems to be no evidence that he actually did.[21] Lucrative concert work was slow in coming: Saint-Saëns had supposedly warned him, 'If you wish to make a name in Paris as a concert performer you must first make a name outside it' — a remark which clearly intimates that Parisian audiences were slow to recognize the merits of performers unless they had made names for themselves elsewhere.[22] By his own account, he played his Piano Concerto, Op. 18, to the celebrated conductor Pasdeloup, hoping to interest him in programming it in the Pasdeloup Concerts, one of the most prestigious series of orchestral concerts in the Paris musical calendar. Pasdeloup expressed no interest in performing the work, but was sufficiently impressed by Esposito's abilities as a pianist to offer him a solo engagement. The young Italian declined the invitation, 'being somewhat hurt by the reception accorded to his Concerto', as he later (1900) revealed in an interview for the *Weekly Irish Times*. He was subsequently to regret this impulsive decision, since an appearance at the Pasdeloup concerts could well have led to further engagements.[23]

Eventually, there were encouraging signs that his circumstances were at last about to improve. According to his friend Alessandro Longo, he had been engaged to play in the concert series mounted by the conductors Colonne and Lamoureux.[24] At this point, events took an unexpected course. On Christmas Eve 1881, Esposito received a surprise visit

19 Edwards, 'Michele Esposito', 706
20 Lorna Watton, *Michele Esposito: A Neapolitan Musician in Dublin from 1882–1928*, unpublished dissertation, Queen's University Belfast (1986), 8
21 Watton, *Michele Esposito*, 8
22 Pine and Acton, *To Talent Alone*, 429. According to van Hoek, Saint-Saëns advised Esposito to tour London, but this statement is uncorroborated elsewhere: see van Hoek, 'Michele Esposito', 224.
23 'Signor Esposito', *Weekly Irish Times*, 8 September 1900
24 Longo, 'Michele Esposito', *L'Arte pianistica* 1, 2 (1914), 2

from his friend, Luigi Carraciolo, who was passing through Paris on his way to Naples. Caracciolo had since been appointed Professor of Singing at the Royal Irish Academy of Music in Dublin (RIAM), the city's foremost private music school. He had, however, experienced some problems with his health since taking up his post and had been granted three months' leave to enable him to recuperate.[25] Esposito confided in his former teacher and colleague that he was experiencing financial difficulties and was eager to secure a teaching post with a regular salary. After returning to Dublin, Caracciolo wrote to Esposito in February to inform him that one of the piano teachers at the RIAM had just resigned and that a position had fallen vacant. Esposito immediately applied for the post. The minutes of the institution's Board of Governors record that 'it was resolved to offer him a temporary engagement on the following terms: that he would give eight hours a week (if required) … and as the Council shall appoint at the rate of £100 per annum, the first engagement [shall] be for 6 months only'. A surviving memorandum from Sir Francis Brady, who negotiated on behalf of the Board of Governors, details that Esposito declined the offer, but having considered the vital necessity of securing the appointment of a piano teacher, and Caracciolo's high personal recommendation of his erstwhile colleague, Brady agreed to authorize Caracciolo to relay a new offer of £40 for six hours a week (and £5 to cover Esposito's travel from Paris to Dublin) for a period of three months. Brady also agreed that, if the appointment continued, a salary of £100 a year for six hours a week would be offered with 10 shillings for additional hours.[26] Even then, Esposito hesitated and was, according to Aiello, tempted to refuse the offer, being fearful of the effect that moving from Paris would have on his career prospects there.[27] On 16 April 1882, he gave another recital at the Salle Pleyel. The notices, according to Cesi's journal *Archivio musicale*, were very positive:

> We reveal, from Parisian newspapers, fine reviews writing of a concert given [by] one of our countrymen Michele Esposito, which do honour to our country. They lavish the most flattering and deserved praises on the young concert pianist; in him they praise his school, his finger technique, his self-confidence, apposite interpretations united by his own *cachet* which serve to reveal his artistic personality. No less complimentary are the assessments and reviews of his compositions.[28]

25   Edwards, 'Michele Esposito', 706; see also Pine and Acton, *To Talent Alone*, 132
26   Pine and Acton, *To Talent Alone*, 132–33
27   Aiello, *Al musicista*, 38
28   Esposito's programme consisted of a gavotte by Rameau, Tausig's edition of Scarlatti's *Pastorale et Caprice*, Beethoven's Piano Sonata, Op. 53, a nocturne by Chopin, Schumann's *Kreisleriana* and the arrangement of one of Schubert's *Marches militaires* by Tausig. Also included in the programme were his First Piano Quartet and five of his piano pieces: the *Capriccio*, Op. 11; the three pieces from Op. 26, *Berceuse*, *Serenata* and *Papillon*; and the *Allegro Appassionato* from Op. 7: see *Archivio musicale* 1 (1882), 216–17.

This encouraging success notwithstanding, Natalia seems to have placed pressure on her husband to accept the RIAM post.[29] Esposito evidently did not feel in a position to refuse, and so, in the spring of 1882, directly after his final Parisian recital, he left Paris for a city that would pose a very different set of challenges. Natalia and Bianca joined him three months later, in July.

29   Aiello, *Al musicista*, 38

3 Working in Ireland, 1882–99

On arriving in Dublin, Esposito probably did not expect to stay there for very long, no doubt regarding his RIAM post as a convenient stopgap until he managed to obtain a better position elsewhere, perhaps in England. In the event, he was to remain for forty-six years. Unfortunately, while Esposito's professional activities in Ireland are quite well documented, we know little about his personal life, or his responses towards his new surroundings. His adaptation to life in a new country was initially made all the more difficult by his ignorance of English, a language he had to get to grips with as a matter of urgency, not least if he were to communicate adequately with his students. (The second language of most Italians at that time was French). Fortunately, Natalia's impressive linguistic skills extended to a command of English (she also spoke fluent French, German and Italian in addition to her native Russian), and she was able to act as a translator for him in the early stages. The young couple took lodgings at 6 Brighton Vale, Monkstown — a pleasant suburb to the south of the city.[1] Esposito's friend and fellow countryman Caracciolo provided much practical help and smoothed his way by effecting introductions of various kinds.[2] According to Aiello, Michele and Natalia made a determined effort to produce a favourable impression on the people that they encountered and were generally successful in doing so.[3]

---

1 Gorman, 'Mario Esposito', 301n. A list of the family's subsequent residences is given in Pine and Acton, *To Talent Alone*, 196n.

2 Unfortunately Caracciolo continued to suffer from ill-heath and was forced to leave Dublin a few years later. His friends staged a benefit concert for him in Leinster Hall in June 1887, but he died a month later: see 'Complimentary Benefit Concert to Signor Luigi Caracciolo', *Irish Times*, 6 June 1887; and 'Sudden Death of Signor Caracciolo', *Irish Times*, 23 July 1887.

3 Aiello, *Al musicista*, 38

Nonetheless, adjusting to their new circumstances must have required a considerable mental effort from both of them. Natalia in particular found the Irish climate difficult and their surroundings probably presented a great deal else that struck them as new and strange. It must also have taken some time to become attuned to the complex conditions prevailing in the country. On the face of it, Dublin was simply another Victorian city in the United Kingdom of Great Britain and Ireland, still possessed of a faded grandeur lingering from its Georgian heyday, with a citizenry ostensibly loyal to the Crown. Yet underneath the apparently placid surface of everyday life, Irish society was deeply divided along religious, social and political lines. The years immediately following Esposito's arrival in the country were marked by growing unrest, leading to increasingly insistent calls for a greater measure of Irish political autonomy and the introduction of Home Rule.

From a purely artistic point of view, musical life in Dublin must have seemed very impoverished in comparison with Paris, or even Naples, for all its shortcomings. Such professional concert life as existed was sustained largely by visiting artists. The city lacked a professional orchestra, as well as a full-time professional opera or ballet company. Although circumstances would improve to some extent during the 1880s — in no small part due to Esposito's efforts — it was widely acknowledged that the outlook for music in Ireland was rather bleak. In 1886, only a few years after Esposito came to Ireland, Charles Larcom Graves, the brother of Alfred Perceval Graves and himself a distinguished man of letters, contributed a piece on the current state of Irish music to the *Musical Times*, which articulated this view in a forceful manner. In Graves's analysis, the sluggish development of native musical infrastructures was not due to any lack of native talent, but rather to local in-fighting which had rendered progress impossible. As a result, such talented musicians as the country produced were left with no choice but to leave, as Ireland offered little scope for a satisfying career:

> I may be allowed to remark how the careers of [Sullivan and Stanford] illustrate the dependence of Irish genius on foreign surroundings. In the present state of affairs this could hardly be otherwise, for the Irish capital does not support a good orchestra, it is sadly in want of a good Concert hall, while the notorious cliquishness of Dublin musical society, owing to a lack of an *entente cordiale* between the chief musical authorities, has sadly hindered the progress of the art in that classic city. Few Irish names are to be found in the ranks of distinguished instrumentalists or executants, and we have already adverted to the lack of a first rate Irish chorus.[4]

These forthright comments elicited a rather heated response from Joseph Robinson, a prominent Dublin musician who had a considerable reputation as a conductor and a teacher at the RIAM. Robinson was understandably anxious to redress the rather negative

4   Charles Larcom Graves, 'Musical Talent in Ireland', *Musical Times*, 27, 524 (1886), 582

picture presented by Graves, pointing to the activities of his own Dublin Musical Society and the concerts it had mounted over the years. Nonetheless, Robinson admitted that he had no choice but to augment the orchestras for these concerts with British players, as skilled local instrumentalists were in short supply. He pointed out that this was scarcely surprising, in view of the poverty of the country and what he described as the 'indifferent' quality of musical education that was generally available. He also identified another crucial factor that accounted for the retarded growth of Irish musical life — the comparative absence of patronage or adequate public support for native musical ventures. Robinson roundly condemned 'the utter indifference shown by the aristocracy and wealthy mercantile class of this city in the advancement of musical art in Ireland' — a remark which clearly suggests that he did not hold a very high opinion of his fellow Anglo-Irish and regarded most of them as philistines. He concluded his riposte with the contention: 'Until these causes disappear, we cannot expect that either patriotism, which is satisfied with brass bands, or an *entente cordiale* between the musical authorities, which exists scarcely anywhere, will remove this reproach.'[5]

The Royal Irish Academy of Music, in which Esposito was to take up his teaching post, was still a fairly young institution, having been founded in 1848. Like many or even most Irish institutions at this period, it was set up by prominent representatives of the Anglo-Irish ruling class and largely reflected its ethos. Although the RIAM's teaching staff was not large and, for obvious reasons, it could hardly hope to compare with larger conservatoires on the continent in terms of resources and prestige, it nonetheless provided some of the best instrumental and vocal tuition that was available in the country. Some of the most notable Irish musicians of the day had been employed there — including Joseph Robinson and the composer Sir Robert Prescott Stewart — but by the time Esposito was appointed, their influence was on the wane.[6] In their desire to appoint the most able teachers, the institution's management began to appoint foreigners, mostly Germans or Italians. Caracciolo was offered a post in 1876 and Carl Lauer, a professor of violin, joined the staff in 1877. Esposito's appointment clearly continued this trend which was maintained throughout the 1880s and resulted in a fairly cosmopolitan staff that contributed notably to musical activity in the city. The young Italian thus took up his post at a time when the institution was undergoing considerable change. During the 1870s and 1880s its managerial structures were radically overhauled to function on a more democratic basis and a concerted effort was made to provide tuition to students from less privileged backgrounds. From 1882, the RIAM's finances improved due to bequests and royal patronage, which made it feasible to offer new scholarships;[7] and when the Royal

5   Letter to the Editor from Joseph Robinson, 24 October 1886, *Musical Times*, 27, 525 (1886), 677–78
6   John F. Larchet, remarked that Esposito took up his post at a time when, 'with the waning powers of Joseph Robinson ... and Sir Robert Stewart, the old order was passing': see Larchet, 'Michele Esposito', 430.
7   See Pine and Acton, *To Talent Alone*, 109ff.

College of Music was founded in London in 1883, an institution designed to serve the whole of the United Kingdom and the British Empire, it became possible for particularly talented Irish students to enrol there for courses of more advanced study.

Esposito gave his inaugural piano recital at the RIAM on 13 June 1882. The programme was almost the same as his last Parisian recital, and was clearly intended to demonstrate his talents as a pianist and composer. By all accounts, the event went very well. From a notice in the *Musical Times* (which described him as an 'able executant') we learn that he played from memory five compositions of his own (his *Capriccio*, Op. 11; his recently published *Tre pezzi*, Op. 26; and the *Allegro appassionato* from the Op. 7 collection), an unidentified nocturne and the A flat Polonaise by Chopin, Beethoven's *Waldstein* Sonata, in addition to compositions by Rameau and Schumann.[8] The Dublin audience and critics were impressed by his pianistic talent, but his extrovert style of performance evidently took some by surprise:

> There was a crowded audience. Signor Esposito comes from the land of song being an Italian. He proved himself an artist of vast technical power and of high accomplishments. He played from memory twelve long pieces. Five of these were compositions of his own .... His technical powers seem adequate to any difficulties. His scale-playing and octave-playing with both hands are perfect. His phrasing is very finished, and he can play — when he so wills — with a delicacy that could of itself hush an audience into silent listening. But we must be pardoned for hinting that we think his double *fortes* pass beyond the limit of human expression, and tend to become a noise. Indeed, extreme force of this sort is a characteristic of his style. Precedent for this style may be sought in the occasional mannerisms of some princely artists — even Rubinstein — but we venture to think the direction is a wrong one in which to go. There is a limit to the powers of the pianoforte. The player should not try to wring out of it effects like those of a great organ or a band of a hundred performers. Force of idea, depth of sentiment, richness of counterpoint, exquisite phrasing, are its real sources of power. Even a treble *forte* should be attained without giving the ear the slightest blow — and to borrow a comparison from another art – has not Doré, the painter, infused immense expression into very small pictures? Bating this peculiarity, the Signor's [sic] playing was beyond question masterly.[9]

The concert was also reviewed in the *Archivio musicale*: his former Italian colleagues were clearly curious to hear news of his latest activities.

Although we have no precise information on the subject, Esposito evidently found his post sufficiently congenial to want to stay in Dublin, and his temporary contract was

8   *Musical Times*, 23, 473 (1882), 401
9   *Freeman's Journal*, 15 June 1882

duly extended. His reputation grew rapidly and he was much sought after as a teacher. In addition to working at the RIAM (which by 1889 brought in about £175 per annum),[10] he supplemented his income by taking students at several Dublin schools, including Blackrock College and Alexandra College. Of the other pianists on the RIAM staff, only the reputedly brilliant but eccentric Alexandre Billet possessed abilities comparable to his own. However, Billet was already sixty-five years of age when Esposito came to Dublin and he seems to have felt rather eclipsed by his younger and dynamic colleague, who in a comparatively short time had succeeded in establishing himself as the city's leading piano teacher.[11] Apart from Billet, however, he evidently succeeded in winning the respect and confidence of his colleagues, as he was appointed to the RIAM Board of Studies in 1883,[12] but was also elected to represent the Professors on the Board of Governors of the institution in May 1888.[13] Interestingly, on the latter occasion, the other principal contender for the position was none other than Joseph Robinson. This event provided a striking indication of the extent to which the balance of power within the institution had shifted in favour of the young guard. Although Robinson's defeat generated a certain amount of acrimony, Esposito nonetheless held this position until 1911.[14]

As a teacher, Esposito seems to have been admired and liked by his students, even if they found him somewhat intimidating. He generally shared his teaching with an assistant, to whom he delegated the responsibility for the initial preparation of pieces with students (such as deciding on fingering and ensuring basic fidelity to the musical text), in addition to the study of technical exercises. The underlying rationale for this system was to spare Esposito a certain amount of drudge and to allow him to concentrate on musical interpretation at a higher level.[15] At the lesson, Esposito took up his position at his own Érard piano, next to that of his pupil, interrupting the student if necessary to demonstrate a point. By all accounts, his lessons were highly stimulating and rewarding. The Irish composer Frederick May, who studied with him for a time, recalled his former teacher as 'much more than a mere pianoforte professor':

> He was a great musical scholar, besides being a fine conductor and a distinguished
> composer, so that lessons from him were a liberal education in music. His beetling

10 Pine and Acton, *To Talent Alone*, 153
11 This seems to be confirmed by a letter Billet sent to the RIAM Board of Governors in which, without mentioning any names, he complained of being undermined and that 'everything has been done to diminish my influence ... ': see Pine and Acton, *To Talent Alone*, 257–58. It appears that students were reluctant to study with him — perhaps because of his eccentric manner. Billet's relationship with the management seems to have deteriorated progressively, and he was eventually pensioned off on grounds of ill-health in 1894.
12 *Freeman's Journal*, 24 February 1883
13 Pine and Acton, *To Talent Alone*, 162
14 Pine and Acton, *To Talent Alone*, 162
15 Enid Starkie, *A Lady's Child* (London, 1941), 237

eyebrows, hawk-like eyes and bushy moustache concealed a kindly nature, although he could be abrupt and sarcastic at times. He was steeped in the literature as well as the music of his homeland, and his eyes always softened when he spoke of the great Italian poets, particularly Dante, whose *Divine Comedy* he regarded as the greatest book ever written. He managed to spare the time too to look through and advise on the juvenile efforts of a young would-be composer, and I remember his somewhat sardonic answer to a query as to whether or not they showed any promise of future development. 'Some develop early, some develop late, and some never develop.' Although he lived in Ireland for so long, his English always remained strongly idiomatic ... [16]

The distinguished Oxford academic Enid Starkie, who later gained international renown for her biographies of Rimbaud and Flaubert, studied as a young girl with Esposito at the RIAM and left a vivid account of these lessons in her autobiography *A Lady's Child*:

He was a very fine musician, probably the finest musician whose services Ireland has ever enjoyed .... I used to feel very nervous when I went for my lesson with him and I never learned to grow out of this fear. There was a second piano in his teaching room, a grand piano, an Érard, his own property, and on this he played in unison with us as we played on the practice piano. This was a nerve-racking experience, and I was always afraid of not being able to keep up with him in the difficult passages and of dropping out of what always seemed to me a contest. When we muddled a run or struck a wrong note he used to open his mouth wide, and horrible sounds gushed out from the back of his throat, as if he were gargling. 'Grrr! Grrr! Stop! Stop! Basta!' he used to roar, banging his hands down on the notes of the piano and making us jump from the music stool with terror. 'Grrr! Grrr! You play ze sentimento but you cannot play ze notes!'[17]

Esposito, though kind-hearted, did not suffer fools gladly and was prone to wild outbursts of temper during lessons. Starkie recalled him as volatile and unpredictable:

We never knew in what mood we were going to find him. Sometimes he was in a gentle and melancholy mood, and then he played with devastating sadness on his own piano and we were inspired to play better than usual, or rather we did not know but that these lovely sounds came from our piano as well as from his Érard. Sometimes everything would go wrong and he would bang loudly on the piano from the very first notes and then get up and stamp round the room in anger. Sometimes, with apparent patience, frigid patience, he would set about explaining everything from the very

16   Frederick May, untitled reminiscences, in Pine and Action, *To Talent Alone*, 391–92
17   Starkie, *A Lady's Child*, 238

beginning, as if to a child just starting music, and I much preferred his open anger to this layer of ice over the boiling lava of the Vesuvius of his native province.

I feared more than anything else the moment when Esposito began to explain everything from the very beginning. I can remember one occasion in particular, when he was in a nasty temper, and he humiliated me with sadistic pleasure. I was then learning the *Liebestraum* of Liszt, and in those adolescent days I thought it beautiful. That day I was playing it with what I thought was deep feeling and emotion, but had I looked over at Esposito I would have seen the sarcastic expression on his face. I thought that I was doing very well indeed, for he was allowing me to play to the end, not stopping me every few bars as he usually did, and he was encouraging me on his piano to further sentimental expression. In my foolish youthful pride I imagined that I was interesting him, and that he was pleased with me, that in fact my playing was moving him, and I laid on the sentiment and the emotion more and more thickly. As I ended I had tears in my own eyes, so touched was I by my playing. When I had played the last chord I looked over at him, expecting approbation, but I only saw on his face an expression of extreme disgust. 'That was beeootifool! Veramente bellissima! Beeootifool!' he said, in exaggerated, mock-admiring tones, looking at me with his most ironic expression, the expression which always made me squirm. I have rarely felt as small as I felt that afternoon, as coarse and vulgar in my emotions. For weeks after that I did not dare ask for anything except Bach, Czerny, or Haydn to study, works into which I could put no romantic expression.[18]

A former student, Thomas Weaving, also recalled how sharp-tongued he could be. On one occasion, a particularly unresponsive pupil wished him a happy Christmas. Esposito retorted: 'I don't wish you a happy Christmas! You've played the same music all this term and it's got worse and worse. Next term you go to the third grade if you do no better.'[19] His manifestations of displeasure were not confined to sarcasm. After hearing a hapless pupil mangle a work by Brahms, he went over to a portrait of the composer which was hanging above the mantelpiece, turned it around to face the wall, and said nothing. In the case of yet another, whose rhythmic sense seems to have left much to be desired, he eventually resorted to beating time violently with a poker.[20] He did not mellow with age. Many years later, when adjudicating for the Sligo Feis Ceoil, he was asked to judge a class of flute bands. After sitting through several hours of hideous cacophony, he announced in his idiosyncratic English: 'I am giving zis prize, not for ze best band, but for ze band zat was ze least worst.' Such a comment risked provoking an outcry from the audience, but

18 Starkie, *A Lady's Child*, 238–39
19 *Irish Times*, 8 October 1956
20 Pine and Acton, *To Talent Alone*, 20

clearly its forbearance had also been stretched to the limit and his forthright comments were received with loud applause.[21] Yet, for all his irascibility, he was greatly respected. The Lurgan-born composer and pedagogue Annie Patterson remarked of him: 'He is the soul of energy and verveful activity and invariably infects even the laziest and most apathetic.'[22] Hamilton Harty, who revered him, remembered him as a man who seemed incapable of mincing his words:

> It was his uncompromising, almost brutal truthfulness which offended a great many who were too petty to appreciate the uprightness and nobility of his character. But, on the other hand, it was that very quality which appealed most strongly to his best friends, and which they revered in him. It was impossible for him to say the thing that wasn't true, even when it would have been most strongly to his advantage to do so. His occasional attempts to be 'diplomatic' and yet perfectly honest were ludicrously unsuccessful. He had a passion for 'telling the truth'.[23]

Harty recalled one particularly striking instance of his teacher's fearless honesty when he went backstage after a concert given by the great Polish pianist Paderewski in Dublin:

> Esposito came to the artists' room to pay his sincere homage to the master pianist. But it was evident there was something on his mind. Finally he could bear it no longer. 'You know,' he said with pathetic craftiness, 'my pupils *always* play a wrong note in that Étude of Chopin and — and — *so do you!*' Paderewski denied the charge with laughing warmth, but, being a great gentleman as well as a great artist, immediately sent for a copy of the piece. But, as usual, Esposito was perfectly right (though the matter was only a trifling one at the most), and the incident ended with a riotously gay dinner party and the strengthening of this deep regard felt by each artist for the other.[24]

In spite of extensive teaching commitments that consumed much of his time and energies, Esposito remained constantly active as a performer. Not long after arriving in Dublin, he took part in a benefit concert for the soprano Elizabeth Scott-Fennell, a colleague at the RIAM who was well known for her performances of Irish airs.[25] Before long, local musicians and performing groups began to invite him to participate in other events. In April 1883, Esposito organized a solo recital in the Antient Concert Rooms, in which Caracciolo, Scott-Fennell and another Dublin vocalist, Walter Bapty made guest

21 *Irish Times*, 31 October 1931
22 *Weekly Irish Times*, 20 April 1901
23 Hamilton Harty, 'Michele Esposito', *The Irish Statesman*, 7 December 1929, 276–77
24 Harty, 'Michele Esposito', 277. Paderewski visited Dublin in 1894 and 1895, and again in October 1902.
25 *Freeman's Journal*, 16 June 1882

appearances. Like his inaugural recital at the RIAM, this was also very well received. The reviewer for the *Freeman's Journal* declared that the Italian 'displayed the power and finish of a master', and noted that he drew 'hearty plaudits from the audience at the end of each piece'.[26] Such solo recitals, supported by colleagues from the RIAM, thereafter became an annual event. He gave readily of his services for fundraising concerts in aid of charitable causes — and continued to do so for the rest of his career. It is not known how regularly he performed outside Dublin, but he appeared to have received occasional invitations to other Irish cities — including one to appear as soloist in the Mendelssohn Piano Concerto in G minor with 'Mr Cohen's Orchestra' in Belfast in February 1884.[27] He also gave public concerts at the Antient Concert Rooms under the patronage of aristocrats such as Lady Power, Countess of Granard and the Baroness de Cussy,[28] and he would often appear as soloist in prominent charity events, such as one organized under the patronage of the Duchess of Carnarvon and the Princess of Saxe Weimar to raise funds for St Patrick's Home for Nurses.[29]

In July 1885, he had the opportunity to give a joint recital in Dublin with his former teacher Benjamino Cesi, who had just returned from a tour of Russia (where he would soon return to live) and was now making a tour of Britain and Ireland. The duo works on the programme included Saint-Saëns's *Variations on a Theme of Beethoven* and a transcription of the same composer's *Danse macabre*. Cesi performed solos by Scarlatti, Handel and Chopin, as well as his own arrangement of the minuet from Thomas's *Mignon* and Thalberg's *Variations sur L'Elisir d'amore*.[30]

Encouraged perhaps by the success of this and other recent public appearances, Esposito gradually expanded the range of his performing activities and organized a series of chamber music concerts. The first of these took place on 1 February 1886 in the Antient Concert Rooms, on which occasion he was joined by his RIAM colleagues Lauer, Griffith and Rudersdorff. The programme, which made no concessions to popular taste, consisted of Raff's Piano Trio in C minor, Op. 102, and Brahms's Piano Quartet in A major, Op. 26. The music of Brahms was relatively unfamiliar in Ireland at the time, and some audience members evidently found the Piano Quartet rather forbidding. The reviewer for the *Freeman's Journal* remarked: 'It is somewhat long, and some passages in it are far from being easy of comprehension, and would require from the ordinary hearer more than one hearing to grasp and properly appreciate their beauty.'[31] The programmes

26 *Freeman's Journal*, 21 April 1883
27 *The Belfast News-Letter*, 23 February 1884. In later years Esposito would visit Belfast to contribute to Edwyn Wolseley's 'Ballad Concerts' at the Ulster Hall in collaboration with Collison, and he was often invited to act as accompanist for instrumentalists at solo recitals: see, for example, *Musical Times*, 43, 708 (1902), 118, for a notice of concert that he gave with the violinist Montagu-Nathan on 10 January 1902.
28 *Freeman's Journal*, 10 and 12 April 1884
29 *Freeman's Journal*, 10 December 1885
30 *Freeman's Journal*, 3 July 1885
31 *Freeman's Journal*, 2 February 1886

for the two subsequent concerts were equally substantial and included piano trios and quartets by Mozart, Beethoven, Schubert, Mendelssohn and Schumann, as well as two works by contemporary composers — Saint-Saëns's Piano Trio in B flat and Rubinstein's Violin Sonata.

Opportunities for him to present further concerts of this nature were greatly increased by a significant development in 1886, when the Royal Dublin Society (RDS), a body established in 1731 to further the growth of agriculture, science and industry, extended its patronage to music and decided to inaugurate a series of 'popular recitals'. It was envisaged that these should promote chamber music — a form of music-making with which Dublin audiences had only a limited familiarity — and a sum of money 'not exceeding £100 and the proceeds of the sale of tickets' was set aside to cover costs.[32] Committees to oversee this new venture were duly appointed and plans were laid. It was decided to hold the concerts in the Society's Lecture Theatre in Leinster House, Kildare Street, and to present them as a weekly series over a period of about two months. Members of the Society were to be admitted free (as were students of the RIAM sometimes),[33] and the price for tickets for the general public was fixed at two shillings. Thereafter, matters progressed swiftly and the inaugural concert in the series took place on 22 March 1886.

In organizing this venture, the committee relied heavily on the advice of Esposito to devise programmes and engage artists. He was naturally invited to participate as a performer: in addition to giving solo recitals, he also gave programmes of chamber music with colleagues from the RIAM in the first and in subsequent series. This arrangement had several advantages. Not least, it provided a platform for these musicians to perform rewarding repertoire of this nature, since similar outlets for their talents were in fairly short supply. It also allowed them to evolve a distinctive performing style and to develop as an ensemble. The programmes on these occasions generally consisted of a chamber work without piano, a larger work with piano (such as a piano trio, quartet or quintet), and a sonata for solo violin or cello with piano. This pattern was established as early as the second concert, when Mozart's Quartet K. 464 in A was given together with Beethoven's Violin, Op. 30/2 in C minor, and Schubert's late Piano Trio in B flat.

The enterprise also had an educational dimension: pre-concert talks (as we would now call them) were given by Arthur Patton and the brilliant polymath John Pentland Mahaffy (who, in addition to his other areas of expertise, also held a doctorate in music) to large audiences of four hundred or more. An article that appeared in the *Freeman's Journal* after the first concert stressed the important role the series could play in raising the general level of musical taste:

32 Hughes, 'The Society and Music', 265
33 Pine and Acton, *To Talent Alone*, 214

... the true art of music is in sore want of such assistance. All the public efforts which have been hitherto made ... have been directed to training *performers*. But it is quite as essential that we, the hearers, should receive training too, until at least we become able to distinguish that which is best in the art when it is placed before us; and further, it is most desirable there should be an adequate exhibition to the public of the noblest productions with which the world has been endowed by its most gifted composers.[34]

The first series of RDS concerts was a resounding success and undoubtedly represented an event of landmark significance in the musical life of Dublin. So popular did the concerts prove that it was proposed to put on two further series in the autumn of 1886 and spring of 1887. As the introductory talks had also proved popular, suggesting that audience members were genuinely eager to learn something about the works being performed, Robert Prescott Stewart was asked to provide analytical notes (in the manner of Grove's programme notes for the Crystal Palace concerts in London) for the recitals between January and March 1887. Even more gratifyingly, some members of the general public requested that works be given more than once, to allow listeners to assimilate them more completely. The Committee readily acquiesced in this proposal and from November 1887 programmes given on a Monday evening were repeated the following Monday afternoon. This practice continued for some years.[35]

The concerts presented by Esposito and his colleagues for the remainder of the decade featured an impressively wide range of music, ensuring that the RDS series could bear favourable comparison with similar concert series in London at the period, such as those organized by Edward Dannreuther.[36] In addition to standard repertoire by composers of the Classical and early Romantic eras, the programmes included much music by living composers such as Brahms, Rubinstein, Grieg, Stanford and Saint-Saëns, as well as others whose names are less well-known today. Interestingly, some of this modern repertoire, such as the Brahms violin sonatas, proved so appealing to audiences that it even came to be programmed by popular request.

The sheer quantity of music that Esposito performed during these years is an eloquent testimony to his exceptional ability to assimilate scores rapidly, and to judge from contemporary accounts, the standard of his playing seems to have been consistently high. His remarkable talents did not go unnoticed by audiences and critics, and engendered something approaching hero-worship. His Beethoven playing was particularly admired: a

34 *Freeman's Journal*, 23 March 1886
35 Hughes, 'The Society and Music', 266
36 See Dibble, 'Edward Dannreuther and the Orme Square Phenomenon', in Bashford, Christina and Langley, Leanne, eds., *Music and British Culture, 1785–1914: Essays in honour of Cyril Ehrlich* (Oxford, 2000), 275–98.

performance of the Beethoven A major Cello Sonata that he gave in 1889 with Rudersdorff, for example, was described as being 'in a manner which might almost be said to be unrivalled.'[37] The reviewer on this occasion also remarked on the enduring popularity of these recitals, noting that they continued 'to attract an assemblage of musical amateurs that overcrowds the little theatre of the Institution every Monday'.[38]

The winter series of 1889 featured three solo piano recitals by Esposito with enterprising programmes that included a selection of pieces by Rameau, Couperin, Frescobaldi, Grazioli and Scarlatti, in addition to more standard repertoire such as Schumann's *Carnival*, Beethoven's Sonata in E flat, Op. 31/3, and shorter works by Chopin. The compositions by Italian Baroque composers were performed in transcriptions by his former teacher Cesi, who had played a prominent role in reviving interest in the keyboard works of Frescobaldi, Galuppi and other neglected figures from this era. The concert met once again with an exceptionally positive reception from the Dublin critics. Much of the music was unfamiliar to them — even Schumann's *Carnival* — but they clearly found the concerts highly enjoyable. The reviewer for the *Freeman's Journal* noted enthusiastically: 'Signor Esposito's playing of all this excessively difficult music was masterly. Not a blemish or imperfection shadowed his performance throughout.'[39]

Esposito's solo recitals in 1889 proved so popular that he was asked to give another series of three programmes the following year (which, because of the established practice of repeats, amounted to six concerts) between 20 October and 24 November 1890. In the same manner as before, he commenced each concert with items of early keyboard music. The first featured Bach's *Chromatic Fantasy and Fugue* and an *Allegro con fuoco* by Paradisi; the second included Handel's popular *Air with Variations* (nicknamed 'The Harmonious Blacksmith'), Couperin's *L'Ausonienne* and Rameau's *Le Tambourin*; while the third introduced further works edited by Cesi, including an *Adagio in D* by Galuppi and Scarlatti's *Fuga del gatto* [Cat's Fugue]. The central item of each programme was a piano sonata — respectively, Weber's Sonata in A flat, Op. 39, and Beethoven's *Appassionata* and *Les Adieux* sonatas — and they concluded with works from the Romantic era by Chopin, Mendelssohn, Liszt (some of his Schubert *Lieder* transcriptions) and Schumann.

By 1890 Esposito had established himself as a leading figure in Dublin musical life, which had already been greatly enriched by his artistic initiatives. It would be interesting to know more about his personal circumstances and inner life during this period, but as so little of his correspondence has survived, information of this nature is almost entirely lacking. He and his wife seem to have enjoyed a good standard of living, judging from the fact that they could afford to employ servants.[40] Nor do they seem to have experienced

37 *Irish Times*, 5 February 1889
38 *Irish Times*, 5 February 1889
39 *Freeman's Journal*, 12 November 1889
40 Watton, *Michele Esposito*, 8

difficulty in making friends, as Natalia maintained a salon which was frequented by writers, musicians and other prominent members of Dublin society. From the few anecdotes which have come down to us, Esposito's wife appears to have been a rather colourful figure and was evidently rather formidable. She insisted on being addressed as 'Madame' and according to her son Mario was an atheist, 'indifferent — even hostile — to religion', no doubt occasioning much scandalized comment on this account. [41] In the course of the 1880s, they had three more children: a second daughter Vera was born on 13 September 1883; Mario, their only son, on 7 September 1887, and Nina, a third daughter, on 2 January 1890.[42] The children grew up speaking English, Italian and French.[43] The three daughters were later educated privately at Alexandra College. Mario seems to have been a remarkably precocious child: his mother, whose philosophical sympathies evidently inclined towards materialism, strongly encouraged his interest in science, even going so far as to install a small laboratory in the house, and generally did everything she could to foster his intellectual development. In a letter of 1959 to the Belgian medievalist Hubert Silvestre, Mario recalled discussions with her about the writings of figures such as Voltaire, Comte and Darwin, and receiving a present at the age of eleven of Alexander von Humboldt's celebrated five-volume *magnum opus* on the natural sciences, *Kosmos: Entwurf einer physischen Weltbeschreibung*.[44] In his teens, however, Mario's interests turned towards philology, under the influence of M. R. Best, a young Celtic philologist who worked in the National Library, and he went on to become a leading expert on the corpus of Latin literature written in Ireland during the Middle Ages. Despite the foreign origins of both their parents, there is no indication that the Esposito children experienced any difficulty in integrating socially, and they quickly grew accustomed to the habitual mispronunciation of their surname by Dubliners who erroneously accented its third syllable (the correct stress is on the second).[45]

In the absence of any definite information, it is difficult to account for the fact that Esposito virtually stopped composing for about fifteen years after moving to Dublin. Between 1887 and 1892 or thereabouts, a slender trickle of works emerged from his pen, all of them for piano: the *Scherzo* in E flat minor, Op. 28, the *Due pezzi*, Op. 29, the *Quattro bozzetti* [Four Sketches], Op. 30, and the two sets of *Progressive Studies* which constitute Op. 31, all of which were brought out by the Dublin publishing and piano manufacturing firm of Pohlmann. Thereafter, he virtually stopped composing again for five years. All of these pieces are of comparatively minor importance. The Op. 28 *Scherzo* reflects Chopin's

41 Silvestre, 'Mario Esposito', 7
42 Sometimes 1891 is given as the year of Mario's birth, but it would seem that Mario was wont to lie about his age: see his letter of 24 October 1958 to Hubert Silvestre, which is quoted in the Epilogue. Elsewhere, Mario confirmed the date of 1887: see Gorman, 'Mario Esposito', 300n.
43 Gorman, *Mario Esposito*, 302
44 Letter from Mario Esposito to Hubert Silvestre, 6 February 1959, reproduced in Silvestre, 'Mario Esposito', 6–7
45 Pine and Acton, *To Talent Alone*, 196

influence not only in its virtuosic style of keyboard writing, which is replete with rapid passagework and chromatic scales in thirds and double octaves, but also in the metrical ambiguity and wide tonal range of the outer sections. The work has a ternary structure, with an expansive central trio. Here Esposito introduces three strains of melody leading to the dominant which are then suffixed by two thematic fragments (designated 'x' and 'y' in Ex. 20), the latter derived from the opening material of the work. The two pieces of Op. 29 are more lighthearted in character, consisting of a dance-like *Serenata* [Serenade] and a sparklingly virtuosic *Impromptu* which has a musette-like trio in the tonic minor.

Ex. 20: *Scherzo*, Op. 28, trio section

The *Quattro bozzetti*, Op. 30, were probably composed as pedagogical pieces and may even have been intended for Esposito's more advanced pupils. The first piece, *Andantino con moto*, evokes a gondolier's song, the barcarolle-like rhythms of the left hand supporting a singing melody in the right laden with decorative acciaccaturas. The rich harmonies of the piece may reflect the influence of the composer's French contemporaries, especially Fauré: indeed, the third sketch in E major recalls the *Berceuse* from the latter's *Dolly Suite*. The second piece is an animated study in neo-Bachian style, while the last is a quick waltz. The *Progressive Studies in Two Books*, Op. 31, were modelled on the kinds of technical exercises which Esposito had practised during his period of study in Naples, such as those of Czerny.[46]

During the 1890s, Esposito maintained the intense performing activity of the preceding decade, which continued to expand in scope. Encouraged perhaps by the success of his solo concerts in Dublin, he organized to give a recital at the Prince's Hall in London on 8 July 1891. He chose a demanding programme, which included Schumann's *Études symphoniques* and Beethoven's Sonata in C minor, Op. 111, and was joined by the violinist Guido Papini for what was probably the premiere of his First Violin Sonata, written in Paris ten years before. The reviews of the London critics confirm that the high esteem in which Esposito was held by their Dublin counterparts was by no means unjustified. The critic for *The Times* (who was probably Fuller-Maitland) wrote a highly appreciative notice:

> Signor Michele Esposito, an accomplished pianist, gave a recital of more than usual interest on Wednesday afternoon in Prince's Hall. Scarcely a single item of his programme could be called hackneyed. Schumann's *Études symphoniques* have, it is true, been heard almost incessantly this season; it is curious to look back at their composer's own low estimate of their fitness for public performance. They were thoughtfully and correctly played in strict and most unusual agreement with the earlier version. Beethoven's sonata op. 111 was given with such intelligence and feeling, and in the beautiful arietta great charm of style was shown. A graceful minuet by Grazioli, and a gigue by Scarlatti which must have been new to most hearers, succeeded the familiar and delightful variations of Handel in D minor; both the former were edited, with a good deal of respect, by Signor B. Cesi. In a melodious violin sonata of his own the player was assisted by Signor Papini. A pretty berceuse, also by Signor Esposito, was not so enthusiastically received by the audience as a less original piece by C. Albanesi, which was encored. The recital closed with a fine performance of Chopin's etude in C minor, the arpeggio study in the second set, a work most rarely heard.[47]

Also in the audience was George Grove, who was struck by the grace and elegance of the Italian's playing:

> I looked in at Esposito's recital three or four days ago. He is the chief piano-teacher at Dublin — an Italian, and I must say he pleased me very much. I heard him play a sonata of his own for violin and P., and the first 2 of the Symphonic Etudes of

---

46 Esposito evidently thought sufficiently highly of Czerny's studies to prepare his own edition of some of them, which was published in 1896 by Piggott.
47 'Signor Esposito's Recital', *The Times*, 10 July 1891

Schumann's. The sonata was full of reminiscences, but very nice to hear, and somehow the Italians have (if not the tremendous technique of Paderewski and other Germans or allies of Germans) a grace and love of beauty *and care for their hearers*, that is very dear to me, and that seems to be fast going out of the piano-playing world. It is very like the difference between Tolstoi and Tourguénieff [Turgenev]. Tolstoi may be more terribly in earnest, but Tourguénieff is the greater and sweeter artist ... .[48]

Papini's appearance on the platform with Esposito on this occasion was by no means an isolated occurrence. The violinist had been a regular participant in the RDS series since their second season, travelling over from London for the concerts. His presence added considerable lustre to the series, as he had an international reputation and worked regularly with some of the greatest instrumentalists of the age, including Hans von Bülow and Anton Rubinstein. He was by all accounts a superb, if somewhat variable performer: Enid Starkie's brother Walter described him as 'an erratic genius', who 'produced a golden tone from his Cremona violin and in his style laid stress on all that was emotional in the music'.[49] Esposito and he clearly had an excellent musical rapport and their appearances as a duo were greeted with special pleasure by the RDS audiences. The critic of the *Irish Times* remarked apropos of a concert held on 2 December 1889:

> Signor Papini is such a general favourite amongst us that the hearty welcome which he received on this his first appearance for the season, was only what we would have expected; and Signor Esposito, whose brilliant performance in his recent pianoforte recitals will not soon be forgotten, has his full share of greeting also.[50]

It was to Papini that Esposito dedicated his First Violin Sonata, Op. 32, and the two men gave the work its Irish premiere at the Dublin Arts Club at 6, St Stephen's Green on 21 April 1894, to which the *Freeman's Journal* devoted a special column.[51] The same newspaper (and probably the same critic) later described the Italian duo as 'Papini the ever-beautiful, Esposito the never-failing'.[52]

In the early 1890s, Papini began to suffer from problems with his health and was eventually prevailed upon to accept a teaching position at the RIAM in 1893 by Esposito,

48 Charles Larcom Graves, *Life of Sir George Grove* (London, 1903), 374. In performing at Prince's Hall, Esposito followed Cesi and Papini who had given a series of concerts there in the summer of 1886: see *Musical Times*, 26, 510 (1885), 480–81 and 27, 522 (1886), 475.

49 Walter Starkie, 'What the Royal Dublin Society has Done for Music', *Royal Dublin Society Bi-Centenary Souvenir 1731–1931* (Dublin, 1931) 61

50 *Irish Times*, 3 December 1889

51 See *Freeman's Journal*, 23 April 1894. The work was performed by the same men for the Leinster Section of the ISM in May 1894 and was given its first hearing at the RDS on 2 March 1896.

52 *Freeman's Journal*, 5 March 1895

who perhaps hoped that a more settled lifestyle might prove conducive to his friend's recovery.[53] Initially, Papini's classes were accounted a great success, but he seems to have quickly lost interest in teaching and increasingly delegated his classes to deputies while he absented himself to fulfil performing engagements abroad. His negligence engendered much dissatisfaction amongst the students and the situation became untenable: he eventually resigned in 1896 after only three years in the post.[54] He returned to London to live, but continued to appear with Esposito in the RDS concerts until 1900. Papini was responsible for bringing about another valuable — and more permanent — addition to the instrumental staff at the RIAM in 1892: the eminent cellist Henry Bast, whose international reputation and breadth of performing experience rivalled his own. It is not clear what induced Bast to accept a teaching post in Dublin, but the prospect of a regular salary may have constituted a sufficient incentive, just as it had done in Esposito's case. He was quickly co-opted to participate in the RDS concerts, and in addition to playing in string quartets, he regularly partnered Esposito in duo sonatas and prompted the Italian to write his only major work for cello in 1898.

The RDS concerts of the 1890s proceeded along similar lines to the earlier series. Much repertoire was naturally repeated, but the programmes continued to include challenging and unfamiliar repertoire by composers such as Rheinberger, Brahms, Rubinstein and Zipoli. The series continued to feature solo recitals by Esposito which made few, if any concessions to middlebrow tastes. His recitals for 1892 as usual featured a very wide range of repertoire, ranging all the way from the Baroque keyboard works to music by living composers. Amongst the works performed were Bach's *Italian Concerto*, Mozart's Fantasy and Fugue in C minor, K394; Beethoven's Op. 111; Schumann's G minor Sonata, Op. 22; and Mendelssohn's *Variations sérieuses*, in addition to music by Scarlatti, Brahms, Liszt and Rubinstein. The final recital of the season, which was given twice on 9 and 16 May 1892, was devoted entirely to the music of Chopin — a composer with whom Esposito was considered to have a special affinity.[55] The programme on this occasion included the B flat minor Sonata, Op. 35; the *Fantaisie* in F minor, Op. 49; the *Scherzo* in C sharp minor, Op. 39; the *Ballade* in G minor, Op. 23; and representative works from the smaller genres.

It was widely recognized that the Lecture Theatre in Leinster House was not an entirely suitable venue for the concerts, as the acoustics were unsatisfactory. Eventually, in 1893 it was decided to undertake extensive remodelling of the interior to effect various improvements. For three years, until 1896, the concerts were consequently held in other venues around the city. Esposito opened the following season with a series of piano recitals in the old library of Leinster House, but this proved far from ideal — the chairs creaked, the space was cramped and it proved very uncomfortable for the audience. The committee

53   Henderson, 'Guido Papini', 234–35
54   Pine and Acton, *To Talent Alone*, 255 and 459
55   *Irish Times*, 22 November 1898

members decided to move the subsequent chamber concerts to a more capacious venue. They settled on the hall of the Royal University in Earlsfort Terrace, but the space there was found to be too cold (a problem exacerbated by inclement weather) and insufficiently intimate for chamber music. As one critic complained, 'All Signor Esposito's undoubted qualities of finish and clearness were lost. The audience, though a fairly numerous one, looked small in the big room, and nobody sat in the gallery.'[56] Finally, the RDS managed to obtain the Royal University's library, which proved more comfortable both for performers and audience, before relocating subsequently to the Council Room of Leinster House. During this time, despite the constant disturbance of routine, the concerts retained an enthusiastic following and were, as the critic of the *Musical Times* noted, 'now so sought for that it is very difficult to obtain admittance'.[57] When the concerts finally resumed in their traditional venue — the first took place on 15 March 1897 — the acoustics were found to be excellent and the space much more comfortable.[58]

From the mid-1890s, Esposito increasingly invited eminent foreign artists to take part in the series, in an effort to boost takings at the box office and also to introduce a greater variety of personnel. In February 1896, for example, the Belgian virtuoso and pupil of Moscheles and Liszt, Arthur de Greef, gave three recitals at Leinster House which included works by Beethoven, Schumann and Chopin. This trend of inviting non-resident musicians would become more marked after 1900. The concerts' programmes continued, as before, to feature standard works from the Classical and Romantic periods, interspersed with a considerable variety of new works such as Arensky's Piano Trio, Mackenzie's Piano Quartet, and Piano Quintets by Dvořák, César Franck, Saint-Saëns and Goldmark.

Esposito's workload at the RIAM increased significantly during this decade. In addition to his usual teaching duties, he took the initiative in setting up a new system of external grade examinations, along similar lines to the ones introduced a few years previously in 1889 by the Associated Board of the Royal Schools of Music. In 1892, a committee was formed to investigate the feasibility of such a venture. By May of the following year, matters had progressed to the point where teachers at the RIAM were requested to submit appropriate pieces for examinations of five grades.[59] Esposito naturally undertook the responsibility for devising the syllabus for the examinations in piano. The syllabi were approved in November 1893 and a prospectus published in January 1894. To begin with, these external examinations were held only in Dublin, but the scheme expanded to other centres in Galway and Belfast. As Esposito taught at many convent schools (where

56 *Freeman's Journal*, 19 December 1893

57 *Musical Times*, 37, 635 (1896), 39

58 The first concert of the 1896 season had to be given in the Library because the Lecture Theatre was not yet ready.

59 For an account of the development of the RIAM local centre examinations during Esposito's time in the RIAM, see Brian Beckett, 'Tested Teaching: The Local Centre Examination System, 1894–1994', in Pine and Acton, *To Talent Alone*, 297ff.

considerable emphasis was placed on music within the curriculum), it was a comparatively easy matter to arrange for these to become the first examination centres. The Loretto Abbey Convent schools in Rathfarnham and Bray, the Loretto Convent, St Stephen's Green, Dublin and the Dominican Convent, Falls Road, Belfast were the first to become involved in this way.[60] In the early years, Esposito did almost all of the examining himself, but after the First World War the number of candidates increased to a point where he required assistance from colleagues.[61]

In 1893 another opportunity to expand his professional activities presented itself, one that would ultimately play an important part in leading him to resume composing. This was the foundation of an Irish chapter of the Incorporated Society of Musicians (ISM), a British organization established by James Dawber and Henry Hiles in 1882 to represent the interests of professional musicians and to foster educational initiatives of various kinds. At first, the ISM grew strongly in the north of England, with music teachers forming the bulk of its membership, but its prestige was greatly enhanced after a conference held in London in 1886, when its ranks were swelled by a number of influential musicians. In 1893 the Duke of Edinburgh became its president and it was proposed to expand its activities to Scotland and Ireland. On 13 September of that year, Esposito attended a meeting chaired by Sir Robert Prescott Stewart to consider the matter, and it was resolved to set up an Irish branch of the ISM immediately.[62] Before long, he was appointed the body's Irish representative — a position that brought him into contact with some of the most distinguished British musicians of the period.[63] He seems to have fulfilled his duties with his usual efficiency and zeal, conscious of the responsibility of his position. In January 1895, it was decided to hold the ISM's annual conference in Dublin and Esposito helped to organize a major concert for the event which acted as showcase for the RIAM and music-making in Dublin as a whole. On this occasion, he performed two of his own piano pieces (his *Berceuse*, Op. 21/1, and the *Allegretto*, Op. 5) and he contributed a *Scherzo fugoso* to an Irish *Toy Symphony* based on traditional airs, a collaborative effort specially composed for the occasion (the other movements were an *Adagio patetico* by James Cooksey Culwick, a set of 'Erin Variations' by T. R. G. Jozé and a *Stretta finale* by Joseph Smith). Many local performers took part, together with musicians from other chapters of the ISM, some playing on toy instruments of various kinds. Esposito's fugue was described as 'a brilliantly outrageous burlesque',[64] in which the composer himself performed on the '*tuba e tremolo*' [sic]. The

60   Watton, *Michele Esposito*, 55
61   Beckett, 'Tested Teaching', 299–300
62   *Freeman's Journal*, 14 September 1893. The Irish chapter was established in November 1893 together with divisions for Leinster, Ulster, Connacht and Munster. Esposito was elected for three years to the Irish council and for two years to the UK general council.
63   Esposito's first official engagement was to represent the ISM at the funeral of Sir Robert Stewart on 27 March 1894.
64   *Freeman's Journal*, 4 January 1895

conference was accounted a great success and provided a valuable opportunity to raise awareness of Irish talent outside the country.

The foundation of an Irish chapter of the ISM and the subsequent expansion of its activities during the 1890s occurred during a decade that witnessed a remarkable revitalization of national cultural life. As is well known, the talents of major literary figures such as W. B. Yeats, George Moore and Augusta Gregory came to increasing prominence at this period, while the selfless work of Douglas Hyde and his associates wrought a transformation in attitudes towards the Irish language and Gaelic culture generally. It was inevitable that these significant developments should stimulate discussion amongst leading Irish musicians, who were acutely aware of the comparative dearth of native compositional talent, and naturally wanted music to occupy a position of comparable prominence to Irish literature. Unfortunately very little detailed research has been carried out on the influence of the Gaelic and literary revivals on musical activity, or indeed on Irish composition of this period generally, but it does appear that there was a growing sense that more should be done to encourage the emergence of a native school of composers. One of the most prominent figures to articulate this view was Annie Patterson, who reiterated it tirelessly in her published writings. Patterson urged composers to seek inspiration in folk music in their efforts to formulate an Irish mode of musical utterance, holding that this was vital if 'a *new school* of composition which shall be distinct as possible' were to come into being — as she told her listeners at the 1901 Pan-Celtic Congress.[65] That she would advocate such a course of action was hardly surprising: the various nationalist schools of composition that had emerged in Eastern Europe only a few decades before had employed the folk music of their native countries with striking success and she no doubt hoped that it would lead to similar results in Ireland. At the same time, she was anxious to resist a rather narrow view that apparently prevailed in some quarters, which held that authentic 'Irish music' should adhere so closely to folk music as to consist of little more than arrangements of traditional airs. Other prominent musicians such as Herbert Hughes similarly opposed such a hopelessly restrictive attitude.[66]

Of Irish composers at the period, Charles Villiers Stanford was undoubtedly significant in suggesting what other possibilities might be open to the native composer in using folk music, although he lived in England and undoubtedly saw himself as being a British composer first and foremost, and an Irish one second. Stanford's own arrangements of Irish folk music, whatever objections may be raised against them on purist grounds, are nonetheless imaginative and skilful, and were highly popular in their day. He also

65 *Weekly Irish Times*, 7 September 1901
66 For a discussion of attitudes to folk music on the part of Irish composers at this period, see Patrick Zuk, 'Music and Nationalism', *Journal of Music in Ireland*, Vol. 2, No. 2, Jan/Feb 2002, 5–10 and Vol. 2, No. 3, Mar/Apr 2002, 25–30; and the same author's 'Music and Nationalism: The Debate Continues', *Journal of Music in Ireland*, Vol. 3, No. 5, Jul/Aug 2003, 12–21. See also Séamas de Barra, *Aloys Fleischmann* (Dublin, 2006), 47ff.

demonstrated how this repertory — or stylized evocations of it — could be used as the basis for more ambitious compositions. His *Irish Symphony* (1887) and the *Irish Rhapsody No. 1* (1901), together with other works such as the comic opera *Shamus O'Brien* (1892) were not only enormously successful, but were accepted by contemporary listeners as authentic expressions of 'Irishness', though they were completely rooted in the mainstream tradition of European art music. Several Irish composers of the next generation such as Charles Wood and Hamilton Harty had no hesitation in turning to Stanford's work for models for their own endeavours in a similar vein.

Patterson's campaign to effect practical improvements in Irish musical life and to promote the work of native composers played no small part in the establishment of the first Irish national music festival, An Feis Ceoil, in 1897. According to the syllabus for that year, the Feis aimed 'at the cultivation of Irish music, and its presentation to the public in a becoming manner', in addition to promoting 'the advancement of musical education and activity in Ireland generally, so as to regain for this country, if possible, its old eminence among musical nations'.[67] The programme of events consisted of concerts and lectures devoted to Irish traditional music, as well as competitions for singers and instrumentalists, classically trained and folk musicians alike. The first Feis was in the nature of a compromise, as there had been a considerable disagreement amongst members of its steering committee (who were largely drawn from the Gaelic League and the National Literary Society founded by Yeats in 1892) over the form that the festival should assume. A sizeable nationalist faction of a somewhat extreme cast wished the Feis to concentrate on traditional music to the exclusion of everything else. At the first public meeting of the Feis committee, which took place in the Mansion House in Dublin on 15 June 1896, Esposito and Patterson raised strenuous objections to this policy. Thanks to their persistent pressuring of their fellow committee members, the syllabus was eventually enlarged. With support from his RIAM colleague Edith Oldham, Esposito succeeded in introducing a composers competition, for which works could be submitted in different categories (cantatas, overtures, string quartets, songs, part-songs and anthems) and which was open to all persons 'of Irish birth and parentage, whether resident in Ireland or elsewhere, as well as those of British or foreign parentage who have been resident in Ireland for three years'.[68] This competition, as we shall see, stimulated Esposito to resume composing after many years of near inactivity. He would also remain closely associated with the Feis as an adjudicator for the performance competitions.[69]

We know nothing about Esposito's attitude to the intensifying Irish cultural and political nationalism of these years, although it was clear that he associated closely with literary and cultural figures of very different political persuasions. It is not impossible

67 Quoted in Éamonn Ó Gallchobhair, 'The Cultural Value of Festival and Feis' in Aloys Fleischmann, ed.,
     Music in Ireland: A Symposium (Cork, 1952), 210
68 *Musical Times*, 37, 644 (1896), 663–64
69 Larchet, 'Michele Esposito', 430

that he kept his views on these matters to himself, considering it to be more prudent for a foreigner to do so. Nonetheless, he was evidently interested in Irish traditional music and believed that it might offer novel expressive possibilities for creative work: this much is clear from an interview that he gave to the *Irish Independent* in February 1906, which appeared under the title 'Irish music — a chance for Irish composers'. His interviewer, the actor and playwright James Cousins, was deeply impressed by the Italian's extensive knowledge of and evident sympathy for Irish culture and was led to declare that Esposito 'had grown into our civic and national life more truly and firmly than many an individual who is Irish only by the accident of birth'. This fact lent considerable authority to his pronouncements on the future of Irish composition.

His remarks to Cousins on this subject are worth quoting at some length here, as they demonstrate that, like Patterson and Hughes, he was anxious to resist narrow and limiting views concerning the sorts of compositions that could be considered authentically 'Irish'. Esposito asked Cousins if he could supply the answer to a question he had often asked, but 'without getting much satisfaction':

[JC] I acknowledged the compliment but, but felt grave doubts on the matter.

'What is Irish music?'

[JC] Well — you see —

'Yes, yes', the Signor went on, with a laugh, and a shrug of his shoulders. 'You all commence that way, but you won't answer my question, "What is Irish music?" Is Brian Boru's March Irish music?'

[JC] It is of course.

'Well, give me the composer's score, and I'll play it. But you can't. You can only give me a melody sixteen bars long; no harmony; no expression. If I give it to sixty performers to play once through, and all playing the same note — well.'

[JC] I quite appreciated his gesture of pain; but suggested that the March might be used as a theme and be treated as Liszt treated the Hungarian melodies.

'Oh, but', he exclaimed, 'where is your Irish music then?'

'I assume', I said, evading the question, 'that you have little sympathy with the advocates of an Irish School of Music.'

'On the contrary', he replied warmly, 'I have every sympathy, but I think there is too much loose thinking on the subject. Some people want us to play or sing nothing but old airs. Others want us to harmonise according to ancient modes. We hear of certain pieces not being "Irish," and we hear it said "That's Irish," because something in a song makes one remember some other air which is regarded as Irish. But there is no standard, why shouldn't modern music be as much Irish as single, primitive melodies?'

Cousins asked if Esposito thought that Irish composers would be better advised not to base their work on folk music:

'No, certainly not', he [Esposito] said, with emphasis. 'I would use up the vast store of thematic material in the melodies.'

[JC] 'According to modern methods?'

'Of course! Music is a universal voice. Every development in the art belongs to the whole world. If your Irish composers use every modern device of the orchestra their music will be none the less Irish.'

'The music that the future will call Irish,' he continued, 'will be written by Irishmen, and will be Irish by virtue of something of his race-consciousness which his music will set free — no matter what his creed or political opinions may be.' Clearly, Esposito considered the view that all Irish composers should use folk music in a very obvious way as the basis for their work to be deeply misguided. The intrinsic quality of musical works had nothing to do with whether they were based on folk music or not, as it was also possible for composers to use this material in ways that were merely naïve and crude. Young Irish composers, Esposito argued, should concentrate first and foremost on acquiring a competent compositional technique — only then would they be in a position to make effective use of the expressive possibilities that folk music provided. As he put the matter succinctly, '[m]y advice to Irish composers is to master their art as musicians to the fullest possible extent; then, go back to the wonderful store of folk-melodies and build them into their music.'[70]

Esposito's personal interest in Irish folk music grew considerably during the 1890s and he started to experiment with arranging it — a development that aroused the keen interest of the *Freeman's Journal*, which devoted an entire column to the discussion of his first published arrangements when they came out in 1897.[71] The *Two Irish Melodies* for piano,

---

70 'Irish Music: A Chance for Irish Composers', *Irish Independent*, 19 February 1906
71 'Five Irish Melodies', *Freeman's Journal*, 11 December 1897

Op. 39, were versions of 'Avenging and bright' and 'Though the last glimpse of Erin' ('The Coulin'), respectively. These were clearly intended for pianists with a modest technique and the second of them was set for the RIAM grade examinations. They were followed by *Three Irish Melodies*, Op. 40, for voice and piano, for which George Sigerson had written the words and which were dedicated to Alfred Percival Graves. The first song 'Hush! O hush!' is a simple lullaby in which the flattened seventh features predominantly.[72] Esposito places particular emphasis on this modal inflexion and heightens the exotic aspect of the folksong in the elaborate piano accompaniment. The second song 'The Heather Glen' is based on the air *An Smactaoin crón* [sic][73] and the third, 'Movourneen Mine', employs a melody from the Bunting Collection entitled 'The Wheelwright'. A further set of *Irish Melodies* for voice and piano was published as Op. 41, which includes a deft arrangement of 'The Lark in the Clear Air'.

Significantly, his next major composition — the first large-scale work he had completed for over fifteen years — was based on Irish subject matter. This was a large-scale cantata for soloists, choir and orchestra entitled *Deirdre*, Op. 38, which he submitted for the 1897 Feis Ceoil composer's competition under the pseudonym 'Allegro Assai'. On the face if it, Esposito's decision to enter this competition seems rather surprising: he was, after all, a highly experienced professional musician in his early forties who had already written and published a considerable quantity of music, rather than a student composer at the start of his career. There are, however, several reasons which may explain this circumstance. First of all, it appears that although the performance competitions of the Feis were expected to attract mostly student entrants, the composers' competitions were not envisaged as taking place on this level. Secondly, Esposito may have felt under some obligation to participate in order to ensure that the competition would feature at least one entry of a decent standard, particularly in its inaugural year — the number of potential participants, one suspects, cannot have been high. Finally, there was the prospect of a public performance for the winning piece — a comparatively rare opportunity which may have been an added incentive. Unsurprisingly, *Deirdre* was duly awarded the Cantata Prize by Ebenezer Prout, the distinguished music theorist and composer, who adjudicated on this occasion.

The text for the cantata was the handiwork of Thomas William Rolleston (1857–1920), a translator and a minor poet who was involved at various times with both the Gaelic League and the Irish Literary Society and who is principally remembered today for his *Myths and Legends of the Celtic Race* (1911). Rolleston's libretto is based on the tale of Deirdre (Derdriu), which is thought to date from the eighth or early ninth century and was preserved in one

72 Apart from being described as 'A Southern Lullaby', no source or title is given for the folk tune.
73 'An smachdín [or smaichtín] crón', *The Complete Petrie Collection of Ancient Irish Music*, III, Charles Villiers Stanford, ed. (London, 1905), tune no. 1582. The Irish title literally means 'a small brown mallet or baton', but, according to P. Dineen (*Foclóir Gaedhilge agus Béarla, an Irish-English Dictionary* (Dublin, 1927), 1063), the phrase *smaichtín crón* refers to 'a kind of tobacco formerly smuggled into Ireland, and hence the name of a popular air'.

of the great Gaelic manuscript collections, the twelfth-century *Book of Leinster*. The action opens at the court of Conchobor (in modern Irish, Conor) mac Nessa, the king of the powerful Ulaid people who gave their name to the province of Ulster. During a drunken revel, the wife of one of Conchobor's bards, Fedlimid, gives birth to a baby daughter. A druid names her Deirdre and prophesies that she will cause great destruction. Some of the assembled company call for the child to be killed, but Conchobor decrees that she be brought up in secret until such time as he can marry her. Years later, the girl sees a raven drinking the blood of a slaughtered calf in the snow, whereupon she declares that the man she desires should have black hair, ruddy cheeks and a white body. When her nurse tells her that Noisi is such a man, she sets out to accost him, wishing to make him her lover. He reminds her of the prophecy but she mocks him for his cowardice, and by recourse to supernatural means, compels him to elope with her. Together with Noisi's brothers, they flee throughout the country, hoping to evade Conchobor's vengeance. His implacable enmity eventually compels them to seek refuge in Scotland, but the king there lusts after Deirdre and they leave for an island in the sea. Conchobor devises a ruse to lure them back to Ireland: he asks Fergus mac Roich to go as an emissary to Scotland and a token of safe-keeping, a task that Fergus accepts in good faith. The exiles agree to return, but are slaughtered on arrival — with the exception of Deirdre, who is forced to live in joyless subjection to Conchobor. When he plans to give her to Eogan mac Durthacht, an accomplice in his treachery, she commits suicide by dashing her head against a rock.

A version of this grim tale of treachery, betrayal and cruelty had been published as early as 1808 by Theophilus O'Flanagan, and further translations and adaptations continued to appear later in the century, some of them by distinguished literary figures such as Samuel Ferguson, Standish O'Grady and George Sigerson. Douglas Hyde published an English verse translation in 1895 (in his collection *The Three Sorrows of Story-telling and Ballades of St Columkille*) which proved very influential and subsequently inspired other contemporary Irish writers to produce treatments of their own, including Lady Gregory, AE (George Russell), Yeats, Synge and James Stephens. Rolleston's version, which appears to have been written specially for Esposito,[74] presents a highly compressed retelling of the original and differs in a few minor, but interesting details. In this version, for example, Deirdre first encounters Naisi [sic] after he has been injured by a wild boar. She falls in love with him while tending his wounds — an episode that clearly recalls Wagner's *Tristan* (Rolleston was himself an ardent Wagnerian). Although the poem is undistinguished in terms of its literary quality, it is nonetheless well suited to musical setting, as it dispenses with as much of the narrative as possible in order to focus on the emotional responses of the principal protagonists, Deirdre, Naisi and Fergus.

---

74 Rolleston's poem was published separately in 1897 by Patrick Geddes of Edinburgh and is described in
    this edition as being written for a cantata entered for Feis Ceoil.

Ex. 21: *Deirdre*, Op. 38, opening chorus

Ex. 22: *Deirdre*, Op. 38, opening chorus, closing section

Rolleston's libretto falls into three sections. The first depicts Deirdre's initial encounter with Naisi and King Conor's realization that he has been betrayed; the second the sojourn of the lovers on the Scottish island and the arrival of Fergus; and the third Deirdre's despair at the slaying of Naisi. This tripartite organization is reflected in Esposito's musical embodiment. Part I is dominated by the chorus whose primary material in C minor ('A blind hand sowed the seed') acts as a form of rondo theme (Ex. 21), supported by secondary material in A flat ('Deep in the trackless forest). These two thematic ideas are well contrasted and convey that essential sense of impending tragedy on the one hand, and the tender femininity of Deirdre on the other. Within the subsidiary paragraph in A flat, a further contrast is created by the brief entrance of the solo soprano, whose music powerfully evokes Deirdre's solitary longing and pain, shifting semitonally from A flat to the remote region of A major. Her climactic high A is skilfully placed to underpin the emotional climax of the passage (at the words 'Her young heart throbbed with longing') and when the soprano is joined by the choir (re-establishing A flat), the rich five-part vocal texture underlines Deirdre's haunting beauty and a sense of her vulnerability. This last is further accentuated by a menacing return of the chorus with stern, hymn-like music in C minor, accompanied by a new idea in the orchestra which is distinctly reminiscent of material from the first movement of Liszt's *Faust Symphony* in its impetuous rhythmic drive (Ex. 22). This leads to a new episode which introduces Naisi in the context of a hunting scene employing the standard Romantic accoutrements of a male-voice choir and horn calls. His ensuing love duet with Deirdre is dramatically interrupted by a solo bass, whose stern recitative relates King Conor's vengeful resolve and imparts a mood of foreboding to the ensuing reprise of the earlier choral hymn, which brings Part I to a close.

Part II opens with a depiction of Deirdre and Naisi's pastoral idyll on their lonely island off the coast of Scotland. Deirdre's tranquil pentatonic musings provide an effective foil to the more anguished music given to Naisi, who is tortured by his betrayal of King Conor (Ex. 23). This material comes to dominate their ensuing love duet and signals the arrival of Fergus, whose ominous calls are heard from afar. Fergus' overtly operatic monologue ('O noble heart') dominates the next section, in which he outlines Conor's proposal for a peaceful solution to the conflict. Ironically, this is predominantly cast in a seemingly innocent C major, which is undermined by Deirdre's fearful interjection in C minor and the orchestral leitmotiv heard previously (Ex. 22). The closing scene, depicting Naisi's naïve trust in Conor's sincerity and Fergus's assurances, is shot through with foreboding and concludes with a poignant aria for Deirdre ('Farewell! O serene glen!') in which she meditates on her uncertain future.

Ex. 23: *Deirdre*, Op. 38, Part II, opening duet

Part III of *Deirdre* opens with an evocation of sunrise on the morning of the lover's return to Ireland. This music unfolds over an extended C pedal lasting thirty-five bars. The chorus gives a brief premonition of the forthcoming battle by the 'last of the clan of Usna' in A minor before the solo tenor sings a lament, centred around A flat minor, over the impending demise of Naisi. The semitonal shift from A flat to A minor, which mirrors a similar move shortly after the opening of Part I, lends vividness to the evocation of the ensuing battle scene that is much more vivid, though the section is perhaps too short to have sufficient impact. As the music subsides in intensity, a reminiscence of Deirdre's closing aria in Part II is introduced to telling effect, though the subsequent evocation of Conor gazing at Deirdre as she kneels among the dead is dramatically less effective. This is rescued by what is arguably the finest music in the cantata, a dirge in E flat minor, which may owe something to the final pages of *La Traviata* (Ex. 24). The influence of Verdi is also manifest in the two powerful climaxes of the coda in which Naisi's angular theme of torment is gradually transformed to suggest a mood of longing and resignation. The last scene evoking Deirdre's longing for death, on the other hand, inevitably brings to mind the close of *Tristan*, and, after the final reprise of the opening chorus, it culminates in a similarly radiant mood.

Ex. 24: *Deirdre*, Op. 38, Part III, Deirdre's aria 'O sword of Naisi'

The composition of *Deirdre* was undoubtedly an event of great importance in the history of Irish music up to this point, and was especially significant in that it reflected the preoccupation of Irish writers at this period with Gaelic mythology. It is interesting to note, however, that in responding musically to the Deirdre legend Esposito made no attempt to employ Irish folk music or stylized evocations of it: the musical language of the work derives exclusively from mainstream European Romanticism. One wonders whether this reflected Esposito's personal conviction that Irish composers should look first to Austro-German, French and Italian models rather than occupying themselves with folk music. If so, such a position would be completely consonant with his insistence that the Feis Ceoil should foster European art music as well as Irish traditional music. Although *Deirdre* is by no means a technically flawless work, it is not unreasonable to suggest that it set new standards of technical excellence and professionalism for younger Irish composers and provided a practical demonstration of the kind of large-scale work it was possible to write on an Irish subject.

From the point of view of Esposito's own personal development as a composer, *Deirdre* also represented a considerable advance on his previous work. In it, he demonstrated for the first time an assured handling of a post-Wagnerian harmonic language which is considerably more complex than that of his earlier scores. The cantata was Esposito's most ambitious work to date and evinces an impressive control of large-scale formal organization. It also reveals a fine instinct for dramatic pacing and a talent for musical characterization — qualities that later stood him in good stead when writing his operas. The rondo design of Part I, which features recurrences of an oppressive C minor, engenders an atmosphere of ineluctable tragedy, while juxtapositions of diatonic tranquillity and chromatic menace in Parts II and III generate remarkable dramatic tension. The vocal writing is also excellently judged throughout: Esposito shows a truly Italianate understanding of vocal gestural resources, even if his setting of Rolleston's English contains occasional misaccentuations. Perhaps the most impressive feature of *Deirdre*, however, is Esposito's ability to depict characters of considerable psychological complexity: Deirdre and Naisi, like Tristan and Isolde, are anti-heroes who are treated with great sympathy and subtlety. Esposito's portrayal lends them a rich suggestiveness which anticipates the later retellings of the legend by Yeats and Synge.

The premiere of *Deirdre* took place on 20 May 1897, the third day of the Feis Ceoil, as part of a concert that also included the third movement of Stanford's *Irish* Symphony and his *Cavalier Songs* as well as the overture to Wallace's *Lurline* (the latter items were conducted by the prominent Dublin choral conductor Joseph Smith). The organization of this concert clearly required a special effort on the part of the Feis Committee, who not only had to engage soloists and secure the services of a suitable choir, but also assemble an orchestra for the occasion. Esposito conducted the premiere himself and rehearsed the forces beforehand. The role of Deirdre was sung by Marie Duma and those of Naisi and Fergus by Ivor McKay and William Ludwig, respectively.[75] The work was very warmly received: Rolleston was called forward for special plaudits and Esposito was highly gratified to be awarded a trophy in the form of a gold harp. 'I shall never forget', he wrote to the committee afterwards, 'how generously the Irish people have treated me, and I shall always strive to be worthy of their encouragement.'[76] The premiere of *Deirdre* did much to establish Esposito's reputation as a composer in Dublin. In his recitals since 1882 he had played relatively few of his own works, with the result that Irish audiences thought of him almost exclusively as a performer. As the critic of *Freeman's Journal* observed:

> To most people who take an interest in music, he is a distinguished pianist, indisputably eminent in that department, and approved more or less warmly

75 *Freeman's Journal*, 21 May 1897
76 *Freeman's Journal*, 25 June 1897

according to individual preferences. But good as he is as a pianist he is many times better as a composer and his cantata *Deirdre* is of his very best work.[77]

Deirdre met with a more mixed reception when it was subsequently performed in London on 26 February 1898 at the Promenade Concerts given by Henry Wood at Queen's Hall. The reviewer of the *Pall Mall Gazette* found the work to be stylistically inconsistent and lacking in inspiration, though he conceded that the performance of the Queen's Hall choir was rather lacklustre.[78] By contrast, the critic for the *Daily News* considered the performance to have been good, but was critical of Rolleston's 'sketchy' libretto and noted that Evangeline Florence, who sang the role of Deirdre, was out of voice.[79] The reviewer for the *Glasgow Herald* detected some Celtic elements in the score, but was more impressed by the Italianate nature of its melodic writing.[80]

Esposito's interest in arranging Irish melodies and the composition of *Deirdre* seem to have resulted in a closer association with prominent protagonists in the Gaelic and literary revivals. In January 1898 he went to London to attend the annual conference of the ISM where, as a result of a paper given by Joseph Seymour about Feis Ceoil, he enjoyed a certain celebrity for having composed *Deirdre*.[81] The 'Irish Toy Symphony' was repeated at the closing concert of the conference.[82] While in London, Esposito was invited to an 'at home' organized by the Irish Literary Society at their rooms in 8, Adelphi Terrace on 8 January, on which occasion Edith Oldham gave a paper comparing the Eisteddfod and the Feis.[83] After the lecture, which was attended by prominent Irish literary figures such as Graves and Sigerson, Esposito played a short programme of his arrangements of Irish folk songs, Op. 40 and 41, assisted by Alex Elsner and Gordon Cleather from the RIAM.[84] This was Esposito's first close contact with the Irish Literary Society in London. Soon after his return to Ireland, he, along with A. C. Mackenzie, Grove and Prout, wrote to recommend that the society pursue a policy of collecting Irish traditional airs.[85] The National Literary Society showed a similar enthusiasm and, with the encouragement of Sigerson, hosted a lecture by Rolleston on Irish songs at which Esposito's arrangements provided a conclusion to the evening.[86] Esposito was now closely engaged with the promotion of Irish culture, and this involvement would soon bring about the composition of his first opera.

---

77 *Freeman's Journal*, 5 March 1897
78 *Pall Mall Gazette*, 28 February 1898. *Deirdre* was heard again at the Dublin Feis of 1903 conducted by the composer; it also received a performance with Arthur Fagge's London Choral Society at the Crystal Palace and in 1907 by the Chicago Choral Society.
79 *Daily News*, 1 March 1898
80 *Glasgow Herald*, 28 February 1898
81 'The Incorporated Society of Musicians', *Pall Mall Gazette*, 5 January 1898
82 On the last day of the ISM conference Esposito appeared as pianist in a performance of his First Violin Sonata.
83 *Freeman's Journal*, 2 January 1898
84 *Reynolds' Newspaper*, 9 January 1898.
85 *Freeman's Journal*, 28 January 1898
86 *Freeman's Journal*, 28 January 1898

4 New Beginnings, 1899–1903

Esposito's involvement in the setting up of Feis Ceoil undoubtedly represented a watershed in his career and caused him to throw himself with seemingly inexhaustible energy into new ventures. Emboldened by the success of the RDS concerts, which had created a sizeable new audience for chamber music in Dublin, he now attempted to realize a long-standing ambition to establish a professional symphony orchestra in the capital. The absence of such an ensemble was keenly felt, as opportunities to hear orchestral music were mostly restricted to rare concerts given by visiting British orchestras. Such local orchestral activity as existed was generally occasioned by Dublin choral societies: *ad hoc* ensembles, augmented by hired professional players from Britain, were formed from time to time to accompany performances of large-scale choral works. During the 1890s, there was increasing discontent with this unsatisfactory situation and it was widely felt that something had to be done. The question was, however, whether there were enough instrumentalists of a proficient standard available to make a professional orchestra seem like a feasible proposition. This issue engendered heated debate during the preliminary discussions concerning the foundation of Feis Ceoil. Charles Villiers Stanford, who had accepted the role of President, was anxious that the new music festival should feature orchestral concerts, contending that they would not only enrich the programme of events, but would also be of educational benefit to up-and–coming Irish composers. A highly regarded conductor with an international reputation, he naturally proposed to conduct these concerts himself, suggesting that one of them could feature Irish works, while the others might feature works by eminent foreign composers who would be invited to attend in person. Stanford did not consider that an ensemble of local players would be adequate for such an auspicious occasion, however, and insisted that it would be necessary to bring a professional orchestra over from Britain. As he explained in his usual forthright manner to the committee:

[If] the committee are unable to raise enough guarantees to engage a first-rate orchestra, [both concerts] will be out of the question. The committee and I will be on the best possible footing if we understand our relative positions clearly from the outset; and I must make it quite clear that if I am to direct any concerts in connection with the Feis the materials must include a first-rate orchestra, or none at all. ... [A]ny middle policy, by which I mean a scratch band and an improvised chorus which has not practised well together, would simply result in a second-rate performance at best, over which I could not, even if I would, preside.[1]

While Stanford's concerns are easy to understand, his proposal to invite the Hallé Orchestra from Manchester aroused considerable controversy. Some committee members baulked at the expense that would be entailed and took umbrage at what they perceived as Stanford's denigration of native talent. Feelings on the latter subject no doubt ran high, given the intensified climate of cultural and political nationalism then prevalent. The Cork-based composer Theo Gmür claimed that there were enough Irish musicians available to form an adequate orchestra and urged the committee to 'let Irishmen do the best they could for themselves without any help from outsiders'[2] Gmür's ardent rhetoric swayed the committee and Stanford's plan was rejected, with the consequence that he promptly resigned.[3] In the event, Gmür's confidence in the capacities of the available Irish orchestral personnel seems to have been vindicated. As we have seen, an orchestra was assembled for the premiere of Esposito's *Deirdre* during the 1897 Feis Ceoil. To judge from the highly complimentary notice of the event that appeared in the *Irish Times*, the ensemble's playing seems to have been of a reasonably good standard, even when one allows for the fact that the reviewer may have exaggerated its quality somewhat out of a desire to be encouraging.[4]

Esposito scored a gratifying personal success directing his own cantata on this occasion, and it is not unreasonable to assume that it rekindled his interest in conducting and prompted him to try and set up an orchestra on a more permanent basis. It must also have struck him that if he wished to write further orchestral works, this was the only way in which he would have a chance to hear them performed. Moreover, there were some signs that sufficient support might exist for an enterprise of this kind. A few months previously, the Dublin Musical Society, which performed choral works, had announced its intention of putting on a series of orchestral concerts that were to be conducted by Joseph Smith. This development was the subject of much favourable comment in the press. As a writer for the *Freeman's Journal* pointed out:

1   'The revival of Irish music', *Freeman's Journal*, 29 March 1895
2   *Freeman's Journal*, 5 April 1895
3   For a fuller account of this episode, see Dibble, *Charles Villiers Stanford: Man and Musician* (Oxford, 2002), 282–84.
4   See the unsigned review 'Irish Music Festival', *Irish Times*, 21 May 1897.

It is an amazing thing that in a city like Dublin orchestral concerts should have so completely fallen away. It is years since we had in Dublin an orchestral concert of high class. We have had to be satisfied with oratorio and cantata from the Dublin Musical Society, frequent ballad concerts, and the excellent chamber music concerts of the Royal Dublin Society. How many Dublin concert goers of the younger generation have heard a Beethoven symphony? It is not that such music is in any way beyond the comprehension of the average concert goer for in London at a shilling a seat people assemble every night in the week during the season at the Queen's Hall to listen to such music. It is not an easy thing to get together a thoroughly good band in Dublin, and modesty may have made the Society too fearful of attempting works of difficulty. But all obstacles seem now to have been overcome ...[5]

An orchestra of seventy-five was assembled for the first concert which took place on 18 November 1896, the programme consisting of the overtures to *Der Freischütz* and *William Tell*, with Beethoven's Fifth Symphony. A second concert, which included Mozart's Symphony No. 39 in E flat and the overtures to *Fidelio*, *Oberon* and *Martha*, was given on 20 January 1897. An auspicious beginning had been made, but unfortunately the venture soon came to an end. The concerts seem to have been poorly attended, and matters were not helped by an acrimonious dispute between Smith and the leader of his orchestra Theodor Werner (a one-time professor of violin at the RIAM and teacher of J. M. Synge), who had apparently insinuated that he was incompetent. Werner may have desired to discredit Smith out of professional rivalry, for he harboured ambitions to launch a series of orchestral concerts of his own. In April 1897 Smith brought a case for alleged libel and slander which was eventually settled out of court, but the in-fighting had evidently done considerable damage. The third concert, given on 3 November 1897 (in which Esposito appeared as soloist in Mendelssohn's G minor Piano Concerto) proved to be the last undertaken by the Society.[6]

Rather more encouraging was the surprising level of interest aroused by the Hallé Orchestra, which gave two concerts at the newly opened Lyric Hall in Dublin on 7 and 8 March of the following year.[7] In view of the poor audiences for the recent Dublin Musical Society events, a writer for *Freeman's Journal* remarked it was difficult to be sanguine about the success of another undertaking aiming 'to interest Dublin in good orchestral work'.[8]

5   *Freeman's Journal*, 10 November 1896
6   See 'Discord among musicians' and 'The libel action between Dublin musicians', *Freeman's Journal*, 16 January 1897, 24 April 1897; and *The Belfast News-Letter*, 'The libel action between musicians settled', 26 April 1897.
7   The dates of 7 and 8 February 1898 given in some other publications are incorrect. The concerts had to be postponed by a month because financial support could not be guaranteed in time: see *Freeman's Journal*, 1 February 1898.
8   *Freeman's Journal*, 5 January 1898

A month later, an article in the same paper excoriated the apparent indifference of the Dublin public even to a first-rate orchestra like the Hallé:

> In a city like Dublin to have to urge, and keep on urging the merits of such performances as are promised, and may be confidently expected, is surely a poor compliment to our supposed musical taste.... There is not a single second-rate English manufacturing town where a visit from the Hallé band would not cause a rush to the booking office almost as keen perhaps as is displayed in Dublin to hear *The Shop Girl* [a popular musical hall farce].[9]

To the relief of all concerned, the concerts were very well attended. The Lyric Hall was full to capacity and the audience responded enthusiastically to Beethoven's Fifth Symphony on the first night and Tchaikovsky's *Pathétique* Symphony (still a comparative novelty) on the second, under the direction of Frederic Cowen.[10] Indeed, the orchestra was so warmly received that it returned to play in Dublin on 15 and 16 November later in the same year.

It was widely agreed that this success gave cause for greater optimism as far as the foundation of a permanent orchestra in Dublin was concerned. As one commentator in the *Freeman's Journal* averred in an article of June 1898, 'the interest manifested in the recent visit of the Hallé Band shows that, once the good band is got together, there will be a worthy audience for it'.[11] The same article also announced that a meeting would be held at the RIAM on 21 June 1898, chaired by Count Plunkett, to discuss the feasibility of the idea. From the outset, it was assumed that Esposito would play a central role and it is a testimony to his standing in Dublin that he managed to inspire confidence in the project to such an extent. As the *Freeman's Journal* declared, 'anyone who knew his character knew that he could not be over-weighted by such an undertaking. This work, which had been started in the interests of musicians of Dublin, was in his mind such a public work that he felt sure it would be taken up, and receive the assistance it required.'[12] Esposito clearly saw the establishment of the orchestra as a matter of civic pride: 'In starting this little Home Rule musical movement the people of Dublin would see it was their duty to support it, and secondly that their enthusiasm must speak out in such a fashion as to make it a permanent and lasting success.'[13]

Idealistic though his motivation may have been, Esposito was under no illusions about just how formidable a challenge the project represented. The principal difficulty was of course financial: professional orchestral players naturally require to be paid. Clearly, it would be necessary to secure substantial sponsorship and Esposito set about solving this

9   *Freeman's Journal*, 1 February 1898
10 *Musical Times*, 39, 662 (1898), 258
11 *Freeman's Journal*, 18 June 1898
12 'An orchestra for Dublin', *Freeman's Journal*, 22 June 1898
13 'An orchestra for Dublin', *Freeman's Journal*, 22 June 1898

problem with his habitual resourcefulness and efficiency. Before the meeting on the 21 June, he circulated a document outlining a plan to secure financial backing to the tune of £2,500 (approximately equivalent to €250,000 today) over a seven-year period. This sum, which was referred to as the Foundation Fund, would be raised from a hundred private donors who would undertake to contribute a total £25 each during this time, paying either a lump sum at the outset, or in instalments over the seven years (in which case they would be required to pay £30). In return, the donors would receive tickets for all concerts for seven years. Each year one seventh of the Foundation Fund would be paid into capital, to be used for the purchase of necessary materials such as scores and orchestral parts and to cover some running costs. The remainder would form a Reserve Fund for contingencies, providing a financial cushion to offset any losses incurred.

Esposito's immediate model for this scheme was the Società Orchestrale della Scala di Milano, which had been set up in 1879 on the basis of financial support obtained in a similar fashion. He clearly felt that such a long-term commitment from sponsors would be necessary if the venture were to stand any chance of succeeding: this arrangement was preferable to relying on annual guarantors who would probably take fright if the orchestra lost money in the early stages, as it almost inevitably would. Building up sufficiently large audiences that would enable the orchestra to pay its way would clearly take some time, particularly in a city like Dublin, which was not as wealthy as major British conurbations such as Leeds, Birmingham or Manchester. As an article in the *Freeman's Journal* explained:

> [Owing] to (1) the absence of any general public knowledge of orchestral music (2) the fact that no orchestra can attain high proficiency until the members have practised together for a season or two, and (3) that fact that there must be considerable initial expenses (such as purchase of music etc), the result of the first season would probably be a failure financially. Guarantors would then be called upon to pay heavily, and would naturally refuse their guarantee the second season. This is what has actually happened in Dublin and other places before this.[14]

At the meeting of 21 June, his proposal was adopted, although James Culwick initially expressed concern that a request for £25 from each sponsor would be perceived as excessive and wondered if it might be more practical to recruit a larger number of donors contributing smaller sums.[15] A steering committee was duly formed to oversee the task of fundraising, which comprised a number of leading figures in Dublin's cultural life: in addition to Esposito and Culwick, its members included Count Plunkett, Edward Martyn

14 *Freeman's Journal*, 1 October 1898
15 'An orchestra for Dublin', *Freeman's Journal*, 22 June 1898

and the former head brewer at Guinness W. P. Geoghegan, who was a friend of Esposito's and a staunch supporter of musical activity in the city.[16]

It soon became clear to the committee that recruiting donors was not going to prove easy, even though a number of prominent figures, such as the Catholic Archbishop of Dublin, William J. Walsh, agreed to contribute.[17] By the start of October, only half the required money had been raised. The committee resorted to publishing an open letter in the *Freeman's Journal* in an effort to raise wider awareness of the project and attract further sponsors. This document provided information about the practical management of the project in a question-and-answer format, presumably in the hope of resolving common queries and dispelling any misconceptions. It concluded by urging 'those who believe in the value of the scheme to add their names to the list of subscribers without delay', as 'Signor Esposito [was] very anxious to begin rehearsals as quickly as possible'.[18] This appeal was not notably successful: by December only £1,650, or so, had been raised and the outlook for the project began to seem bleak. At this point, there was an unexpected glimmer of hope: a wealthy anonymous donor (possibly Edward Martyn, who provided generous financial support for other musical initiatives in the city)[19] undertook to contribute £500 if the total funds could be brought up to £2,000 by 31 December.[20] By 15 December, the fund had reached £1,841 9s, with some donors making pledges of between £1 and £5. Further urgent appeals for support were issued.[21] By 22 December the total stood at £1895 14s — tantalizingly close to the necessary amount.[22] There was much rejoicing when the provisional Committee met on 2 January 1899 to discover that this sum had since risen to £2,024 15s, enabling the Society to accept the generous donation of £500.[23] The Dublin Orchestral Society (DOS), as the fledgling orchestra was named, could now plan its first season.

A new committee was formed to manage the orchestra's finances and oversee practical matters, such as the hiring of personnel, booking venues, advertising and the printing of tickets and programmes. Its active members included some of Esposito's most loyal supporters, including his friend W. P. Geoghegan, Edith Oldham and Edward Martyn. Meetings were generally held at the RIAM, although in the early stages other venues such as the Antient Concert Rooms were also used. When one considers that Esposito continued to

---

16 See *Freeman's Journal*, 21 July 1898 and *Musical Times*, 40, 672 (1899), 89–90. For Geoghegan, see Stanley Dennison and Oliver MacDonagh, *Guinness 1886–1939: From Incorporation to the Second World War* (Cork, 1998), 21 and 31.

17 *Freeman's Journal*, 1 October 1898

18 *Freeman's Journal*, 1 October 1898

19 It seems likely that Edward Martyn helped finance the DOS throughout its existence: see 'An Irishman's Diary', *Irish Times*, 15 May 1928.

20 *Freeman's Journal*, 8 December 1898

21 *Freeman's Journal*, 15 December 1898

22 *Freeman's Journal*, 22 December 1898

23 *Freeman's Journal*, 4 January 1899

fulfil his regular teaching duties during this period, as well as performing and composing, his workload must have been enormous. His first task, naturally, was to recruit suitable players. He was fortunate in being able to secure the services of an able orchestral leader in the person of Adolph [Adolf] Wilhelmj, the son of the great German violinist and virtuoso August Wilhelmj, who settled in Dublin in 1899 having previously taught violin for four years at the Belfast Conservatoire. Recruiting personnel for the string sections does not appear to have proved very difficult, as there were quite a few proficient players in the city. RIAM colleagues such as the violinist Patrick Delaney, the violist Octave Grisard, and the cellist Henry Bast provided a nucleus of reliable members, which was supplemented by other local players of a good standard. Securing competent wind and brass players presented a much greater challenge, as they were in short supply nationally. In Britain, orchestras often borrowed players from the police force or army bands, and Esposito had recourse to a similar expedient.[24] Some of his wind players came from the Royal Irish Constabulary band and regimental bands stationed in the city.[25] Other instrumentalists were recruited from the pit orchestras of various Dublin theatres and members of the teaching staff at the Dublin Municipal School of Music also participated. By these means, the membership of the orchestra was raised to sixty-one, of which forty were string players (12 first violins, 10 second violins, 8 violas, 5 cellos and 5 double basses).[26]

Players were paid at different rates depending on their rank. The leader and the principal cellist, together with the principals of the woodwind and horn sections, received the highest fees. The leaders of the second violin and double bass sections and the principal trumpet and trombone players received twenty percent less than this; while the remaining rank-and-file players received forty percent less. According to Richard Pine and Charles Acton, it is not very clear from the society's accounts what these fees worked out at in practice, but it would appear that the average payment was about £1 8s per concert. In the event that the concerts made a financial loss, players were guaranteed to receive at least half fees. Since many of the orchestra's members had regular professional engagements by night, it was agreed that all of the society's concerts would take place on Sunday afternoons. This arrangement naturally had its drawbacks, but it was unavoidable if the concerts were to take place at all.[27] Esposito was to be paid £20 per concert and

24 Although today it is hard to imagine a shortage of wind and brass players, wind instruments were often not taught in conservatoires in the nineteenth century. For some years after the foundation of the Royal College of Music in London in 1883, the college orchestra had to engage the services of wind and brass players from the Crystal Palace and Philharmonic Orchestras. This situation persisted until teachers of wind instruments joined the staff and began to train student players: see Dibble, *Charles Villiers Stanford*, 169 and 216.

25 *Musical Times*, 44, 729 (1903), 705–07

26 Pine and Acton, *To Talent Alone*, 230–31; also *Freeman's Journal*, 27 April 1899 and *Musical Times*, 40, 672 (1899), 90

27 'Michele Esposito', *Musical Times*, 44, 729 (1903), 705

the Society engaged the services of a secretary who was paid £30 a year.[28] Even allowing for the fact that the orchestra would not perform continuously throughout the year, the costs involved in running it were still considerable: a correspondent for the *Musical Times* estimated somewhere in the region of £1,000 per annum.[29]

From the outset, Esposito was determined to ensure that the orchestra's programmes would contain music of genuine substance, as his RDS concerts and solo recitals had always done. There is no doubt that he saw the orchestra as having an educative function and hoped that it would enable Dublin audiences to familiarize themselves with mainstream repertoire that they had not hitherto had the opportunity to hear. Ambitious plans for future programmes formed in his mind. After meeting Sir George Grove at Queen's Hall after the performance of *Deirdre* in February 1898, he explained to the former Director of the RCM that, having played almost all the sonatas of Beethoven to the Dublin public, he wanted to introduce them to the symphonic works.[30] He voiced a similar resolve in a letter later that year: 'It will be uphill work for me but nothing will ever be done if one does not try and seriously [sic].'[31] He was equally determined to ensure that the quality of orchestral playing would be as high as possible. According to the *Musical Times* correspondent, Esposito initially proposed to hold no less than thirty-four rehearsals for each programme: this number is probably much exaggerated, but it is possible that the general rehearsals for the first season's concerts were preceded by intensive sectional rehearsals.[32] The task, as Larchet later remarked, of welding this 'motley gathering of ... performers into a homogenous entity' required every ounce of Esposito's patience and determination. Some sense of the practical difficulties with which he was faced can be gathered from the fact that many of the instruments owned by the wind players were constructed at an older concert pitch, which was about a semitone too high.[33]

The Dublin Orchestral Society's first season in 1899 was advertised as being under the patronage of the Lord Lieutenant and Countess Cadogan, which clearly gave it a certain social *cachet*. This gesture of official support may have been additionally welcome, as there had been some objections to the concerts on religious grounds, as holding them on a Sunday was perceived to violate the Sabbath day. This opposition was successfully overcome by the Archbishop of Dublin who attended them in person when it was possible for him to do so.[34] Five concerts were given during the series in the 'Large Hall' of the Royal University, spaced out at intervals between 1 March and 7 June.[35] The programme

---

28 Pine and Acton, *To Talent Alone*, 228
29 *Musical Times*, 40, 672 (1899), 90
30 Percy Young, *George Grove 1820–1900: A Biography* (London, 1980), 263
31 Letter from Esposito to Grove, 7 December 1898, GB-Lcm
32 *Musical Times*, 40, 672 (1899), 90
33 Larchet, 'Michele Esposito', 430–31
34 Larchet, 'Michele Esposito', 431
35 The Aula Maxima at the University's Earlsfort Terrace premises was referred to in this manner in the *Irish Times* advertisements for the series.

for the inaugural concert consisted of the overture to Gluck's *Iphigénie en Aulide*, Mozart's Symphony No. 40, a rarely played concertante work by Mendelssohn, the *Serenade und Allegro giojoso*, Op. 43 (in which the solo piano part was played by one of Esposito's pupils, Harry Charles), Beethoven's *Egmont* Overture, Wagner's *Faust* Overture and a selection of movements from Bizet's *L'Arlésienne* Suite No. 1. The concert received a long and detailed notice in the *Irish Times*, which makes for interesting reading and is worth quoting at some length here. The reviewer (who, to judge from the prose style, may have been Annie Patterson) opens by expressing indignation at the comparatively small audience for an event of such historical significance in the annals of Irish music. We are also allowed to gather that the writer found the audience disappointingly unresponsive, because it was largely composed of people who were unfamiliar with classical music and consequently had little appreciation of what they were hearing:

> We confess that we are not satisfied with the attendance at the first concert. A very fine programme was placed before the public. ... The performance, to those who could best appreciate it, represented a signal chapter in the history of musical art. ... Not for many years, if ever before, has such an entertainment been afforded to the public, and with such limited recognition. If we are to be placed in the possession of an Irish orchestra — and the performances of last night have demonstrated that we can be — there must be upon the part of the musical community a far heartier comprehension of the work which is being done in their service. No musician present can have failed to acknowledge the high ability of the orchestra, conducted with conspicuous ability by Signor Esposito. But we should have expected to find an audience of thrice the volume, and far more sensible of the quality of the work which it was privileged to enjoy than it proved itself to be.[36]

To judge from the review, the audience's enjoyment was dimmed somewhat by excessively resonant acoustics of the 'Large Hall', which made it unsuitable for a symphony concert. And although the quality of playing throughout the evening appears to have been highly variable, the critic found much to praise and admitted to having been pleasantly surprised: 'We did not expect a great performance of the works advertised for production, but we say frankly that what was done far exceeded the expectations of those who came to hear.' Esposito managed to coax a sensitive account of the Gluck overture from the ensemble, and some spirited playing in the Mozart symphony — the reviewer characterizes the performance of the finale of the latter work as 'masterly' and 'magnificent'. On the other hand, the Beethoven and Wagner overtures seem to have been beyond the technical capacities of the orchestra, with the result that the performances were rather crude and

36 'The Dublin Orchestral Society', *Irish Times*, 2 March 1899

incoherent. But in the final summing-up, the critic leaves the reader in no doubt that a promising beginning had been made:

> But taking together the incidents of the whole concert, it is our duty to declare that its performances far exceeded the level of achievement that had been expected. In tuning the orchestra was as nearly perfect as possible. Signor Esposito has taught its members the precise value of time, and no musician who was present at the concert last night can fail to recognise in him an absolute master of the forces under his command. We candidly say that he has most signally proved an ability hitherto unexpected. He worthily takes his place at the head of an orchestra from which great things will be expected in the future, and which, by its performances of last night, has more than justified the hopes which those who promoted it have entertained. The success of the Dublin Orchestral Society is in our deliberated judgement assured, and it is now in a better position then ever to appeal to and rely upon the cordial support of the musical community of Ireland. We do not say that the performances of last night approached perfection. But they unquestionably mark a step in advance, and afford the earnest of greater achievements in a nearer future than most had imagined.

The second concert took place three weeks later on 22 March. The *Egmont* Overture was again included in the programme, together with Mendelssohn's *Hebrides* Overture, the overture to Cherubini's *Medea*, Beethoven's First Symphony, Saint-Saëns's *Danse macabre* and Tchaikovsky's *Nutcracker* Suite. The solo item on this occasion was played by Wilhelmj — a *Romance* for Violin and Orchestra from a *Konzertstück* by his father. The audience was small, but enthusiastic. Once again, Esposito's conducting elicited highly favourable comments in the press; as the reviewer for the *Freeman's Journal* remarked: 'First we knew him as an excellent pianist; then he astonished us as a composer of originality and distinction; now he turns out to be a first-rate conductor besides.'[37] The remaining concerts took place on 26 April, 25 May and 7 June. The programmes for these repeated a few works that had already been heard, and featured a range of standard classics such as Haydn's Symphony No. 104, Beethoven's Second Symphony, Mendelssohn's *Italian* Symphony and the overture to Weber's *Euryanthe* as well as more modern works such as the prelude to Saint-Saëns's oratorio *Le déluge*. In the April concert, which was held in the Theatre Royal, Esposito appeared as soloist in Mendelssohn's G minor Piano Concerto. Between this and the fourth concert, the DOS performed at the concert of works by prize-winning composers at Feis Ceoil on 18 May 1899. On this occasion, Esposito conducted the premiere of a new orchestral work of his own, the *Poem*, Op. 44, for harp and small orchestra, which he had composed as an entry for one of the composers' competitions

37 *Freeman's Journal*, 23 March 1899

and which had won first prize in its category. He conducted the piece again at the DOS's fifth concert of the season, having re-scored it for larger forces.[38]

The second DOS season got underway on 1 November 1899 and ran until 2 May 1900. This time, the major symphonic works programmed included Beethoven's Fourth and Eighth Symphonies and Brahms's Second Symphony. Henry Bast appeared as soloist in the A minor Cello Concerto of Saint-Saëns; Ernest Schelling, a young American pianist who had studied with Moszkowski and Paderewski, performed Chopin's Second Piano Concerto; Wilhelmj played two movements from the Bruch Violin Concerto in G minor; while Esposito himself played the solo part in two performances of the Schumann Piano Concerto. Of modern works, Dvořák's concert overture In Nature's Realm [V přírodě] and Humperdinck's overture to Hänsel und Gretel (both composed only a decade or so previously) were featured. These concerts received generally favourable reviews, notably from Annie Patterson, who was evidently concerned to be as encouraging as possible. If she is to be believed, the standard of playing had improved since the first season: her notice of the concert of 25 January 1900 singles out the brass and wind players for special praise.[39] Nonetheless, the number of empty seats in the hall remained at alarmingly high levels. Despite the support of prominent Dublin society figures such as the Lord Lieutenant (the orchestra was invited to perform at a State concert at Dublin Castle on 6 March 1900 in front of an audience that included the Duke and Duchess of Connaught),[40] the concerts were not well attended. It seemed doubtful whether it could continue to operate for much longer, and only four concerts were announced for the third season commencing in November 1900.[41] An article in the Musical Times warned ominously that 'this series will bring to a termination the existence of the Society unless the support accorded by the public is very much greater than heretofore. It is most desirable for the honour of our city that such a thing should be averted.'[42] Some weeks before the season got underway Annie Patterson published a feature article on Esposito in the Weekly Irish Times, in which she presented his views on the difficulty of maintaining a professional orchestra in the city — that it would be impossible for the DOS to carry on without state support:

> In the first place Signor Esposito says that no orchestra can be supported alone by the public of the town in which it is permanently. There must be reserve funds at the back; in fact the orchestra must be paid for, either by the corporation of the town in question, or by private individuals. In London, Paris, and Berlin, 'possibly', says the Signor, 'a good orchestral society may pay its own way, because in these cities there is always a large population', who are continually contributing their quota of

38 Musical Times, 40, 677 (1899), 480
39 Weekly Irish Times, 10 February 1900
40 Freeman's Journal, 7 March 1900
41 Freeman's Journal, 13 June 1900 and Musical Times, 41, 692 (October 1900), 681
42 Musical Times, 41, 692 (1900), 681

audiences to all that is popular or noted in the metropolis which they happen to be visiting. In Dublin matters are no doubt different. Here we are all the year round, to a great extent consisting of the same professional people, the same connoisseurs, the same critics. The burden of supporting any one or all musicians' undertakings generally falls upon a few generous-souled and enthusiastic amateurs, and when these have done what they can — and they really are most liberal and willing to help as far as they may, in reason, be expected to do — the rest lies with the public. But, from many causes, too numerous to be dealt with now, public support for classical music must always be more or less of a fluctuating and uncertain description. In fact, the high class concert is a luxury which must be *purchased* by the few, and if the price exceeds the resources of that few, then, as in Germany, France and Italy, the Government must step in to the rescue and, by giving a grant, place the undertaking upon a basis that will enable it to maintain its high standard of artistic and educational excellence without coming to grief financially.[43]

There seemed little hope that the government would provide such a subvention in the near future, and in the meantime Esposito had no choice but to find other ways to boost the takings at the box office. For the next series of concerts, vocal items were included in the programmes in the hope of widening their popular appeal. At the first concert on 21 November 1900, the celebrated American baritone Denis O'Sullivan (1868–1908) sang a *scena* from Verdi's *Don Carlos* and arrangements of Irish songs by Stanford and Esposito; while at the second, Florence Schmidt performed arias from Mozart's *Idomeneo* and an excerpt from Massenet's oratorio *La vierge*. The purely orchestral items performed this season included Mozart's *Jupiter* Symphony and Sullivan's overture *In Memoriam*, and Esposito's *Poem* was given a further hearing. Nonetheless, the concerts continued to lose money and a public meeting was held at the Leinster Lecture Hall, Molesworth Street on 11 April 1901 to consider the Society's future.

This was presided over by the Lord Chancellor of Ireland, Sir Ignatius O'Brien (later Lord Shandon) and according to the report in the *Irish Times* it drew a large crowd, with leading Dublin cultural and intellectual figures such as Edward Martyn and John Pentland Mahaffy in attendance. It opened with the presentation of a detailed report on the state of the Society's finances since it commenced operations, which revealed that the average cost of each concert had been roughly in the region of £150. The cost of mounting the five concerts of the first season had come to £897 18s 1d, leaving a deficit of £259 6s 8d which had to be borrowed from capital. The proceeds from the eight concerts of the second season were much lower — a mere £313 14s 7d, as poor weather and the outbreak of the Boer War had exercized a highly disruptive effect on concert attendance generally in the city. The expenses for the season amounted to a colossal £1,265 11s 6d, which required

43 *Weekly Irish Times*, 15 September 1900

£550 17s 8d to be borrowed from capital. The third season was much less ambitious in its scope, as we have seen. This time, the box office takings came to £176 4s, while expenses came to £584 12s 11d. Under the rules of the DOS, £387 5s 1d could be allocated to offset the deficit, which meant that the loss on this occasion was only £21 3s 10d. The total deficit incurred over the three years thus amounted to £831 10s. Despite this sombre news, it is interesting to note that Esposito received encouraging reassurances that the Society still enjoyed a large measure of support. The Lord Chancellor made an extempore speech in which he stressed the civic importance of the Society and the vital necessity of its continuance:

> In his opinion, having regard to the fact that [the Society] had [had] only three seasons, and that it was more or less a pioneer movement, and as such had to battle its way, it had nothing to be ashamed of and nothing to fear. (*Hear, hear.*) The Society had an able and gifted conductor, himself a distinguished musician who had been a citizen of Dublin for almost a generation, and who had got under his control, and created by him [*sic*], a large and powerful band composed of gifted and excellent musicians. That in itself was an achievement of no little moment. (*Applause*) He did not think it was desirable in a meeting of that kind if you believed at all in what you were doing to sound a creaking or despondent note. A Society that intended to live and was worthy of living should always look to the future with vigour, boldness, and courage. ... Ireland was a musical country, and the Irish were a musical people. ... There was no reason why a Society like that should not look for encouragement and support in every direction. He did not believe that music should ever be narrowed to the dominions of class or party, or creed. (*Hear, hear.*) It looked for support from all who took an interest in music ... . They were sometimes told by those of an economic turn of mind, 'Why can't we be satisfied with an occasional importation from other countries of distinguished bands, and players?' Well, they were always glad to hear good music wherever it might come from, and good bands and musicians who had come from other parts of the world were welcome. ... But they had a right — had they not? — to a good orchestral band of their own. (*Hear, hear.*) The cities of England were not satisfied with being told they could have fine bands and great musicians from London; they said, 'Why should we not make an effort and have fine orchestral bands of our own?' Manchester was not so satisfied, and Dublin, equally with Manchester, should make an effort to have a first-class orchestral band. (*Applause*)[44]

These rousing words were followed by a vigorous speech from Mahaffy, in which he was eloquent in his praise of the orchestra's contribution to musical life in the city and urged

44 'Dublin Orchestral Society', *Irish Times*, 12 April 1901

that an effort be made to save it. He declared that was the 'solemn duty' of those present 'to do everything they could' to ensure that the Society could continue its work 'on a sound basis'. A resolution was passed to the effect that 'a committee be formed to raise funds, increase the membership and to take any other steps necessary' to accomplish this aim. This committee was duly formed, and it was resolved that funding should be sought from Dublin Corporation on the grounds that the activities of the DOS had a valuable educational dimension. There was call from some quarters to seek patronage from the wealthy, such as Countess Cadogan and the Duchess of Connaught,[45] but in the end the Committee resolved to appeal once again to the Dublin public for a new round of subscriptions both to pay off the Society's overdraft and to pay for a new season of concerts.[46] However, by September 1901, the Society had not received the support it had hoped for (despite the circulation of 8,000 leaflets to householders) and announced in the press that it would discontinue its activities unless funds were urgently found.[47]

Throughout this difficult period, Annie Patterson continued to write articles in support of the DOS and its conductor, doing as much as she could to keep the issue of the orchestra's predicament at the forefront of public awareness. Shortly after the meeting on 11 April, she wrote an interesting article for the *Irish Times* in which she reflected on the apparent lack of support for native musical ventures. During 1900 and 1901, the Hallé Orchestra had been brought over to Dublin three times by the impresario Mrs Page Thrower. Although the ticket prices were rather high by Irish standards, the concerts attracted large and enthusiastic audiences. (Thrower, incidentally, still did not make a profit, such were the expenses involved.) This fact clearly indicated that a sizeable number of people in Dublin were willing to pay considerable sums to attend orchestral concerts — but many of these, evidently, did not attend the DOS performances. In some cases, their absences could probably be explained on grounds of snobbery; but Patterson also intimates that the DOS had been subjected to unfavourable comparisons with the Hallé. As she quite reasonably points out, the comparison between the two ensembles was unfair: the British orchestra possessed the resources to hire the finest players, enabling it to perform to a very high standard. Esposito's orchestra was struggling for its very survival only a few years after its foundation, and its financial predicament had become all the more acute on account of the lack of public support. If this situation continued, there could be little hope of improvement:

> Many people who know nothing of the working expenses of such an undertaking are inclined to cavil at the fact that the Dublin Orchestral Society had been obliged to draw largely on the capital subscribed at its inception. The need for so doing had

---

45 'Dublin Orchestral Society', letter from 'Dublinensis' to the Editor, *Irish Times*, 11 April 1901
46 'The Dublin Orchestral Society', *Irish Times*, 5 May 1901
47 *Irish Times*, 19 September 1901. At this stage, subscriptions to the value of only £140 had been raised together with £29 in private donations.

come from the fact that the public have not attended the concerts as was reasonably expected they might have done. Comparisons of one local orchestra with other and longer established bodies are unfair. The public should remember that, considering its organization, the DOS has really made remarkable strides towards a high standard. Years of steady and patient rehearsal are always necessary before an ensemble such as may be heard at the Crystal Palace Concerts, for instance, is attained. But when it is remembered that competent critics have noticed a steady advance in excellence of rendition of orchestral works at every recurrent concert of the DOS, as especially when it is borne in mind that the Society gives a certain amount of steady employment to all our chief local performers, it seems the bounden duty of every citizen to do "his little best" to keep alive such a combination in our midst, or, by hearty support, enable it to go on towards perfection.[48]

Patterson alluded to the plight of the orchestra again in an *Irish Times* feature article surveying the state of Dublin musical life on 21 September 1901, decrying the fact that it could be allowed to 'die for want of funds'.[49] The newspaper also carried a lengthy letter from James Culwick on the same day, which extolled Esposito's 'superhuman' exertions and urged Dubliners to realize the value of the DOS before it was too late. Interestingly, Culwick, like Patterson, attributed the poor attendance at concerts to a misplaced snobbish conviction that they were not sufficiently fashionable to be worth attending.[50]

In the end, enough financial support was mustered to allow a fourth season to go ahead. Sufficient funds had been raised for four concerts and the players agreed that, should the takings at the door be insufficient at these concerts, their services would be given free of charge for two further concerts (to bring the season's total to six).[51] On 4 November 1901, a deputation from the Society attended a monthly meeting of the Dublin Corporation and appealed for an annual grant, contending that the existence of the orchestra would help raise the standard of musical education amongst the general population.[52] This proposal met with some opposition: given the dire levels of poverty prevalent in the capital at the time, tasks such as slum clearance and the provision of municipal housing were understandably deemed to be more deserving of public funding.[53] Nevertheless, the Corporation adopted the motion, although it finally undertook to provide a grant of £50, rather than £260 as had originally been requested.[54]

---

48 'Music of the Day', *Irish Times*, 20 April 1901
49 'The Prospects of Musical Dublin', *Irish Times*, 21 September 1901
50 James Culwick, letter to the Editor, *Irish Times*, 21 September 1901
51 'Musical and Dramatic Notes', *Irish Times*, 19 October 1901
52 'Dublin Corporation: Monthly Meeting', *Irish Times*, 5 November 1901
53 *Irish Times*, 5 November 1901
54 'Dublin Orchestral Society: General Meeting', 4 October 1902

The first concert of the fourth season took place on 20 November 1901. The programmes this time contained a proportion of works that the orchestra had played previously, but also introduced many new items. Esposito's student Annie Lord gave the Dublin premiere of Tchaikovsky's First Piano Concerto on 11 December in a programme that also included Beethoven's *Coriolan* Overture and his Eighth Symphony, as well as Wagner's *Faust* Overture. This was followed by a concert on 24 January 1902 that mostly consisted of Wagner excerpts, including the overtures to *Der fliegende Holländer* and *Tannhäuser*, the preludes to Acts I and III of *Lohengrin*, the prelude to Act III of *Tristan und Isolde* and the *Walkürenritt* from *Die Walküre*. Esposito's interest in Wagner's music dated, as we have seen, at least as far back as his Paris years; but the design of this programme may have been inspired by an all-Wagner concert that Richter had recently given with the Hallé in Dublin. The programme on 19 February featured Mendelssohn's *Scottish* Symphony and the overture to Smetana's opera *The Bartered Bride*. A further concert featuring the music of Wagner was given on 24 March — 'in response to a generally expressed desire', according to the commentator for the *Musical Times*.[55] This time the items played included extracts from *Lohengrin*, the 'Entrance of the Gods into Valhalla' from *Rheingold*, the prelude to Act III of *Tristan*, and the overture to *Die Meistersinger*, as well as the overture to Mozart's *Le nozze di Figaro* and two arrangements of Irish airs for cor anglais and orchestra made by Esposito himself.[56] The final concert on 18 April was advertised as a 'Tchaikovsky Concert'. Its second half was given over to two works by the Russian composer, the *Nutcracker* Suite and the *Pathétique* Symphony; while in the first half, the overture to Gluck's *Iphigénie* and the ballet music from Schubert's *Rosamunde* preceded the premiere of a new work by Esposito, his concert overture *Othello*, Op. 45.

The range of repertoire explored by the DOS over these four seasons is impressive, as is the increasingly ambitious nature of its programmes. Whatever the shortcomings of the performances may have been — and they were no doubt considerable — one cannot help but admire Esposito's achievement, particularly given the orchestra's straitened financial circumstances. And when one considers that his activities as a conductor must have consumed a great deal of whatever spare time he had left over from teaching and administration, it is altogether remarkable that the four years between 1899 and 1903 proved to be his most productive period to date as a composer, despite having experienced a protracted period of ill-health in 1902.[57] In addition to completing five orchestral

---

55 *Musical Times*, 43, 711 (1902), 333
56 The scores of these arrangements appear to be lost. It is possible that one of them may have been a version of Esposito's First Irish Rhapsody for violin and piano, Op. 51, which was composed in 1901. According to the catalogue of works in Aiello's monograph, this piece was arranged for cor anglais and piano in 1902: see Aiello, *Al musicista* 74.
57 The minutes of a meeting of the RIAM Board of Governors held on 4 June 1902 state that Esposito was presented with a cheque for £26 5s 'as a special mark of our appreciation of [his] service & in consequence of his long illness': see Pine and Acton, *To Talent Alone*, 576, note 52. The nature of the illness is not specified.

scores, one of them a symphony, Esposito composed three important chamber works, piano pieces and an opera. It is difficult to establish precise dates of composition for several of these compositions, and one cannot always assume that the order of their opus numbers necessarily reflects the order in which they were completed. Disappointingly, a considerable proportion of this music is lost, as the scores were never published and the manuscripts have since disappeared. The most frustrating losses in this respect are four of the five orchestral works, the symphony being the only one of them to have survived.

There can be little doubt but that the foundation of Feis Ceoil and the Dublin Orchestral Society were directly responsible for reviving Esposito's interest in creative work, which had lain more or less dormant for a long period preceding the composition of *Deirdre*. Between them, they provided a strong practical incentive for him to tackle projects of a more ambitious nature than small-scale piano pieces and songs. The *Poem*, Op. 44, would be the first purely orchestral composition he had completed since his First Piano Concerto, written twenty years previously. This was written for a Feis Ceoil competition that had been established in commemoration of the German harpist and composer Charles Oberthür, who had died a few years previously in 1895. Three of Oberthür's former students donated funds to award a composition prize for concertante works for harp and small orchestra.[58] The prize was offered at the Feis Ceoil in Belfast in 1898 but was not awarded, leading it to be offered at the Dublin Feis Ceoil the following year. As we have seen, Esposito conducted the premiere of the *Poem* in May 1899. It subsequently received further performances both under the composer's own baton and that of his former *protégé* Hamilton Harty. A fairly lengthy, but rather colourful description of the piece appeared in the *Freeman's Journal* after the premiere, from which it seems clear that it was cast in one movement and had the character of a fantasia. The reviewer noted the 'modern' character of its harmonic language and had much praise for its imaginative instrumentation:

> Signor Esposito knows how to make his strings speak. The grace, weirdness, and passion that he draws from them at the opening, and the lively fancy with which they enrich the sober melodies of the winds, are fine specimens of orchestration. Then there is the solitary note on the horn so splendidly led up to which so beautifully interrupts the stream of hurry and passion, and with a few characteristic notes of the oboes leads to the ease and quiet so finely expressed in the melody assigned to the clarinet; the characteristic deliveries of the oboes, clarinets and flutes, and the fanciful effects of the harp, which in a soft, playful way come in like the eddies and low murmurings of a current in the deep flowing stream of melody from the winds. The orchestra played the piece *con amore* with evident desire on every

58   The Oberthür Prize was the initiative of Edith Davies of Belfast, who, together with two other Oberthür pupils set up a fund to endow it: see 'The Feis Ceoil: General Meeting in Dublin', *The Belfast News-Letter*, 24 June 1899.

instrumentalist's part to bring out all the beauties of so charming a composition. The audience warmly applauded, and the composer was several times called forward to receive the expressions of their enthusiastic approval.[59]

It would be interesting to know if the 'modern' harmonic idiom or the orchestral sonorities owed anything to contemporary French music, but the reviewer's remarks are too vague to allow one to form any definite impression of the *Poem*'s stylistic orientation.

According to Aiello, the concert overture *Othello*, Op. 45, was written in 1900 and received its first performance at a DOS concert on 18 April 1902.[60] Esposito was not the first composer to base a symphonic work on Shakespeare's tragedy: the Czech composer Zdeněk Fibich had written a tone poem *Othello, after Shakespeare*, Op. 6, in 1873 and his compatriot Antonin Dvořák composed another as his Op. 93 in 1892. It is also possible that Esposito's imagination was fired by Verdi's great operatic treatment of the same subject. Our knowledge of the piece is solely dependent on a programme note written for a performance of the work given by the Hallé Orchestra in 1922. To judge from this, it was cast as an extended sonata form structure prefaced by a lengthy slow introduction. This opened in D minor and introduced two ideas: a horn motif associated with the idea of fate and another evoking Desdemona, which were subsequently transformed into the first and second subjects of the sonata-allegro proper. The first subject, a depiction of Othello's jealousy, was characterized by its 'relentless fury'. A second contrasting thematic idea associated with Desdemona made its appearance on the oboe, 'falling strewn and helpless through the sharp chords'.[61] The development was occupied with 'a warm, expressive and more tranquil exposition of what seems meant for the lyrical theme', which reminded the writer of the programme note of the second subject of the first movement of Tchaikovsky's *Pathétique* Symphony.[62] The opening violence erupted anew in the recapitulation, which concluded abruptly, 'with the voice of the oboe silenced swiftly and pitiably in the closing bars'.[63] From this account, it seems clear that *Othello* was a turbulent, dramatic work in the mould of earlier nineteenth-century symphonic poems such as Tchaikovsky's *Romeo and Juliet*. It certainly seems to have made a vivid impression at its premiere, leading the critic for the *Musical Times* to describe it as 'a work of great power'.[64]

According to the catalogue given in Aiello's book, the work that was eventually titled *Oriental Suite*, Op. 47, was also completed in 1900, but for reasons that are not clear it did not receive its first performance until 1 March 1905, at the third of that year's DOS

59 *Freeman's Journal*, 19 May 1899
60 Aiello, *Al musicista*, 73
61 Programme booklet for Hallé Orchestra concerts, 23 March 1922, 507–08
62 Hallé programme booklet, 508
63 Hallé programme booklet, 508
64 *Musical Times*, 43, 711 (1902), 333

concerts. It seems to have been very well received at its first performance and the critic for the *Irish Times* was full of praise for its striking orchestral effects:

> It was with great pleasure that the audience listened to Signor Esposito's unnamed Suite for Orchestra. The note on the programme, of course, explained the ideas which the composer intended to illustrate. His fancy has been inspired by an Eastern legend, which allows full scope for melodic phraseology, and for the employment of all sorts of orchestral devices. The whole is a piece of very clever baroque musical fancy, a *pasticcio* of luxuriant orchestral impressions ... . [65]

To judge from this account, it is possible that Esposito consciously set out to write an orchestral showpiece, not unlike Rimsky-Korsakov's *Scheherazade*, with gorgeous and exotic instrumental coloration as well as a definite underlying programme. Unfortunately no further information about the piece has so far come to light and it only seems to have received one further performance, which took place in Russia in July 1914.[66] We know even less about the *Fantasia*, Op. 48, for two pianos and orchestra. The date of composition of this work is uncertain, but it was evidently complete by late 1903, as an allusion is made to it in a *Musical Times* feature on Esposito which appeared in the November issue of the periodical that year.[67] It was first performed by the DOS with the pianists Edith French and Annie Lord on 25 February 1904. This concert was not reviewed in the *Irish Times* and the notice that appeared in the *Musical Times* merely mentions that the *Fantasia* was included on the programme. We consequently have no idea of what the piece may have been like — not even how long it was or whether it was in one or more movements.

Of the two orchestral compositions dating from this period that have survived, the first to be written was a work originally entitled *Symphony on Irish Airs*,[68] but which is now generally referred to as the *Irish Symphony* or the *Sinfonia Irlandese*, Op. 50. Like the *Poem* for harp and orchestra, this score had been prompted by a new Feis Ceoil composer's competition inaugurated in 1901 for symphonies based on Irish folk tunes. This idea was apparently inspired by Dvořák's *New World Symphony* and its use of Negro melodies, although one wonders whether Stanford's *Irish Symphony* had been a more obvious model. Interestingly, Stanford adjudicated the competition and Esposito's work was announced as the winning entry in February 1902.[69] The symphony was first performed during the Feis on 7 May that year by the DOS under the composer's direction. The orchestra performed it again at the opening concert of their winter season, and it was repeated at

65 *Irish Times*, 2 March 1905
66 Aiello, *Al musicista*, 56
67 *Musical Times*, 44, 729 (1903), 705–07
68 It was so described in the programme on the occasion of its premiere: see the advertisement on page 4 of the *Irish Times*, 7 May 1902.
69 *Musical Times*, 43, 709 (1902), 188

the annual conference of the ISM in Dublin on 31 December. On this occasion, it shared the programme with Culwick's *Concert Overture* and an Organ Concerto by the eminent English music theorist and composer Ebenezer Prout, who was Professor of Music at Trinity College, Dublin. It met with a resounding success on the occasion of its first performance, and was described by the reviewer for the *Musical Times* in glowing terms as 'a masterly work of very great power and beauty'.[70]

Although Esposito's symphony is less distinguished than Stanford's *Irish Symphony*, lacking the latter's imaginative exuberance and sheer technical finesse, it is nonetheless a work of considerable charm which undoubtedly merits an occasional revival. It is, moreover, of notable historical importance, as it represents one of the very few attempts by an Irish composer at this period to write an extended orchestral work based extensively on folk tunes. The style of the music is not altogether dissimilar to that of Dvořák in its diatonic lyricism and its modally tinged harmonic language. The first movement is a sonata-allegro featuring three themes enunciated in the keys of D major, F sharp minor and A major, respectively (the first of these is shown in Ex. 25) — a procedure which may owe something to the corresponding movement of Brahms's Second Symphony. The initial phase of the development reworks these ideas in interesting ways, but the remainder of the movement is perhaps less persuasive. The introduction of a new folk tune in F major militates against the attainment of sustained symphonic momentum and this idea is subsequently overused. A false recapitulation of the opening material in the very remote region of A flat major also strikes the listener as somewhat contrived. More successful is the Scherzo which was particularly warmly received by the audience at the first performance. The outer sections of this have the character of an energetic jig. The principal thematic idea, shown in Ex. 26, perhaps lacks the rhythmic élan of Stanford's hop-jig in nine-eight time in his *Irish Symphony*, but Esposito nevertheless derives witty effects from the persistent oscillations between tonic and submediant harmonies. A subsidiary idea, sounded over a drone bass, provides an effective contrast. The trio is dominated by a theme with the character of a reel (which also moves between harmonic reference points of I and VI) and is framed by references to a hop-jig fragment.

Ex. 25: *Sinfonia irlandese*, Op. 50, I, first subject

Ex. 26: *Sinfonia irlandese*, Op. 50, II, opening

The structure of the slow movement is quite unconventional, peculiar even. Its main theme, an extended melody suggestive of a lament (Ex. 27), vacillates ambiguously between F sharp minor and A major. It is immediately restated in a more turbulent guise in F minor before F sharp minor is restored. After a forceful climax in this key, this idea is dispelled by the introduction of two entirely new strands of folk melody in the tonic major (Ex. 28). These ideas constitute a gentle, protracted coda to the movement; and it is only in the last ten bars that the minor mode is restored with a reference to the opening melody. The last movement is a kind of rough-hewn rondo that presents a medley of Irish themes — a march in D, a reel in C (which bears a striking resemblance to Percy Grainger's as yet unpublished *Molly on the Shore*) and a fanfare in E flat. Towards the close, the martial theme prevails: Esposito presents it in a series of imitative entries that build up a rich contrapuntal texture before its final vigorous restatement in the tonic D major.

Ex. 27: *Sinfonia irlandese*, Op. 50, III, main theme

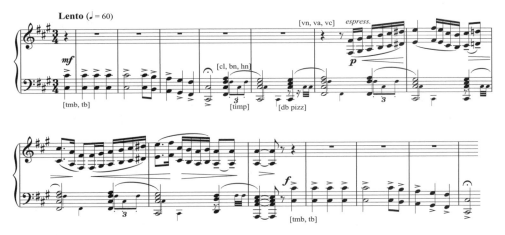

Ex. 28: *Sinfonia irlandese*, Op. 50, III, subsidiary idea

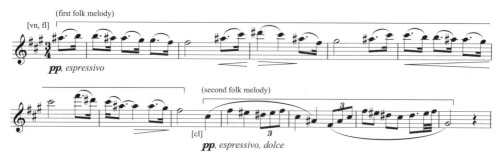

The other surviving orchestral work from this period is an altogether slighter affair, although still very attractive. The *Irish Suite*, Op. 55, which met with a highly enthusiastic reception on the occasion of its first performance by the DOS on 9 December 1903, is in five movements and is based on Irish melodies throughout. The first movement, which is in ternary form, contrasts a lively opening idea and a contrasting melody in dotted rhythms. The second movement, marked *Allegretto vivace* is a simple rondo structure in which both melodies, in F major and D minor, respectively, are pervaded by pronounced modal inflexions. The beautifully orchestrated slow movement is in ternary form and features an expansive Irish air in D minor, the opening of which is shown in Ex. 29, and a brisk theme given to the winds which returns in a livelier guise in the coda, this time marked *vivace*. The fourth movement has the character of a minuet and seems redolent of the eighteenth century, while the finale, a reel, is based on repetitions of an ostinato figure in E minor. This forms the basis of an attractive set of variations, which ends cheerfully in the major.

Ex. 29: *Irish Suite*, Op. 55, III, main theme

Two of the three major chamber works that Esposito wrote during these years have survived — the String Quartet in D major, Op. 33, and the Sonata for Cello and Piano in D major, Op. 43. Both of these scores were published and have consequently been preserved; the Piano Quintet, Op. 42, which remained in manuscript, has disappeared.[71] The String Quartet, like the *Poem* for harp and orchestra, was entered for a composers' competition at the 1899 Feis Ceoil. According to the work-list given in Aiello's monograph, this had been composed over

---

71 According to the catalogue of works in Aiello's monograph, the Piano Quintet was composed in 1898, but no further information is given except the rather curious detail that the composer transcribed the work for wind quintet thirty years later in 1928. This score has also disappeared and there is no record that either version was ever performed.

a decade previously in 1886, although it is possible that Esposito revised it before submitting it.[72] The quartet won first prize in its category and was judged by Stanford, who acted as adjudicator, to be 'very good, and the best thing sent in'.[73] This favourable estimate of the work's qualities was subsequently echoed by the critic for the *Freeman's Journal*, in whose opinion it represented 'the best and most important composition which the Feis Ceoil has so far invoked'.[74] The score was dedicated to the composer's friend W. P. Geoghegan.

Ex. 30: String Quartet in D major, Op. 33, I, opening

72 Aiello, *Al musicista*, 92
73 *Belfast News-Letter*, 28 January 1899
74 *Freeman's Journal*, 1 May 1899

Like the *Irish Symphony*, the First String Quartet cannot be adjudged a complete success, but it nonetheless has many features of interest. The first movement is conceived on an ambitious scale and has a monumental quality that may owe something to the example of Beethoven's quartets from his middle and late periods. As in the First Violin Sonata, the underlying sonata structure is handled in a rather unconventional way. This is particularly evident in the management of tonal relationships. The main theme, shown in Ex. 30, persistently features a flattened leading note, C natural, which emphasizes the subdominant region. The stability of D major is further undermined when these C naturals provide the conduit from D to the unexpected pedal B at bar 14 (Ex. 31) and subsequent references to the principal theme feature the same pitch C as the peak of their thematic contours, emphasizing a dissonant minor

Ex. 31: String Quartet in D major, Op. 33, I, 14ff.

ninth. Apart from these local harmonic divagations, however, the exposition is confined to the tonic for almost seventy bars, which militates against the attainment of the kind of tonal dynamism that one might expect at this point. Curiously, the first significant tonal shift that occurs is once again to the subdominant — although this ushers in a protracted phase of tonal instability. The lyrical cast of the musical material evinces similarities with Dvořák's string quartets, but the functional ambiguity of the opening twenty eight bars (are they introductory or does the movement get properly underway at bar 29?) surely owes something to Beethoven's procedures in some of his late quartets.

The development section handles these thematic ideas with considerable inventiveness and is notable for its concentrated motivic economy, with extensive use being made of sequences of rising semitones deriving from the B–C motif that featured in the exposition. Its tonal organization moves through a series of minor thirds from A minor to C major/minor to E flat major/minor, allowing the pitch C, which was so prominent in the exposition, to reassert its dominance at the development's core. The subsequent move to E flat introduces a false recapitulation of the thematic material commencing in bar 29 (thus confirming that the opening bars were, in fact, introductory) before dropping a semitone to D for the recapitulation proper. The movement concludes with a lengthy coda of Beethovenian proportions, in which the principal thematic ideas are subjected to further elaboration and are worked up to a strenuous climax.

The quartet's second movement is an altogether lighter affair, being an elegant *Intermezzo*. Its principal theme is notable for its capricious changes of tonality from F major to G minor, and then to D minor, which is eventually revealed as being the tonic key. This mood of whimsy also pervades the Trio, which is in a quicker tempo. Here Esposito introduces new material which is gradually transformed to provide an accompaniment to the *Intermezzo* theme on its reappearance and subsequently forms the basis of an attractive, quirky coda. The deeply felt *Adagio* that follows is strikingly contrasted in mood. Its harmonic language is undoubtedly indebted to Liszt and Wagner, as the chromaticism of the ambiguous opening progressions reveals (Ex. 32). Indeed, the movement's key, B major, and the extraordinary passage of eighteen bars before the first definitive cadence (much of which unfolds over a supertonic pedal) reminds one of *Tristan*. An impassioned subsidiary theme moves to the dominant, F sharp major, as it rises to a climax. The juncture at which the opening material returns (once again over a C sharp pedal) is obscured by the prevailing harmonic lability. The music eventually cadences unambiguously in B major ten bars from the very end, whereupon the subsidiary idea forms the basis of a brief valedictory coda. The finale, which is a lively sonata-rondo with some unusual structural features, dispels the preceding mood of pathos. Although this is an engaging movement which features some effective contrapuntal writing, the quality of its thematic invention is somewhat less distinguished and it cannot be said to provide a wholly satisfactory conclusion to the quartet as a whole.

Nonetheless, this shortcoming does not render the work unviable and it would be well worth an occasional revival.

Ex. 32: String Quartet in D major, Op. 33, III, opening

The Sonata for Piano and Cello in D major, Op. 43, was written in 1898 or thereabouts and was dedicated to Henry Bast, Esposito's RIAM colleague and chamber music partner for many years. Bast gave the first performance at an RDS concert on 20 February 1899 with the composer at the piano, and the sonata was subsequently performed in London on 8 December 1904 by the pianist Archie Rosenthal and the cellist Arthur Trew.[75] This work is undoubtedly one of the composer's finest achievements. It represents a notable advance on the G major Violin Sonata, demonstrating a much more sophisticated handling of formal organization and tonal relationships. These aspects, and the general richness of the sonata's musical fabric, have a kinship with the music of Brahms. The first movement is pervaded by an opposition between two contending tonal areas — a feature that may owe something to the German composer's procedures in works such as the A major Violin Sonata, Op. 100. The initial statement of the opening theme in D major (Ex. 33) is immediately followed by a counterstatement in F sharp minor before a return to the tonic. Both of these keys prove to be of cardinal importance in the movement's overall design.

---

75 *The Times*, 9 December 1904

The second subject appears initially in the dominant, but A major eventually yields to F sharp minor at the end of the exposition. Esposito then presents the opening theme once again in the tonic and its opposing mediant, creating the impression the exposition is being repeated. This proves deceptive, as the attainment of F sharp minor marks the beginning of a protracted development section which is one of the most complex in all of Esposito's surviving works. In its course, the structural importance of F sharp is reasserted: it is brought into prominence as the dominant of B minor during a tranquil central episode and as the key in which the entire development comes to a close, only to be negated at the last by the return of the first subject in D major. The key of F sharp major is also triumphantly established at the climax of the second subject in the recapitulation, before the movement subsides into the coda. The slow movement, which is in B minor, is a straightforward ternary structure that affords a measure of emotional and dramatic relief after the drama of the preceding movement. The sonata's finale, like that of the D major String Quartet, is an unconventional sonata-rondo structure in which the order of the thematic material is reversed in the recapitulation. This proceeds in a buoyant and optimistic mood, but closes unexpectedly in a more subdued fashion with a final reprise of the rondo theme marked *molto più lento*, its former dynamism now transformed into wistful introspection.

This period also saw the composition of several new piano works. The most substantial of these is the *Suite*, Op. 34, which was published by Breitkopf und Härtel in 1902 in two parts. This work was undoubtedly prompted by Esposito's interest in early Italian keyboard music and reflects the fin-de-siècle vogue for neo-Baroque keyboard suites of the kind written by Grieg, Stanford and Debussy. It is far more than an exercise in pastiche, however: its seven constituent movements are unified by a motto theme comprising a tetrachord (Ex. 34), which recurs in subtle transformations and creates the impression of an unfolding programmatic narrative, resulting in a work of considerable formal complexity. This idea is announced in the first two bars of the opening *Prélude* (Ex. 35), in which it is then elaborated into a restless *moto perpetuo*. The second movement, *Agitato-Tranquillo*, is based on further transformations of the motto, first as a *Scherzo* in D minor (Ex. 36) and with a contrasting slow section. The *Badinage* that follows is a ternary structure. Once again, the thematic material for both sections derives from the motto theme. The outer section employs it in the form D–E flat–G–F (Ex. 37); while the trio is particularly ingenious, featuring a tenor melody in the left hand deriving from the pitches D flat–E flat–G flat–F, which is accompanied by semiquaver figurations also derived from the motto (Ex. 38). The idea also pervades the *Nocturne* in D flat (Ex. 39), notably in the repeated left-hand progressions as well in the highly ornate melody in the right hand. In the rondo-like *Valse* that follows *attacca*, the motto is subject to two contrasting and highly characteristic interpretations, the first, a lilting tune in B flat with the motto presented as a syncopated inner voice, the second a more melancholy strain in C minor. The *Petite sérénade* returns to G major and the original succession of pitches for the motto, creating the impression that the work is drawing to a close. This turns out not to be the case: one further movement is yet to come. The concluding *Rêverie* (Ex. 40) provides a dreamy epilogue in a radiant B major, far from the original tonic, based on a final 'transcendental' version of the motto: D sharp–E–G sharp–F double sharp.

Ex. 33: Sonata for Piano and Cello in D major, Op. 43, I, opening

Ex. 34: Suite, Op. 34, 'motto' theme

Ex. 35: Suite, Op. 34, Prélude, opening

Ex. 36: Suite, Op. 34, Agitato-Tranquillo, opening

Ex. 37: Suite, Op. 34, Badinage, opening

Ex. 38: Suite, Op. 34, Badinage, central section

Ex. 39: Suite, Op. 34, Nocturne, opening

Ex. 40: Suite, Op. 34, Rêverie, opening

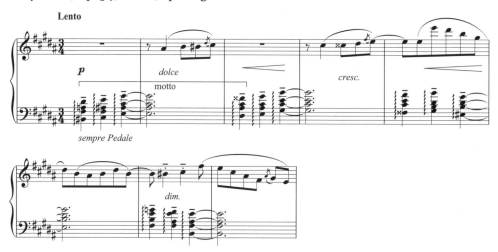

The other piano works from this period are of comparatively minor importance. The *Tarantella*, Op. 35, for piano duet was written for student performers and was dedicated 'to the pupils of Sion Hill Convent, Blackrock, Co. Dublin'. It is based on two effectively contrasted thematic ideas: the first makes prominent use of angular intervals, especially the opening tritone (Ex. 41), while the second is thoroughly reminiscent of Italian opera (Ex. 42). Esposito was evidently fond of the piece, as he transcribed it for orchestra in 1905. The *Deux nocturnes*, Op. 36, are more ambitious in scope than the *Quattro notturni*, Op. 13, of 1879 and make considerable technical demands on the performer. The harmonic language of the second nocturne is notable for quirky modulations and piquant dissonances, a characteristic passage being shown in Ex. 43. The *Deux valses*, Op. 37, are also quite virtuosic in nature and display a similar harmonic inventiveness, the second waltz being particularly attractive.

Ex. 41: *Tarantella, Op. 35, main theme*

Ex. 42: *Tarantella, Op. 35, subsidiary idea*

The remaining works that Esposito composed during these years continue his exploration of the expressive potential of Irish folk music. In addition to publishing arrangements of folk tunes, he completed several pieces of a more sophisticated nature that evoke the folk idiom. The two Rhapsodies for violin and piano, Opp. 51 and 54, which date from 1901 and 1902, respectively, and were both subsequently orchestrated, are clearly indebted in their general approach to the example of Liszt's celebrated Hungarian Rhapsodies, like many other folk-inspired works by European composers at this period. The first of these has the character of a virtuoso showpiece, although it also features passages of poignant emotional introspection. It opens with a *Caoine* [Lament] in D minor which emulates the prolix ornamentation of traditional Irish *sean nós* singing and is contrasted to telling effect with another melody in the major mode. This slow section leads to the main body of the rhapsody in A minor, which comprises a number of sections based on various folk melodies in alternating tempi. The Rhapsody, Op. 54, was a prize-winning work at the Feis of 1903 and was dedicated to the English violinist John Dunn, formerly a professor of violin at the RIAM (albeit only for a short period). Its opening *Andante* in E minor, which features several cadenzas, is followed by pastoral central section in G. The work concludes in E major with a lively jig.

Ex. 43: No. 2 of *Deux nocturnes*, Op. 36, opening

In the same year, Esposito also completed a substantial vocal composition, *Roseen Dhu*, Op. 49, to words by Alfred Percival Graves, which is described on the published score as an 'Irish Vocal Suite adapted from old Irish airs'. The title *Roseen Dhu* is an anglicization of the Irish *Róisín Dubh*, meaning 'little dark rose' or 'dark Rosaleen'. This soubriquet evokes a wealth of historical associations which may require a few words of explanation for non-Irish readers. In the eighteenth century, Gaelic poets (especially those from Munster) cultivated a literary genre known as the *aisling* (meaning 'dream' or 'vision'), which was ostensibly a love poem but was frequently used to convey a covert political subtext expressing the hope of the disenfranchised Catholic majority for deliverance. Typically, the poet would describe an encounter with a *spéirbhean* [sky-woman] of remarkable beauty who would identify herself as Ireland and prophesy the liberation of the country through a return of the Catholic Stuart kings to the English throne. Various names came into currency for these female personifications of Ireland, one of which was *Róisín Dubh*. Graves provided Esposito with a sequence of lyrics based on this personage, which present a loose narrative sequence. The events depicted have only the most tenuous connection with the historical context just described, however, and his poems trivialize the original conception, turning it into a sentimental love story. The action is set during the turbulent period after the accession of the Catholic James II to the English throne in 1685, an event which precipitated bloody conflict in Ireland. The imaginary Jacobite hero of Graves's poems participates in a celebrated episode that took place in 1690 during the first phase of the Williamite War of 1690–91 — the successful defence of the city of Limerick against an assault by a formidable multi-national force brought over by William of Orange to subdue the country. The 'argument' prefacing the score presents the following synopsis of events:

> The Singer, an Irish patriot serving under James II, describes how, after a dream, of impending disaster, he sees the King's ships ride safely into harbour. He then meets and falls in love with Roseen Dhu and hopes against hope that she returns his affection but is not assured of it until, passing her home on a sudden call to arms, without having had time to bid her farewell, he hears her passionately lamenting that he has gone without knowing she loved him. But the alarm proves a false one. He returns and they are joyfully affianced. Then the war summons sounds in earnest. Roseen will not be left behind her lover but rides with him into Limerick City and there falls at his side in the very hour of Victory.

The seven songs of Esposito's cycle depict the emotional responses of the protagonist at crucial junctures in the action — an approach essentially similar to that adopted by Arthur Somervell in his settings of lyrics from Tennyson's *Maud*. Esposito evidently envisaged the songs as a hybrid between folk song arrangements and art songs, retaining the artless character of the melodies but imbuing them with something of the expressive intensity and seriousness of German lieder. The individual songs traverse a considerable emotional range: 'The shadow of a dream' for instance, is imbued with romantic melancholy, while others, such as 'My rose of hope' (Ex. 44), are more expansively lyrical and optimistic in tone. One's impression that *Roseen Dhu* was modelled on the great lieder cycles of Schumann is reinforced by the fact that Esposito arranges the songs according to a carefully chosen tonal scheme based on sequences of rising major and minor thirds — an intervallic pattern much in evidence in the prelude to the first song (Ex. 45). The outer pairs of songs, which are predominantly solemn in mood, are written in keys a minor third apart (C sharp and E, and C and E flat, respectively), while the middle three songs, which explore the theme of love, present a succession of keys related by major thirds (E, A flat and C). Although Esposito's harmonizations and accompaniments are skilful and imaginative enough, his decision not to introduce contrasting material of his own invention allows him little scope to respond in a flexible manner to the narrative scheme and militates against the dramatic effectiveness of the cycle. As each song presents a succession of verses set to the same folk tune, the cumulative effect is rather monotonous.

Ex. 44: *Roseen Dhu*, Op. 49, 'My rose of hope'

Ex. 45: *Roseen Dhu*, Op. 49, 'The shadow of a dream'

The cycle was first performed in London by the baritone Denis O'Sullivan on 11 November 1901. O'Sullivan had previously appeared in a DOS concert in 1900 and would collaborate with Esposito on two stage works over the next two years. O'Sullivan, who was very popular with Irish audiences, had come to prominence during the 1890s when he sang in London with the Carl Rosa Opera Company. His dramatic and interpretative gifts were highly regarded and he won great renown for his performance of the rebel Shamus in Stanford's opera *Shamus O'Brien*, singing the title role during its long run in London before touring the work throughout Britain, Ireland and America. He was a regular visitor to Dublin and Esposito probably became acquainted with him when he was invited to sing at the RIAM in May 1900.[76] Their professional relationship appears to have deepened into a friendship, for Esposito worked closely with O'Sullivan over the next four years and composed several works expressly with him in mind.

Esposito's association with O'Sullivan led him to venture into new creative territory and compose his first stage work, a one-act operetta *The Post Bag: A Lesson in Irish*, to a libretto devised by Alfred Percival Graves. The circumstances surrounding the genesis of this score are somewhat obscure. It was commissioned by the Irish Literary Society and was subsequently performed under the auspices of that organization on 27 January 1902 at St George's Hall in London. The production was managed by O'Sullivan, who played the part

76 Pine and Acton, *To Talent Alone*, 224

of Seaghan. Joseph O'Mara, a popular Irish tenor who had also made his reputation singing in Stanford's *Shamus O'Brien*, played the role of Phelim while the remaining principal role of Kitty O'Hea, was sung by the soprano Evangeline Florence. Presumably for reasons of economy, the orchestral accompaniment was rendered on two pianos, one of which was played by Esposito. At the Irish premiere, which took place in the Gaiety Theatre on 14 March with the same performers, Esposito directed a pit orchestra. The previous evening, the operetta had been given in a private command performance at Dublin Castle by invitation of the Lord Lieutenant. It was subsequently revived by the Irish Stage Society of the London branch of the Celtic Association, which arranged a production at the Royal Court Theatre in London on 3 July 1908. On which occasion it featured in a double-bill with Graves's play *The Absentee*, for which Herbert Hughes had written incidental music.[77]

The central character of *The Post Bag* is Kitty O'Hea, a girl from Connemara. At the opening of the opera, she is eagerly awaiting a letter from her lover Brian O'Blake, who has gone to America to look for employment. Phelim O'Shea, the postman, arrives without his postbag, dressed in his Sunday best. In O'Blake's absence, he has been hoping to woo Kitty, but his efforts have so far been unavailing. Presently, another young man with designs on Kitty arrives on the scene, Seaghan the Smith, who is also dressed to impress. Kitty, keen to have some amusement, decides to play Phelim off against Seaghan before turning both of them out of the house. From her ensuing soliloquy, we learn that Kitty has retained her love for O'Blake but despairs of ever seeing him again. Phelim returns, this time in his postman's uniform complete with postbag. He hands her a letter which turns out to be from O'Blake. Kitty starts to read it: it begins in English, but the more private contents are in Irish which Kitty finds more difficult to understand. Not knowing what to do, she calls back the postman, asking him to translate it for her, pretending that it is from her cousin Nora. Phelim, who sees through her deception, decides to misrepresent the contents of the letter. He tells Kitty that it is from O'Blake, and not Nora, but that he cannot bring himself to read it as it reveals her lover in such a bad light. Kitty begs him to translate it even if she must learn the worst. Phelim pretends that O'Blake has taken up with another girl in New York and has written to suggest that Kitty take another man instead. Kitty is naturally horrified. Phelim then tries to renew his suit with greater enthusiasm and departs, leaving her to lament her fate.

77 'Our London Letter', *Irish Independent*, 17 June 1908, *Freeman's Journal*, 6 July 1908 and *The Times*, 4 July 1908

Ex. 46: *The Post Bag*, Op. 52, Kitty's aria 'They call me the luckiest lass alive'

In the next scene, Seaghan the Smith returns. Having being informed by Phelim of O'Blake's putative treachery and abandonment of Kitty, he tries to press his suit, singing some of his more amorous lines in Irish. Seeing that Seaghan speaks Irish, Kitty asks him if he would translate O'Blake's letter for her, pretending that it is from a friend, as she wishes to assure herself of the accuracy of the previous translation. Unbeknownst to Kitty, Seaghan cannot read — but he tries to turn the situation to his advantage and exposes Phelim's duplicity in the hope of winning Kitty's affection. His translation presents an alternative, if equally colourful version of events. O'Blake is writing to Kitty to tell her about a grave misfortune he had suffered. He had been on board a ship which foundered when it struck an iceberg. Clad only in his nightshirt, he had managed to jump from his bunk onto the iceberg, clutching a bottle of whiskey, from where he had to listen to screams of the crew as they drowned in the freezing ocean. Having emptied the contents of the whiskey bottle, he inserted the letter into it and cast it into the sea, hoping it would float to Ireland. The missive concludes with O'Blake's dying wish, a mysterious postscript, instructing Kitty not to 'demean' herself with the postman, but, with O'Blake's blessing, to yield to the smith instead. Kitty is understandably baffled by the discrepancy between the two translations. Contrary to what one might expect, the whiskey has left no hint of stain or smell upon the letter and she questions Seaghan about the whereabouts of the bottle. At this moment, Phelim enters, but realizing that Kitty has confounded their deception, tries to wrest the letter from Seaghan in a pathetic attempt to save his honour. In the resulting fray, the letter is torn to pieces and Phelim throws the scraps into the fire, but Kitty, who has retained the envelope in her pocket, catches sight of the writing, in English, on the inside flap of the envelope and realizes that O'Blake is on his way back to her. Just at this moment, O'Blake arrives, blowing his cow horn. Recognizing that the game is up, both men escape by jumping out the window (though Phelim has to return to through the door to gather his postbag from the table). United with her lover at last, Kitty throws herself into his arms.

As will be clear from the foregoing account, *The Post Bag* is a lighthearted farce reminiscent of the popular 'kitchen comedies' that later became staple fare at the Abbey Theatre. Graves's libretto, which is couched in colourful Hiberno-English, was undoubtedly conceived with the dramatic gifts of O'Sullivan and O'Mara in mind, as both excelled in playing comic stage-Irish characters. Although this style of acting would probably be regarded with disfavour today, it was relished by audiences at the period and within its own terms of dramatic reference Esposito's operetta is strikingly successful in setting this libretto to music. The work makes extensive use of Irish folk tunes, both as a basis for individual songs and for ensemble pieces. The whole of the first scene is based essentially on contrasting jig themes, while a contrasting slow reel accompanies the ridiculous overtures of Phelim and Seaghan. Kitty's buoyant aria in the second scene, 'They call me the luckiest lass alive', is also based on a jig (Ex. 46), as is Phelim's song in the third scene 'Atlas, for having a differ [sic] with Jupiter'. It is perhaps not surprising, given O'Sullivan's extensive role in both the production and the performance of *The Post Bag*, that the character of Seaghan should have the most memorable music. His first number ('Just as the Post-man told me'), is a deft reel in D major, which allows ample scope for comic stage business; a second number, a sombre air in D minor ('Oh, beauty's brightness!') is harmonized with the full panoply of Esposito's rich late-Romantic harmonic vocabulary; while the third, 'The Iceberg' (in which Seaghan farcically describes O'Blake writing from his hut on an iceberg after the sinking of the 'good ship Tarrycumdiddle') has the character of a ballad. Esposito's extensive use of quick dance tunes frequently leads him to adopt a style of word-setting reminiscent of the humorous patter songs that feature in the works of Sullivan and other popular operetta composers of the period such as Clay and Cellier. There are other witty musical touches. Kitty's lament in Scene 4, for example, suggests a parodic reminiscence of Schubert's *Gretchen am Spinnrade* (though Kitty sews rather than spins). At one crucial dramatic juncture, her reading of O'Blake's English postscript to his letter is delivered in a monotone while the orchestra rises to a triumphant

Ex. 47: The Post Bag, Op. 52, Letter scene

climax in B major (Ex. 52). After this tonal highpoint, which constitutes the climax of
the opera, a sense of reality is restored for Phelim and Seaghan who make their hasty
departure to the accompaniment of a further reel in the more prosaic key of B flat. From
a musical point of view, *The Post Bag* is a far more successful and interesting work than
Roseen Dhu, even if one occasionally wishes that Esposito had allowed himself a greater
degree of latitude in his handling of the traditional melodies. Interestingly, some of the
most inventive music in the opera is found in the transitions between the solo numbers,
when he allows himself to depart from quoting folk songs in their original forms. The
work demonstrates considerable dramatic flair, which was to be more fully realized in
Esposito's next opera, *The Tinker and the Fairy*.

5 Dublin or Naples? 1904–14

In the decade leading up to the First World War, Esposito's professional life proceeded on much the same lines as in previous years. He remained productive as a composer and continued to teach at the RIAM in addition to making regular appearances as a pianist and conductor. Since a detailed description of his activities during this decade would make for unduly repetitive reading, the account that follows is confined to giving an overview of their scope.

Gratifyingly, the DOS managed to survive throughout these years — although not without a struggle. In early 1903, the orchestra had once again found itself in parlous financial circumstances. The *Musical Times* reported after a concert on 24 February that the Society's funds had been 'quite exhausted', as the money taken at the doors had been insufficient to pay the expenses. Fortunately, an anonymous benefactor (who may well again have been Edward Martyn) came to the rescue and promised to cover the expenses incurred by the last two concerts of the season.[1] These duly went ahead, and after the final concert on 6 April another initiative was launched to place the DOS's finances on a sounder footing. The average cost of mounting a season of five concerts was somewhere in the region of £650, whereas the box office takings generally only came to £125. The modest annual grant of £50 from Dublin Corporation cleared only a small portion of the deficit. Clearly, it was necessary for the society to redouble its efforts to attract patrons willing either to pay an annual subscription or to make a donation. By April, £325 had been raised by this means, and plans were drawn up for the next season in the confidence that the estimated shortfall of £150 would be covered by additional subscriptions — an assumption which seems to have proved correct.[2] Having secured this extra revenue, the

1   *Musical Times* 44, 722 (1903), 259
2   *Musical Times*, 44, 728 (1903), 657

Society fared rather better over the next few years: indeed, after the 1906–07 season it could announce that it was free of debt, having cleared a £47 9s deficit carried over from 1904–05 and paid all expenses.[3]

The programmes that Esposito devised for the DOS concerts between 1903 and 1907 were remarkably enterprising and featured a substantial quantity of new or unfamiliar works alongside more well-known fare. Amongst the works in the former category were Richard Strauss's *Burlesque* for piano and orchestra, Saint-Saëns's Fifth Piano Concerto (with Annie Lord as soloist), Elgar's incidental music to a play co-authored by W. B. Yeats and George Moore, *Diarmuid and Grania*,[4] Alexander Mackenzie's orchestral ballad *La belle dame sans merci* and Sibelius's *Swan of Tuonela*. In subsequent years, the programmes included such exotic novelties as the Prelude to d'Indy's opera *Fervaal*, Massenet's incidental music to Leconte de Lisle's play *Les Erinnyes* and Dukas's *L'apprenti sorcier*. As in previous years, the music of Wagner was well-represented by excerpts from *Tristan, Parsifal, Die Meistersinger* and the *Ring* cycle. Unsurprisingly, there was also a considerable quantity of works by Beethoven: the orchestra introduced the *Eroica* and *Pastoral* symphonies into its repertoire, and gave the first performance of the Ninth Symphony (the instrumental movements only) in Dublin in over thirty years during its 1907–08 season. In addition to making occasional appearances as a soloist, Esposito conducted several of his own orchestral compositions: as we have seen, his *Fantasia* for two pianos and orchestra was given in 1904 and the *Oriental Suite* received its first performance in 1905.

On the whole, the DOS concerts seem to have been fairly well attended and although the Society's balance sheet showed a slight loss at the beginning of 1908, it does not seem to have engendered a great deal of anxiety.[5] Later that year, Esposito expanded the scope of the orchestra's activities to introduce a new series of orchestral concerts held in the Antient Concert Rooms on Sundays, which were aimed at working-class audiences.[6] The orchestra was scaled down to between thirty and forty players for these events, which were of a somewhat shorter duration than standard symphony concerts, generally lasting about an hour and a half. Initially, the programmes consisted of popular staples, but as time went on less familiar items were introduced. The venture was supported by prominent figures in Dublin society (such as the Lord Lieutenant and Archbishop Walsh) and proved highly successful — so much so that it continued the following year.[7] In January 1909, Esposito put on one of these concerts in collaboration with the renowned Moody Manners

---

3   The payment of this debt was made possible by donations amounting £174 1s: see 'Dublin Orchestral Society General Meeting: A Lively Discussion', *Irish Times*, 19 January 1907.

4   This is the title of Moore and Yeats's play: Elgar's incidental music, however, is always referred to as *Grania and Diarmid*.

5   *Musical Times*, 49, 780 (1908), 113

6   This initiative emulated a similar series of popular orchestral and choral concerts which were established in May 1887 by the philanthropist businessman Edmund Hay Currie and took place at the People's Palace, Mile End in London.

7   *Musical Times*, 52, 817 (1911), 191

Opera Company (one of the co-founders of which, Charles Manners, was half-Irish and had studied at the RIAM) to raise funds for the victims of the earthquake that destroyed the Sicilian city of Messina on 28 December 1908, in which at least 60,000 died. It is an indication of the level of public support for these concerts that he managed to raise a hundred guineas — in token of which he received a letter of appreciation from the Italian ambassador in London that was published in the Irish Times.[8]

Indeed, their popularity was such as to draw attention to the lack of a suitable venue for symphony orchestra concerts in Dublin — a long-standing problem which was only resolved decades later, and then only partially, with the conversion of the Great Hall of the former Royal University in Earlsfort Terrace into the National Concert Hall in 1981. At one of the Sunday concerts in February 1908, Esposito made a speech urging that something be done to improve matters. According to the Irish Independent, he was not sanguine about the possibility of a new hall being built with public money, and was of the opinion that the most practical solution would be to form a private syndicate to take over the Antient Concert Rooms and renovate them. This proposal aroused the interest of Edward Martyn, who regarded it as feasible.[9] The following year, Esposito's strictures concerning the unsuitability of existing Dublin venues for large-scale musical events were echoed by the eminent Irish tenor John McCormack, who had just returned from a highly successful sojourn in America. At a banquet organized in his honour at the Gresham Hotel, McCormack spoke enthusiastically about the marked improvements in Irish musical life that had come about in recent years, but felt constrained to add:

> ... there is one fact that I deplore when I come to this city. That is the unfortunate absence of a public hall worthy of the capital of our country (applause). The Rotunda and the Antient Concert Rooms are buildings with many historic associations, but Dublin ought to possess a hall larger and better equipped than these (hear, hear). For many purposes it would be useful, and for none more than for the development of musical functions of various kinds for which there is no proper accommodation at the present time in Dublin. I hope something will be done before long to provide such a hall.[10]

Esposito, who was present at the banquet, responded to McCormack's pronouncement by declaring that he and others had tried to realize this aim and had even arranged for plans for a new concert hall to be drawn up, but had been unable to obtain the necessary financial support. As the report of the Freeman's Journal explained:

8   Irish Times, 26 January 1909
9   Irish Independent, 7 February 1908
10   Freeman's Journal, 1 October 1909

Referring to the want of a decent concert hall, he mentioned that he, with other gentlemen, had made an effort to get one; and went so far as to have plans drawn of a projected hall; but when the want of funds was mooted the supporters of the project disappeared (*laughter*). He believed that it lay entirely with the Corporation to build a hall. It would certainly be a source of revenue to the city, and after a short time the cost of the building could easily be wiped out (*hear, hear*).[11]

Unfortunately, in spite of Esposito's efforts, no such support was forthcoming from the Corporation and his hopes to see this particular aspiration realized came to nothing.

In spite of the success of the Sunday concerts, the Society found itself in financial trouble once more at the end of 1908. The secretary, C. W. Wilson, announced that the Society was in deficit to the tune of £189 13s 10d and warned that it was 'on the verge of bankruptcy'.[12] This stark reality was further emphasized by the Lord Lieutenant, the Earl of Aberdeen, who made an appeal at the DOS concert on 9 December for extra funds.[13] Matters were exacerbated the following year when the Dublin Corporation decided to withdraw its annual £50 subvention.[14] Once again, the orchestra's future seemed doubtful and the press rallied in support. As a writer in the *Irish Independent* pointed out,

> [t]he [Dublin] Orchestral Society is the only source from which we get classical music adequately rendered. The Sunday concerts have been very successful, and a glance at the audience will show how many people have come, through them, to care deeply and intelligently for the noblest forms of the most spiritual of the arts.[15]

Esposito stubbornly refused to admit defeat and struggled to keep the orchestra going throughout the rest of 1909 and 1910. The accounts for 1910 showed a deficit of £49, even after a generous private donation by Leopold Dix of £189.[16] At the Annual General Meeting of the Society on 31 January 1911, chaired by Edward Martyn, it was noted that University College, Dublin[17] had refused further use of their Great Hall, which meant that the DOS would be forced to hire more expensive venues.[18] In January of the following year, the society continued to report a financial loss and launched another public appeal for funds. This time £200 was raised. When Dix presented the final accounts for the year, donations from members and subscribers amounted to £304 and other ticket subscriptions to £286

---

11 *Freeman's Journal*, 1 October 1909
12 'Dublin Orchestral Society: General Meeting', *Irish Times*, 5 February 1909
13 'Dublin Orchestral Society: Wagner Concert', *Irish Times*, 10 December 1908
14 'Dublin Orchestral Society: General Meeting', *Irish Times*, 5 February 1909
15 'Are Dublin folk musical?', *Irish Independent*, 5 February 1909
16 'Dublin Orchestral Society: Annual Meeting', *Irish Times*, 2 February 1911
17 University College Dublin was one of the new constituent colleges of the National University of Ireland, which replaced the Royal University in 1908.
18 'Dublin Orchestral Society: Annual Meeting', *Irish Times*, 2 February 1911

6s. Ticket sales at the concerts came to £149 4s 5d which, after the total expenditure of £712 19s 3d, left a small balance. Nonetheless, the situation remained worrying: the committee recognized that unless a further annual subvention of £250 was forthcoming the Society might have to curtail its activities.[19] By January 1913, however, the spectre of financial insolvency had disappeared: the Treasurer announced that donations, subscriptions and ticket receipts (£642 8s 6d) had exceeded expenses (£640 14s 7d) by the tiny sum of £1 13s 9d. This margin of profitability was precariously small, but it nonetheless seemed little short of miraculous that the orchestra had managed to break even. The Sunday concerts continued to enjoy good houses at the Antient Concert Rooms as the music critics of the *Irish Times* regularly noted,[20] and the DOS seasons went ahead as usual, though in a variety of different venues. Esposito continued to introduce new works to the Dublin public: Elgar's *Enigma Variations*, Tchaikovsky's *Francesca da Rimini*, Charpentier's *Impressions d'Italie*, Franck's Symphony in D minor and much mainstream repertoire by composers such as Mendelssohn, Schumann, Berlioz and Borodin, in addition to music by lesser-known figures such as Leo, Svendsen, Leone Sinigaglia and Goldmark.

In addition to his appearances as a conductor, Esposito continued to perform as a solo pianist and chamber musician. His involvement with the RDS had ceased for a period between 1900 and 1903 for reasons that are not entirely clear: the *Irish Times* announced that he had 'severed his connection with the Royal Dublin Society' and intended 'to give recitals on his own account'.[21] This he duly did, at the premises of the Antient Concert Rooms under the management of Pigott & Co, the first recital taking place on 16 November 1900.[22] In January 1901, he and several of his associates (including Wilhelmj, Delaney, Grisard, and Bast) reconstituted their former chamber ensemble and gave eight afternoon concerts under the auspices of a newly formed society, the Dublin Chamber Music Union. Throughout 1901 and 1902 the members of the ensemble gave regular concerts under the Union's auspices, varying the programmes to include piano music, concerted chamber works (including music for wind as well as strings) and songs, many of which were sung by the RIAM professor, Gordon Cleather. By 1903, however, the rift with the RDS committee had evidently been healed and the Chamber Music Union ceased to exist after its last concert on 20 March. Esposito was invited back to give two solo concerts in close succession, on 2 November 1903 and 8 February 1904. Shortly thereafter, he began

19 'Dublin Orchestral Society: Annual Meeting', *Irish Times*, 26 January 1912
20 For a typical example of such a report, see 'Sunday Orchestral Concert', *Irish Times*, 12 February 1910.
21 'Signor Esposito's Recitals', *Irish Times*, 16 November 1900
22 According to Anthony Hughes, audiences for the RDS concerts had started to decline and the Society incurred a substantial deficit of £400. Hughes suggests that the drop in attendance resulted from the audiences' overfamiliarity with Esposito and his colleagues, and indicates that there had also been some disagreements over fees: see Hughes, 'The Society and Music', 267. In November 1900 it was announced that the RDS Chamber Concerts would cease. Only three months later, however, the RDS indicated that the series would resume, featuring an entirely new ensemble led by Emile Verbrugghen: see *Irish Times*, 9 November 1900 and 4 January 1901.

to appear once more in chamber music recitals with his usual associates, though not to the same extent as before. In contrast with earlier years, the RDS seasons now featured a far greater proportion of visiting artists, which was undoubtedly a healthy development and one which had been long overdue. An impressive constellation of eminent virtuosi came to Dublin during these years, including Busoni and Paderewski, and of the finest chamber ensembles of the period, such as the Brodsky and Rosé String Quartets. This worked to Esposito's advantage, affording him opportunities to work with some of these instrumentalists. He performed with the quartets of Adolf Brodsky and Hans Wessely, for example, partnering their members individually in duo sonatas and the ensembles as a whole in works such as the Schumann and Brahms Piano Quintets. In 1911 he appeared as a guest pianist in a recital by Wassily Sapellnikoff (1867–1941), joining the Russian virtuoso in a rendition of Saint-Saëns's *Variations on a Theme of Beethoven*.

With colleagues from the RIAM and Sigismund Beel, an American violinist who was a regular fixture of Dublin musical life between 1902 and 1910, Esposito formed a new chamber group, the Beel-Esposito Quintet. This ensemble gave concerts along similar lines to those in which he had participated during the 1890s. After the death of Henry Bast, his place was filled by the English cellist Clyde Twelvetrees, who was appointed Professor of Cello at the RIAM in 1902 and remained in Dublin until 1922, when he became principal cellist of the Hallé Orchestra. Esposito and he seem to have become close friends and frequently gave duo recitals together. When Beel ceased visiting Dublin, this ensemble disbanded, and Esposito took to performing piano trios with Wilhelmj and Twelvetrees instead.

Esposito's solo recitals remained as enterprising as ever: they continued to include early Italian keyboard works, but also included such novelties as five Debussy *Préludes* in one of his programmes for 1911, a mere two years after their publication. The audiences for the RDS concerts tended to be rather conservative and regarded new music with suspicion. Much to their dismay, Esposito's prize pupil Annie Lord frequently performed works by Debussy and Ravel: Walter Starkie recalled 'the look of horror that came into the faces of some of those steadfast Mozart and Mendelssohn lovers' when they were subjected to manifestations of musical modernity. 'Such music', as Starkie remarked, 'ruffled the calm surface of the minds of those charming people, who would have wished the world to continue changeless in the little theatre'.[23] Fortunately for them, Esposito also played standard repertoire that was probably more to their taste, including much Beethoven and Chopin. RDS *habitués* also had the opportunity to hear him deliver the occasional lecture. On 9 March 1906, for example, he gave a talk on Italian keyboard music from the Baroque period, which was illustrated with examples played on a harpsichord made by Ferdinand Weber in Dublin around the year 1770; while on 10 February 1911 he lectured on 'The

23 Starkie, 'What the Royal Dublin Society has Done for Music', 62

Origins of Opera', demonstrating his considerable knowledge of early operatic repertoire by Caccini, Peri, Cavalieri and Monteverdi.

As the subject matter of these talks might suggest, Esposito's interest in early music seems to have intensified at this stage of his life. An *Irish Times* advance notice for one of his RDS recitals in 1903 mentions that he had made a trip to Italy earlier that year, in the course of which he had an opportunity to acquaint himself with music by Alessandro Scarlatti that was still in manuscript — though under what circumstances it is not clear.[24] A profile of the composer that appeared in the *Musical Times* shortly afterwards notified readers that he was currently 'compiling and editing a volume of clavier music by Italian writers of the 16th, 17th and 18th centuries', and had procured from 'one of the Conservatories in Italy some manuscripts, hitherto unpublished, of several fine compositions by Alessandro Scarlatti – Toccatas etc. and some very fine variations, which, he says, have more unity running through them than anything down to Beethoven's Variations in C minor'.[25] The fruits of this editorial activity were presented in a volume entitled *Early Italian Piano Music: A Collection of Pieces Written for Harpsichord and Clavichord*, which he completed in October 1905 and which was published by Oliver Ditson of Boston in 1906. Esposito's project had presumably been stimulated by his awareness of important recent initiatives by Italian scholars in the domain of early music, one of the most notable of which was the publication of three hundred keyboard sonatas by Domenico Scarlatti in 1906 in an edition prepared by his erstwhile student at the Real Collegio, Alessandro Longo. Much of the music in Esposito's volume had been published already elsewhere, but the pieces by Alessandro Scarlatti — the 'Aria' from *Toccata Seconda*, the 'Minuetto' from *Toccata Quarta*, the 'Tema con variazioni' from *Toccata Settima*, the *Toccata Ottava* and *Nona* and the Fugue in F minor — were completely unknown.[26] The collection comprised many items that Esposito had programmed in his recitals for many years, including pieces by Ercole and Bernardo Pasquini, Rossi, Frescobaldi, Marcello, Durante, Zipoli, Martini, Galuppi and Paradies. Domenico Scarlatti, son of Alessandro, was represented by nineteen sonatas and the *Cat's Fugue*, and works by Clementi were also included. The volume was clearly designed for pedagogical use: the prefatory matter included biographical sketches of the various composers, many of whom would have been unfamiliar to music students, as well as a preliminary introduction about the mechanism and historical development of the clavichord and harpsichord.[27] The volume provides a fascinating insight into the

24 'Royal Dublin Society: Music Recitals', *Irish Times*, 31 October 1903
25 'Michele Esposito', *Musical Times*, 44, 729 (1903), 707
26 In his introduction, Esposito states that his editions of these had prepared from manuscripts housed in the Conservatorio di Musica Giuseppe Verdi in Milan.
27 Esposito's anthology was reprinted under the title *Early Italian Keyboard Music: 49 Works by Frescobaldi, Scarlatti, Martini and Others* by Dover Publications, New York, in 2005, though with the omission of some introductory matter.

performance practice of the period, for in many cases Esposito provides alongside the original text a version which is reconceived in terms of the modern grand piano.

His labours in this field did not lead him to neglect original composition and he completed a number of substantial works in the decade before the outbreak of World War I. This period, however, was not as productive of new compositions as the previous years had been and the scores that Esposito managed to complete were generally on a more modest scale than the preceding orchestral and chamber works. His next two opus numbers consist of arrangements of Irish airs for violin and piano, which need not detain us here. The *Two Shelley Songs*, Op. 58, were completed in February 1905. These represent a rare contribution by Esposito to the emerging repertoire of English art songs. Both are compositions of substance and exude a mood of sadness and regret. The first poem, 'Time long past', dwells on images of irreparable loss and human mortality. Esposito's sombre setting is pervaded by the sonority of a dominant minor ninth, which obstinately refuses to resolve to the tonic even at the end — an appropriate musical image for unsatisfied yearning. The poetic persona of the second poem, 'To night', is burdened by an oppressive sense of the futility of human existence: he longs for extinction, yet recoils from the horror of death. This song is on a larger scale and is highly adventurous tonally, moving from C major at the opening to F sharp minor for the third verse to depict the unwelcome presence of 'the weary Day turn'd to her rest, Lingering like an unloved guest.' C minor makes a dramatic return for the last stanza, but turns to the major to convey the exalted mood of the conclusion.

The *Three Ballades* for piano, Op. 59, were completed in March 1905 and were dedicated to the distinguished German pianist, Agnes Zimmerman, who was resident in London and gave several recitals in Dublin for the RDS. Esposito performed them for the first time at an RDS recital on 2 November 1908. The influence of Brahms is immediately evident in the first and third pieces of the set, particularly with regard to the style of keyboard writing and the prevailing heroic mood. As one might expect from the title, the pieces have the character of fantasias and suggest a covert programmatic content. The first ballade, in E major, is striking for its unexpected modulation to D major, rather than the dominant for the subsidiary theme (Ex. 48). The entire piece is generated from the interplay of these two ideas, presented in a range of tonal areas, some of them very remote. The second ballade, an expressive *Lento*, is rather simpler in style and more Chopinesque in its decorative figuration. There are two principal ideas, one in A flat, the other in F minor. The piece grows steadily in textural complexity until this intensity is dispelled by a brief cadenza and a final reprise of the A flat material. The final ballade in E minor is cast in a more conventional ternary form. The robust outer sections feature emphatic cross-rhythms (Ex. 49), to which the more introspective and lyrical central section in B major affords an effective contrast.

Ex. 48: No. 1 of *Three Ballades*, Op. 59

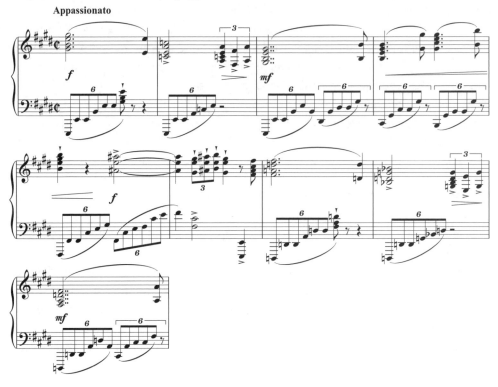

Ex. 49: No. 3 of *Three Ballades*, Op. 59

The following year, 1906, saw the completion of a substantial chamber work, the Second
String Quartet in C minor, Op. 60, which Esposito entered for a competition organized

by the Reale Accademia Filarmonica in Bologna. The jury (which included the composer Ermanno Wolf-Ferrari) judged the work the best of the sixty-seven entries submitted and awarded it first prize. Esposito received £40 (2,000 lire) in prize money and a performance of the quartet was organized by the Reale Accademia in 1908.[28] It was not given in Dublin for another eight years, but drew prolonged applause from the RDS audience on the occasion of its Irish premiere on 2 February 1914.[29] The work was dedicated to the Wessely Quartet. It was subsequently revived by the Brodsky String Quartet, which performed it on 19 February 1923 at the RDS.

The quartet's first movement is remarkably concentrated in its formal organization and motivic working-out. Much of the material is derived from two melodic strands stated simultaneously in invertible counterpoint by the first violin and cello at the opening (Ex. 50). The descending chromatic stepwise motion of the bass heard in bars 1 to 11 pervades the harmony and melodic contours of the entire movement. This idea is especially prominent in the latter part of the development and in the tortuous chromaticism of the turbulent coda. The *Adagio espressivo* in A flat is somewhat reminiscent of the corresponding movement in Dvořák's *American* Quartet, although Esposito's tonal scheme is more wide-ranging. This is cast as a ternary structure, the central section of which commences in C sharp minor but soon moves to a tranquil D major. The vigorous Scherzo makes considerable demands on the virtuosity of the performers and employs sharply contrasted dynamic levels that generate considerable dramatic urgency. The lyrical trio juxtaposes two attractive ideas, one suggestive of Neapolitan popular song, the other featuring a yearning suspension above the subdominant (Ex. 51 and Ex. 52). The headlong impetus of the finale, which is in sonata form, is only temporarily held up by a more melodious second subject. Once again, Esposito's skill as a contrapuntist is much in evidence. The quartet as a whole is imaginatively composed for the medium, though, perhaps at first hearing, less directly appealing: its spare textures and rather austere mood are in stark contrast to the expansiveness of its predecessor. Nonetheless, it is in some ways a work of greater subtlety than the First String Quartet, particularly in its formal organization. It is eminently worthy of revival and compares favourably with those late quartets of Dvořák and Stanford's quartets of the same period (Op. 99 and Op. 104).

28 A subtitle on the title page of the published miniature score of the quartet reads 'Premiato al Concorso Internazionale della R. Accademia Filarmonica di Bologna 1906', but the results of the competition were not announced until April 1908: see *Irish Times*, 27 April 1908.

29 *Irish Independent*, 3 February 1914

Ex. 50: String Quartet in C minor, Op. 60, I, opening

The following year Esposito entered a French composition competition held under the patronage of the Prince of Monaco, for which he submitted his Second Violin Sonata in E minor, Op. 46. According to the work-list given in Aiello's monograph, this had been composed in 1899,[30] which would account for its earlier opus number, but Esposito may have revised the sonata before sending it off. The adjudicating panel (which included such distinguished musicians as Vincent d'Indy, Jacques Thibaud, Alfred Cortot and Pablo Casals) placed Esposito's work first out of sixty-eight entries when the results were announced in 1907. Apart from earning him 2,000 francs (about £80), the prize brought with it publication of the winning sonata by Astruc in 1907 and the prospect of a performance by Thibaud and Cortot, who were then both at an early stage of their careers.[31] Esposito gave the English premiere of the work with Sigismund Beel in the great hall of the Hotel Majestic in Harrogate on 2 January 1908 during the annual conference of the ISM and the two men repeated their performance for the RDS on 20 January.[32] The sonata was then taken up by the young English violinist, May Harrison, who played it in London at the end of March;[33] and shortly thereafter Beel gave it again with Herbert Fryer at the Bechstein Hall in May of the same year.[34]

Ex. 51: String Quartet in C minor, Op. 60, III, trio section, principal theme

---

31 This account is based on the information given in Aiello, *Al musicista*, 53. (Aiello, incidentally, gives the work the incorrect opus number of 68 and misspells the surname of Cortot). It has not proved possible to determine the exact title of the competition or to find out which body was responsible for organizing it: the most likely candidate is the Société Nationale de Musique. The published score of the sonata merely bears the inscription 'Œuvre couronnée au Concours International de Musique (Paris 1907)'. Otello Calbi gives the title of the organization in a garbled macaronic form as 'Società Music. Nouvelle [sic] di Parigi' (see Aiello, *Al musicista*, 96), whereas the *Irish Times* identifies it merely as 'Société Musicale' (18 January 1908).

32 *Musical Times*, 49, 780 (1908), 104

33 *The Times*, 1 April 1908

34 *The Times*, 5 May 1908

Ex. 52: String Quartet in C minor, Op. 60, III, trio section, subsidiary theme

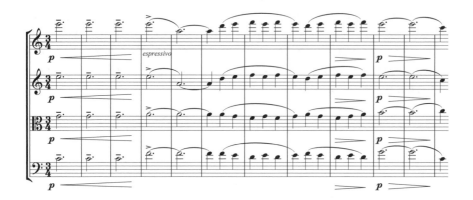

The work represents a considerable advance on the composer's previous violin sonata and is not dissimilar in style to the D Major Cello Sonata that was composed around the same time. As in the latter score, a concern to achieve a taut structural organization and close motivic integration is in evidence throughout. Much of the material in the first movement is derived from the motif of a semitone — comprising the notes B and C — which is announced at the outset (Ex. 53). A train of semitonal progressions in the bass leads to the introduction of a contrasting idea, an extended melody, which is shown in Ex. 54. Semitonal inflexions pervade the rest of the first subject group and the bridge passage: even when the dominant of the relative major G is reached — the tonality of the second subject — its stability is threatened by the continuance of extensive semitonal movement in all the parts. The second subject is one of Esposito's most memorable inventions and is announced in a three-voiced polyphonic texture in which semitones retain their prominence (Ex. 55). The development opens with a reference to the opening material, as if an expositional repeat is about to get under way. Much of the musical argument here is also dominated by the semitone motif, and significantly, the music spends a considerable amount of time in C minor, a region surely determined by the movement's opening gesture. As one might expect, the pitch C inexorably leads to the establishment of its companion note B, the dominant of E minor, which heralds the recapitulation. Nonetheless, when the recapitulation eventually commences, Esposito continues to emphasize C in the bass, accompanying it with new harmonies that suggest a move to the Neapolitan region, before restoring the principal melody in E minor (Ex. 56). For the reprise of the second subject, Esposito obscures the tonality E major in a similar fashion until a dominant pedal is established. The inspired coda, which is more lyrical in nature, affords a brief respite from the highly charged music that has preceded it, though the ubiquitous semitonal movement ominously reasserts itself before the close.

Ex. 53: Sonata No. 2 for Violin and Piano, Op. 46, I, opening

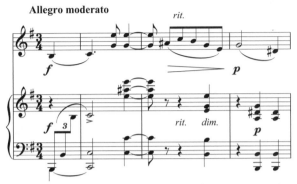

Ex. 54: Sonata No. 2 for Violin and Piano, Op. 46, I, subsidiary theme

Ex. 55: Sonata No. 2 for Violin and Piano, Op. 46, I, second subject

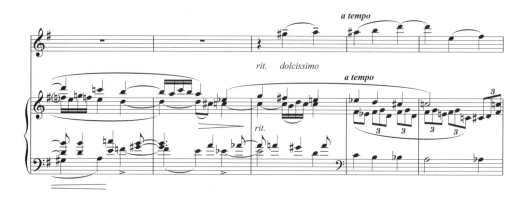

Ex. 56: Sonata No. 2 for Violin and Piano, Op. 46, I, recapitulation

The second movement, *Andantino*, is effectively a conflation of a Scherzo and slow movement. The playful opening idea alternates a *pizzicato* figure in the violin with a quirky response from the piano (Ex. 57), but as the first section proceeds, these gestures increasingly take on an exaggerated and burlesque character. The middle section has the character of a conventional slow movement, in which the opening violin figures are worked up to an emotional climax before resuming their original guise in the last eleven bars. The competition judges would almost certainly have been impressed with this unusual and unconventional movement and it was also singled out for special notice by the London critic of *The Times* (probably Fuller-Maitland), who remarked on its 'clever use of *pizzicato* chords', which gave the principal theme a 'pleasant flavour of originality'.[35] The finale is more overtly melodious and has a straightforward sonata structure. On the whole, it is much less complex than the preceding movements, but is nonetheless highly attractive and has well-contrasted thematic material, the second subject group being especially notable for its skilful employment of metrical augmentation and striking harmonic progressions.

35 *The Times*, 1 April 1908

Ex. 57: Sonata No. 2 for Violin and Piano, Op. 46, II, opening

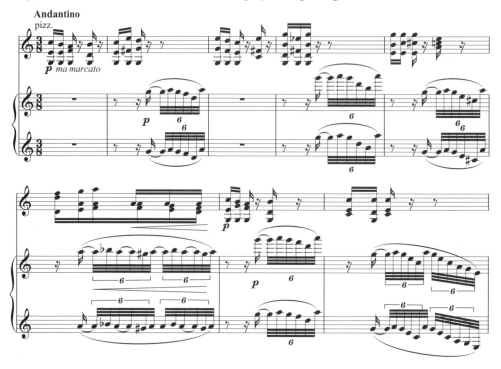

Esposito's other major projects during the first decade were both connected with the stage. After *The Post Bag*, O'Sullivan and Esposito collaborated on one further dramatic enterprise. Sometime in 1903 or 1904, O'Sullivan's wife, Elizabeth Curtis O'Sullivan (who wrote under the pen name 'Patrick Bidwell') wrote a musical play *Peggy Machree*, which she described as a 'romantic comedy with music'. Its improbable plot, set in 1740, recounts the adventures of a young noblewoman, Lady Margaret O'Driscoll, who escapes from a convent on her birthday and disguises herself as an Irish country girl (or, as described in the press, a 'colleen') by the name of Peggy Machree. As a joke she agrees to participate in a mock-marriage at Downkilty Fair with her lover, a naval officer, Barry Trevor (a role designed specially for O'Sullivan). Later, however, Lady O'Driscoll discovers that she has been married in earnest, as the marriage ceremony has been performed by a real priest rather than a friend of Trevor's. The couple part when Trevor goes off to war; but meet many years later when, disguised as a strolling player, he turns up in time to rescue Lady O'Driscoll from a runaway horse. His disguise is soon penetrated and after his discovery of her, the couple fall in love again, only to realize they are already man and wife. This rather unlikely plot formed the basis of a stage work resembling an updated ballad opera. O'Sullivan asked Esposito to arrange a number of songs based on Irish airs selected by him and his wife, and the composer also appears to have supplied some original music.

Additional numbers were provided later by the Canadian-born composer Clarence Lucas, who conducted the first production.

Peggy Machree opened in Grimsby on 7 November 1904 and was subsequently taken on tour around Britain. The production came to London's West End for five weeks and scored a considerable success. Esposito's music found general favour: the reviewer for the Times remarked that 'there is a quality in every number not usually heard on our lyric stage; something quaint and haunting, something a little melancholy even in the merriest songs'.[36] After the London season the play went back on tour around the British Isles, generating substantial revenues for O'Sullivan and his wife. In August 1905, Peggy Machree played to full houses at the Gaiety Theatre, with the American actress Claudia Lasell in the role of Peggy and Leslie Stiles as Trevor.[37] In November 1907, O'Sullivan departed for America to perform in an American production at McVicker's Theatre in Chicago, which opened on 5 January 1908.[38] While playing in Columbus, Ohio, he was suddenly taken ill with appendicitis and died at the end of January after an unsuccessful operation.[39] He was only thirty-nine years of age. The tour of 'Peggy' came to an abrupt end, but the piece was revived by his compatriot, the tenor Joseph O'Mara (who also played the role of Barry Trevor), for his tour of the USA in 1908.[40] To judge from an interview O'Mara gave to the New York Times, Esposito either adapted the songs to suit the tenor's vocal range or may have written some new material especially for him — it is not clear which.[41] The production was a major hit at New York's Broadway Theatre when it was mounted at the end of December and received highly enthusiastic coverage in the Irish press.[42] As a result, three numbers that Esposito had arranged for the show were published by the John Church Company in New York in 1908.

Esposito's next project was one of greater artistic substance — an opera based on a play by the Gaelic scholar and activist Douglas Hyde, who came to national prominence for his attempts to promote the revival of Irish through his work with the Gaelic League. Hyde was a writer of considerable distinction, who, in addition to producing notable translations of Irish poetry, enjoyed a considerable success as a playwright. His first play in Irish, Casadh an tSúgáin [The Twisting of the Rope] had been warmly received when it was put on in Dublin in 1901. This success encouraged him to compose a second play on a fairytale-like subject, An Tincéar agus an tSidheóg [The Tinker and the Fairy], whose central character is one of the fairy-folk (or aos sí) of Irish legend and mythology. The play, translated into English by Belinda Butler, was first staged privately in the garden of the novelist George Moore

36 The Times, 29 December 1904
37 'Gaiety Theatre: "Peggy Machree"', Irish Times, 29 August 1905
38 New York Times, 6 January 1908
39 New York Times, 2 February 1908
40 New York Times, 22 December 1908
41 New York Times, 18 October 1908
42 See Robert Potterton, 'Joseph O'Mara', North Munster Antiquarian Journal xxxii (1990), 85ff.

before an invited audience of three hundred guests on 19 May 1902.[43] On this occasion, Hyde himself played the part of the Tinker and the role of the Fairy was taken by Sinéad Ní Fhlannagáin, who later became the wife of Éamon de Valera.[44] Esposito was asked to provide songs and incidental music, and seems to have assisted in the production.[45]

It would be interesting to know how Esposito came into contact with Hyde, or, for that matter, to learn more about his relations with other literary figures who were prominent during the Revival, but unfortunately, reliable information on these matters is exceedingly scant. What can be said with reasonable certainty, however, is that Esposito's wife and his daughter Vera appear to have been acquainted with several Irish writers, including John Millington Synge. Natalia is known to have translated *Riders to the Sea* into French and Russian around this time,[46] and Vera acted in productions of two of Synge's plays.[47] Hyde may have frequented Natalia's salon and met her husband there — he would, in any case, have been an obvious composer from whom to commission incidental music for the play. At some point, Esposito conceived the idea of composing a more extended operatic treatment and Hyde was evidently willing to give him permission to do so.

Given the precedents of *Deirdre* and *The Post Bag*, it is perhaps not surprising that Esposito should turn once again to Irish subject matter for his second opera. During the previous decade, several Irish composers had written operas on Irish subjects or in the Irish language, amongst them Annie Patterson, Thomas O'Brien Butler and Robert O'Dwyer.[48] These works were consciously conceived as contributions to an emergent repertoire of Gaelic art music and it is possible that they might have prompted Esposito to compose something along similar lines. Getting an opera put on in Dublin represented quite a challenge, however, as no professional opera company was based there at the period: such operatic fare as was on offer was provided entirely by visiting British companies. This fact no doubt explains why Esposito delayed for several years before composing his operatic setting of Hyde's play.

In 1908, however, the prospects of securing a production unexpectedly improved due to a succession of chance circumstances. Three years previously, the Irish singer Barton

43 Hyde's play was later translated by Lady Augusta Gregory as *The Tinker and the Sheeog* and published in 1903.

44 Janet Eggleston Dunleavy and George W. Dunleavy, *Douglas Hyde: A Maker of Modern Ireland* (Berkeley, 1991), 221–22

45 According to Ní Fhlannagáin, the composer seems to have cut a faintly comical figure at the first performance, exhorting the actors in his excitement to 'singa – singa': see Pine and Acton, *To Talent Alone*, 564, note 154.

46 Synge mentions these translations in his correspondence during 1904, but neither seems ever to have been published. The Russian translation was entitled *Zhertvï Mori* — literally, 'Victims of the Sea'; Natalia does not appear to have settled on a suitable title for the French version: see Maurice Bourgeois, *John Millington Synge and the Irish Theatre* (London, 1913), 259–60, 261.

47 See Chapter 6.

48 For an account of operas by Irish composers at this period, see Axel Klein, 'Stage Irish, or the National in Irish Opera, 1780–1925', *The Opera Quarterly* 21, 1 (2005).

McGuckin, who had made a considerable reputation as leading tenor with the Carl Rosa Opera Company,[49] had founded a new amateur choral society in Dublin. Shortly afterwards, this was renamed the Dublin Amateur Operatic Society (DAOS) and in May 1906 it gave performances at the Theatre Royal of Gounod's *Faust* and Balfe's *The Bohemian Girl*.[50] In May of the following year, the company put on a short season of four operas, Bizet's *Carmen*, Benedict's *The Lily of Killarney*, Mascagni's *Cavalleria rusticana* and a revival of the previous year's production of *The Bohemian Girl*, with a chorus of two hundred and an orchestra of sixty players.[51] However, by September 1908, pressure seems to have been placed on McGuckin to resign from his position as conductor,[52] and Esposito was invited to take over his role.[53] Esposito no doubt welcomed the opportunity to conduct in the theatre, but motivation for accepting the position undoubtedly transcended mere self-interest. For one thing, he was acutely aware (as McGuckin had also been) of the absence of opportunities for young singers to get stage experience in Ireland; and having successfully established a professional orchestra, he was eager to see whether it might be possible to found a professional opera company. He outlined his vision in an interview printed in the *Freeman's Journal* before the commencement of the company's 1909 season:

> ... we want to give the singer with a good voice a proper chance – to establish a training school for operatic repertoire work. As it is, the singer has only one resource, to join an opera company, beginning by singing in a chorus. That means several years of hard work, and perhaps at the end of the time the voice goes, and a promising career is blighted, all for want of an early opportunity of efficient training in operatic work ... [A] great deal depends on the support we meet with. If next week's performances are properly supported, we will do something more next year. People who come can count on a pleasant night and on hearing good music, and — as we hope — may be helping to make Dublin the future home of a National Opera. ... My aspirations are to found the Society on a firm basis, and do for dramatic music what the Orchestral Society has done for symphonic music, and make it the beginning of a National Opera, which will give a chance to Irish composers.[54]

In its first season under Esposito, the DAOS presented two operas, Verdi's *Ernani* and Gounod's *Faust*: Esposito conducted the week's performances and brought over H. G.

49 McGuckin was particularly noted for his principal roles in several new British operas produced in London during the 1880s, including Goring Thomas's *Esmeralda*, Alexander Mackenzie's *Colomba* and *The Troubadours*, and Hamish MacCunn's *Jeannie Deans*.
50 *Irish Times*, 2 May 1906
51 *Irish Times*, 4 May 1907
52 Letter from McGuckin to the Editor of the *Irish Times*, 22 September 1908. After giving up the conductorship of the DAOS, McGuckin returned to London, where he died in 1913: see *Irish Times*, 18 April 1913.
53 *Irish Times*, 24 October 1908
54 *Freeman's Journal*, 27 March 1909

Moore from the Covent Garden Opera Company to act as stage manager. These drew favourable notices in the press, and the takings at the box office were sufficient to allow a second season to go ahead in March 1910. This time three operas were performed — Bellini's *Norma*, Weber's *Der Freischütz* (for which Esposito provided recitatives) and the new operatic version of *The Tinker and the Fairy* with Nettie Edwards and J. C. Browner in the principal roles. Once again, the reviews were generally complimentary, though the responses to Esposito's opera were somewhat mixed. The performances were not especially well attended, however. On the last night of the run, which concluded with a performance of *Der Freischütz*, there were repeated calls for Esposito to take a bow onstage, but he had left the theatre immediately after the final act — one gathers in a fit of despondency. The manager was eventually obliged to appear in front of the curtain in his stead: he thanked the audience for their support, but explained that the company was unlikely to survive unless it enjoyed greater public support.[55] After this season, Esposito subsequently relinquished his position as conductor. The Society quickly declined and by 1911 had ceased to exist.

Disheartening though the failure of this venture may have been, it had at least provided Esposito with an opportunity to realize what is arguably his finest work on stage. His musical embodiment of Hyde's drama has the simplicity and artlessness of a folktale. As the curtain goes up, an old woman is discovered onstage, repining bitterly at her fate. We learn that she is a denizen of the supernatural realm, but has been condemned by her jealous rival the Fairy Queen to grow old and die unless she can persuade a mortal man to kiss her on the last day of her existence. That fateful day has come at last. A youth appears in the wood: she tries to seduce him, but he shuns her and flees. A gipsy vagabond enters — a 'tinker', to use the word commonly employed in Ireland. This time the Fairy works her wiles with greater success, and inveigles him into kissing her. Faintly bemused, the Tinker does so, whereupon the Fairy is transformed into a young beauty. She promptly falls in love with her rescuer and, wishing to repay him for his noble deed, offers to join her lot to his. The Tinker is initially afraid and tries to dissuade her, emphasizing the harshness of his everyday life. His arguments are unavailing. The couple embrace, but as they kiss, mysterious fairy music is heard. The Fairy is torn between returning to her natural element and remaining in the mortal world; being unwilling to re-experience the indignity of senescence, she abandons the Tinker in spite of his sorrowful pleas. The Tinker is left to meditate ruefully on his loss: he packs his belongings and departs.

Frustratingly, the orchestral score of *The Tinker and the Fairy* appears to have been lost, but even a study of the vocal score reveals that the work is undoubtedly one of the most successful of the various attempts to compose operas on Irish subjects at this period. It amply demonstrates Esposito's dramatic flair and his instinct for pacing and effective

---

55 See *Freeman's Journal*, 4 April 1910, and *Irish Times*, 4 April 1910. There are some minor discrepancies between these accounts.

characterization, and contains some of the most inventive and memorable music that he ever composed. The score of his original incidental music to Hyde's play has also disappeared, so it is impossible to ascertain the extent to which he incorporated or reworked existing material in the operatic version.[56] Whatever the case may be, the opera is especially interesting from a stylistic point of view, as it represents a bold attempt to fuse a chromatic harmonic idiom which is obviously indebted to Wagner with a diatonic modality deriving at least to some extent from the inflexions of Irish folk song. Esposito contrasts these sound-worlds to telling dramatic effect in a manner strikingly reminiscent of Glinka's *Ruslan and Lyudmila* or the later operas of Rimsky-Korsakov, employing chromaticism to characterize the supernatural elements and diatonicism to portray the human realm. The appearances of both the Youth and the Tinker are dramatized by the use of folk-like ideas (Ex. 58), which afford a marked contrast to the anguished, highly chromatic music given to the Fairy when she contemplates the curse that has been laid on her (Ex. 59) or her imminent death— although Esposito also employs music of a more diatonic nature to evoke her lost youth.

Ex. 58: *The Tinker and the Fairy*, Op. 53, opening scene

Ex. 59: The Tinker and the Fairy, Op. 53, opening scene

The Tinker and the Fairy is also indebted to Wagner in its employment of leitmotifs which are developed extensively, lending the score a truly symphonic richness and breadth. Like Wagner's mature operas, the work is seamlessly through-composed, rather than conceived as a sequence of individual numbers. This enables Esposito to achieve some powerful long-range climaxes as he builds towards dramatic highpoints, such as the moment when the Tinker yields to the Fairy's entreaties, and kisses her. This scene, which contains some of the finest music in the opera, is largely wrought from a leitmotif representing the power of love. Little by little, this idea gains ascendancy over the material associated with the curse and is progressively purged of disruptive chromatic elements as the fairy is magically restored to her youthful form. A passionate love duet ensues in B major (a choice of key that surely recalls Tristan), which has an impressive urgency and sweep. The unexpectedly poignant dénouement of the final pages is deeply affecting: here, our initial sympathetic engagement with the Fairy is now transferred to the love-stricken Tinker, who implores her not to return to her supernatural world. As the Fairy disappears to the mysterious strains of a female chorus, the dejected Tinker is left alone on stage, whereupon the orchestra provides a reprise of the music which led to his transformational kiss, but now imbued with a powerful sense of sorrow and loss.

Unfortunately, the stage realization of The Tinker and the Fairy appears to have been far from ideal, and the reviews, though respectful and appreciative, strike the reader as somewhat muted in their praise. The anonymous critic for the Irish Times remarked that 'it would not be fair to the composer to pretend that [the] performance was all that the music deserved', as the soprano entrusted with the role of the Fairy, Nettie Edwards, was nervous and not in particularly good voice. As far as the music itself was concerned, the writer averred that it was 'pleasant rather than deep' and lacked memorable melodic invention, the principal interest residing mostly in the orchestral writing.[57] The deficiencies of the performance evidently prevented the work from making its full effect and, sadly, it does not seem to have been revived subsequently. Staging a revival at this remove would necessitate the re-orchestration of the opera from the vocal score — a labour that would be amply justified in view of the work's superb craftsmanship and dramatic power. The Tinker and the Fairy was to prove Esposito's last opera. There is evidence to suggest that he subsequently considered collaborating with George Moore on another based on the Deirdre legend, but nothing came of this venture.[58]

Although we know next to nothing about Esposito's personal or inner life during this period, a number of circumstances suggest that he became increasingly disillusioned by his professional circumstances as the decade drew to a close, despite the high esteem in which he was held. His importance in the cultural life of his adopted country had been

57 'New work by Dr Esposito', Irish Times, 30 March 1910
58 See Robert Hogan et al., The Modern Irish Drama: A Documentary History, vol. 2, The Abbey Theatre: Laying the Foundations, 1902–1904 (Dublin, 1976), 10.

acknowledged by the conferral of an honorary DMus on him by the Royal University of Dublin in July 1905;[59] and his activities as a composer, performer and teacher had earned him national renown. In spite of this, a series of unfortunate incidents precipitated a marked deterioration of his relationship with the management of the RIAM in the years leading up to the First World War. Ironically, this had been caused by proposals to elevate him to a position of greater authority within the institution.

The administrative burden involved in running the RIAM had grown considerably, on account of increased student numbers and the burgeoning system of local centre examinations. The Academy had never had a Director — unlike most conservatoires in Britain and on the continent — a functionary who attended to day-to-day business, interviewed applicants, arranged examinations and public concerts, inspected classes, and so forth. Early in 1909, the Governors of the RIAM met to discuss a proposal that such a post be created and offered to Esposito. Because of budgetary constraints, it was only possible to make it a part-time position: it was envisaged that Esposito would be required to work in this capacity for two hours a day during term, for which he would be paid an extra £200 per annum. He would retain his existing teaching position, for which he would continue to be paid separately. This proposal, which may have been originated with Esposito himself, met with a very mixed response. Some of the Governors did not consider Esposito to possess sufficient business acumen for such a post; others felt that the institution simply could not afford the extra expense involved. They may also have wondered whether it was wise to concentrate so much power in Esposito's hands, affording him a position of even greater influence in Dublin's musical life. Esposito was asked if he would be prepared to give up certain additional fees, such as those he received for examining, in the event that he was offered the position: he refused, being understandably concerned to increase his income. In the end the Board decided to defer consideration of the matter for twelve months (by a majority of eleven votes to five), whereupon Esposito resigned as the professors' representative on the Board of Governors. He was persuaded to withdraw his resignation, but the episode seems to have left a lingering residue of ill-will. [60]

The extent of Esposito's dissatisfaction can be gauged from the fact that he considered moving back to Italy and returned to visit Naples for the first time in over thirty years. Initially, one of the principal motivations for this trip had been a desire to see his friend Martucci, with whom he had apparently continued to correspond regularly since leaving Italy.[61] During the intervening years, his erstwhile fellow student had come to international prominence as a pianist, composer and conductor, and in 1902 had returned to Naples to become the Director at the Real Collegio, now renamed the Conservatorio San Pietro a

59 Some friends made him a gift of his doctoral robes, in addition to presenting him with a full score of Tristan and a service of table silver: see Musical Times, 46, 750 (1905), 528.

60 See Freeman's Journal, 28 January 1909; 'Royal Irish Academy: Appointment of Officials', Irish Times, 28 January 1909; and Pine and Acton, To Talent Alone, 272–74.

61 Aiello, Al musicista, 50

Majella. Martucci was equally eager to see Esposito and urged him to come to Italy. Esposito eventually promised to visit him in July 1909. Sadly, the meeting never took place: Martucci was in poor health and died prematurely on 1 June at the age of fifty-three.[62] Esposito made the journey to Italy nonetheless and arrived in Naples on 24 July, where he was reunited with his mother, now an old woman of eighty. He took the opportunity to visit Castellammare and went on to Sorrento to spend time with his former student Alessandro Longo. Several years later, Longo wrote of their meeting in his journal *L'Arte pianistica*, recalling how 'on two gentle afternoons we made music and spoke long about art; such a grateful recollection I have kept stored away in my memory'.[63] Revealingly, when the post of Director at the Naples Conservatoire was advertised after Martucci's death, Esposito applied. His application was unsuccessful, however, presumably because his name was completely unknown to the appointing panel.[64] Esposito had no choice but to return to Ireland.[65]

   In the end, the idea of creating a new post for him at the RIAM was not pursued — no doubt to Esposito's great disappointment. Trouble flared up again two years later, when he became involved in an unseemly altercation with one of the governors, Albert Foot, at a meeting of the Board on 25 January 1911. The exact details of the incident are somewhat unclear, but Esposito later claimed that his ire had been roused by an extraordinary proposal of Foot's to 'make a clean sweep of all the professors' — meaning presumably to replace those who sat on the Board of Studies, because he was dissatisfied with the way in which it was run.[66] The minutes for a meeting of the Board of Governors on 22 March 1910 present the following account of what happened next:

> Dr. Esposito, rising in his seat & raising his voice & leaning across the table towards Mr. Foot, in a loud voice called across the table (at the head of which the Chairman Mr. Irwin was seated) to Mr. Foot 'That is Mr. Foot's opinion' — & then laughed derisively & said, continuing in a loud voice, 'Who minds Mr. Foot' — or 'Nobody minds Mr. Foot — whereupon Mr. Foot said 'We don't want any Italian tricks here' or 'any of your Italian tricks here' — Dr. Esposito then rushed over to the Pianoforte where his hat &c were and said 'I will not sit any more at this Board with Mr. Foot' & the Chairman endeavoured to calm Dr. Esposito, who ran to the door the Chairman urging him to come back, but Dr. Esposito again refused & went away.[67]

Esposito promptly wrote to the Secretary tendering his resignation from the Board of Governors, being deeply disappointed by the Chairman's failure to reprimand Foot. He was

62 Aiello, *Al musicista*, 50
63 Alessandro Longo, 'Artisti italiani all'estero: Michele Esposito', *L'Arte Pianistica* 1, 3 (1914), 7
64 Longo, 'Michele Esposito', 2
65 Aiello, *Al musicista*, 52
66 Pine and Acton, *To Talent Alone*, 275
67 Pine and Acton, *To Talent Alone*, 275

asked to withdraw his resignation, but refused. The Board of Governors promptly found itself at loggerheads with the Board of Studies, which reproved the governors for failing to censure Foot's outburst and refused to put any other person forward to represent them in his place. Realizing the seriousness of the position, the Board of Governors called for an apology from both Foot and Esposito. Foot quickly responded with his, but Esposito decided to go one step further and tender his resignation from the institution altogether, giving three months' notice. This, as everyone realized, was a dreadful situation. The Board delayed for three weeks before acknowledging his letter, in the hope that he might compromise and offer an apology. Esposito's friends Leopold Dix and W. P. Geoghegan wrote to the Board expressing the view that his resignation would be a calamity for the institution. This fact was universally acknowledged and finally, after the Board formally expressed its regret at Esposito's decision, the Italian was persuaded to withdraw his resignation and offer an apology to Foot in his turn. The Board must have been deeply relieved when this crisis was eventually resolved, but it undoubtedly caused lasting damage. Esposito made his feelings of rancour plain in a final symbolic gesture: having been unanimously re-elected as the professors' representative on the Board of Governors, he declined to take up the position again.[68]

It is interesting to note that in the wake of this episode Esposito's thoughts seem to have turned increasingly towards Italy. Between 1910 and 1913 he spent his summer vacations there, visiting Florence, Siena and Bologna. His sojourn in the latter city in 1912 was notably productive from a creative point of view, as he completed a number of compositions for piano which were allotted the opus numbers 62 to 65. The *Three Pieces* for piano, Op. 61, may date from this period too, although their striking stylistic heterogeneity leads one to think that two of them might have been composed at an earlier stage of Esposito's career. As the individual titles make explicit — *Alba* [Dawn], *Zenith* [Midday] and *Tramonto* [Dusk or Sunset] — this set of pieces evokes the daily progress of the sun. The first piece, *Alba*, may owe something to Debussy: as we have seen, Esposito had programmed some of the French composer's *Préludes* in his solo recitals. Here Esposito depicts the rise of the sun and progressive intensification of the light by a series of harmonic moves through keys arranged in ascending major thirds — A major, F major, D flat major and A major. Each of these shifts is dramatized by a rise in dynamic level, starting *pianissimo* and culminating in a radiant *fortissimo*. The piece is essentially an improvisation on a single thematic idea heard at the outset (Ex. 60). This is based on an A major triad with an added sixth and Lydian D sharp: the two motifs marked *x* and *y* assume increasing importance later. *Alba* is undoubtedly one of the most experimental pieces that Esposito ever composed, both in terms of its harmonic language and its structural organization. By contrast, *Zenith* and *Tramonto* are more traditional in conception. In *Zenith*, the heroic cast of the first thematic idea and the nocturne-like character of the second are clearly reminiscent of Chopin — a composer whose pronounced influence can be felt in much of Esposito's earlier work. The piece is constructed from two principal thematic ideas, which

68 Pine and Acton, *To Talent Alone*, 274–79

are treated in rather unusual ways: the second idea, for example, is originally introduced in the tonic region of D flat major before being restated in a more ornamented form in B major (Ex. 61). In the recapitulation it undergoes further transformation and is combined with the first subject in a climactic passage marked *con passione*. The melancholy third piece of the set, *Tramonto*, features a number of harmonically adventurous passages based on whole-tone scales and augmented triads.

Ex. 60: *Alba*, from *Three Pieces*, Op. 61/1, opening

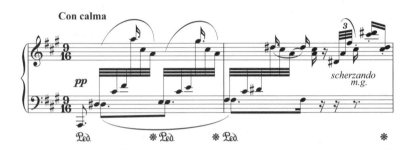

Ex. 61: *Zenith*, from *Three Pieces*, Op. 61/2

The quirky *Impromptu* in A flat, Op. 62, also features some piquant chromatic colouration, particularly in its rapid semitonal shifts from one tonal region to another, although the second subject, in E flat minor, is somewhat conventional. *Remembrance*, Op. 63, is also notable for the elusive nature of its harmonic language. One particularly striking passage, which punctuates the statements of the two main thematic ideas, features consecutive diminished triads with an added seventh (Ex. 62). *A Village Fête*, Op. 64, as the title might suggest, evokes rustic festivities. This attractive miniature is punctuated by jubilant evocations of pealing bells and has a subsidiary theme reminiscent of a popular Neapolitan song. Both *Remembrance* and *A Village Fête* were given their first performance by Esposito at an RDS concert of 16 November 1914. The *Three Pieces*, Op. 65, were obviously intended as pedagogical material, but demonstrate once again Esposito's ability to write rewarding music for young players.

Ex. 62: *Remembrance*, Op. 63

In addition to these piano pieces, Esposito also completed two works of a more substantial nature. The first of these was the Third Violin Sonata in A major, Op. 67, which was first performed by the composer and the Italian violinist Achille Simonetti at the RDS on 11 January 1915.[69] Simonetti, who had studied in Genoa and Paris, settled in London in 1891, where he came to prominence as a chamber musician through his appearances with the London Trio. He moved to Dublin in 1912, replacing Wilhelmj after the latter's resignation from the RIAM, and remained in the city for five years. In addition to assuming the responsibility of leader of the DOS, he performed regularly with Esposito and Clyde Twelvetrees in what came to be known as the Dublin Trio.[70] By all accounts, he and Esposito got on extremely well, despite their very different temperaments. Walter Starkie gave an amusing account of their relationship:

> Simonetti was typically Italian but the exact antithesis to Esposito. Esposito came from Naples, Simonetti came from Turin: Esposito was nervy, fiery, passionate, and outspoken; Simonetti was gentle, ironical, indulgent, and long-suffering.

69 *Irish Times*, 12 January 1915
70 *Musical Times*, 54, 839 (1913), 44

Both made ideal partners in chamber music, because their varying qualities compensated each other. Esposito always dominated their arguments, because, when he did not convince with words, his eyes, blazing defiance, and his Olympian frown fulminated his opponent. Simonetti, when worsted, would throw up his hands resignedly and pick up his fiddle. Their partnership at times reminded me of when Handel conducted and Corelli led the orchestra in Rome and the fiery German would abuse the lyrical Archangelo [sic], whose playing was too soft and lyrical for the former's tempestuous music. But why, after all, expect Raphael to thunder like Michelangelo? Both Esposito and Simonetti, however, had one accomplishment in common: like Rossini, they were past masters of the culinary art, and I could never make up my mind which of the two prepared the better dish of spaghetti.[71]

Ex. 63: Sonata for Violin and Piano in A major, Op. 67, I, opening

---

71   Walter Starkie, untitled reminiscences, reproduced in Pine and Acton, *To Talent Alone*, 294ff.

The sonata Esposito composed for Simonetti is on a much more expansive scale than his previous contributions to the medium and continues the harmonic and structural experimentation of his recent piano music. In the opening movement, Esposito employs a tripartite tonal scheme once more in the exposition, this time centring on the regions of A major, F sharp minor and E major. The opening material of the first subject, shown in Ex. 63, persistently oscillates between major and minor modes and features pervasive cross-rhythms which obscure the prevailing compound duple metre. The tonic is only finally established with the introduction of a secondary idea in bar 13. The principal themes of the exposition are vividly characterized and are elaborated with considerable polyphonic skill. Up to the middle of the development section the music remains within the stylistic parameters of late Romanticism, but at this point Esposito introduces a passage of remarkable complexity, in which the listener's sense of tonal reference points and metrical regularity are attenuated (Ex. 64).

Ex. 64: Sonata for Violin and Piano in A major, Op. 67, I, development section

The curious slow movement and the Scherzo are similarly replete with harmonic surprises, if of a less extreme kind. The former, marked *Allegretto moderato*, is a solemn minuet in F sharp minor, the sense of gravity being enhanced by suspensions in the piano part. Esposito's handling of the overall tonal design is masterly, notably in his move to the Neapolitan, F major, shortly before the reprise of the principal theme. The atmosphere of earnestness evaporates with the Trio in the tonic major: its limpid, gently flowing triplets continue during the reprise of the minuet and bring the movement to a tranquil close. The third movement, *Andante cantabile*, is a rondo in which the reprises of the rondo theme are presented with increasingly elaborate piano textures. By contrast with the preceding movements, the finale is perhaps more conventional in nature, but its structural organization is decidedly unusual. It is in sonata form, but lacks a development section proper: instead, a harmonically unstable second subject substitutes for the customary phase of protracted tonal instability. The recapitulation ensues immediately upon the conclusion of this paragraph, with the first-subject material extensively transformed in its *pianissimo* restatement in the tonic minor, followed by a highly curtailed reprise of the second subject. Like all of Esposito's chamber music, the Third Violin Sonata is a highly appealing work that is effectively written for the medium. It is also particularly interesting from a stylistic point of view, inhabiting as it does the sound worlds of both late Romanticism and early Modernism.

The other large-scale score that Esposito completed during these years came into existence because of his involvement with the ISM, for which he continued to act as an Irish representative. In 1912, the General Council of the Society invited him to compose a work for piano and orchestra to be performed during its annual conference in London at the end of the following year.[72] Esposito responded with a Second Piano Concerto in F minor, Op. 68 — his first new orchestral composition in almost a decade. The concerto was completed during the summer of 1912, during a productive sojourn in Bologna. In the event, the premiere was given in Dublin rather than London, perhaps because Esposito wished to give the piece a trial run before performing it in London at the end of that month. This took place in the Gaiety Theatre on 16 December 1913, on which occasion the DOS was conducted by Simonetti.[73] The piece was well received by the audience, although the performance seems to have been less than ideal on account of Simonetti's inadequate control over the orchestra.[74] The score of the concerto, like that of its predecessor, has been lost, but the reviewer for the *Irish Times* gave the following description of the work:

> The first movement is written in F minor and in six-four time. Its principal subject is of a free, one might almost say wild, character; but it embodies a strong purpose and

---

72 'Dublin Orchestra Society: Concert at the Gaiety Theatre', *Irish Times*, 18 December 1913
73 *Irish Independent*, 17 December 1913
74 'Dublin Orchestra Society: Concert at the Gaiety Theatre', *Irish Times*, 18 December 1913. The accounts of Simonetti's conducting on this occasion are at variance with one another: the reviewer for the *Irish Times* described his direction of the orchestra as 'eminently successful'.

appeal. In the second subject of this movement are found some of the most beautiful passages for both piano and orchestra, although the latter is kept somewhat in the background, so that the solo instrument may have more prominence. The scoring for the orchestra, however ... has not been neglected, and forms quite a study in itself, if one could spare attention from the piano part. The subject is cleverly amplified, and a skilful use is made of materials previously heard in an orchestral summary of them with which the movement concludes. The movement is described as *allegro maestoso*.

The second, a slow movement, is put in the rather unusual nine-eight time. This movement is extremely melodious, and includes a kind of dialogue between the orchestra and the piano, leading to a section played quickly, while the dignified conclusion of the movement is of a most impressive character. Dr Esposito received a great ovation at the conclusion of this movement. Brightness is the prevailing characteristic of the third and last movement. An extensive use is made of arpeggio and scale passage, and the resources of the orchestra are called into play in great variety. The character of the movement alternates between sternness and brightness, while it is concluded in brilliant style.

Not alone is Dr Esposito to be congratulated on the great merit of his composition, but also on the manner in which he played it. The composer put his whole heart into giving his work and adequate interpretation, and never has he played in better style, both as regards manual dexterity and the clear tone he obtained. At the conclusion of his playing, Dr Esposito had to return three times to acknowledge the applause which greeted his performance, and he was evidently highly gratified at the impression his new work had made.[75]

Esposito performed the concerto for a second time at a concert of music by ISM members given in Queen's Hall in London on 31 December, with the New Symphony Orchestra and Sir Frederic Cowen as conductor. The responses of the British critics towards the work were more mixed than those of their Irish counterparts. The critic for the *Times* opined that it had praiseworthy features, but suggested that it was diffuse and over-long:

Mr Esposito's Concerto ... rather damped the ardour. If it had been in one movement it would not have been the spoil-sport it was. The first movement is practically a concerto in the condensed form which Liszt made popular. It has a middle slow movement based upon a charming church-like tune, which is well worked into the recapitulation. But not content with this the composer has added

75 'Dublin Orchestra Society: Concert at the Gaiety Theatre', *Irish Times*, 18 December 1913

a separate slow movement, a very weak-kneed affair, and a finale with a long fugato upon a rather poor theme.[76]

The reviewers for the Musical Times and the Telegraph inclined to a similar view, although the reviewer for the Standard declared that the work deserved a second hearing.[77] To judge from these comments, the concerto seems to have been conceived on quite a monumental scale and was perhaps the most ambitious large-scale instrumental work that Esposito had ever composed — a consideration which makes the loss of the manuscript all the more regrettable.

In the years immediately before the outbreak of war, Esposito's life was considerably enriched by his deepening friendships with two men who had a deep respect for his abilities and opened up valuable new professional opportunities for him. The first of these was a scion of a prominent Anglo-Irish family, Stanley Cochrane (1877–1949), whose father, Sir Henry Cochrane, had been a co-founder of the highly successful firm of Cantrell and Cochrane, a purveyor of bottled mineral waters and other beverages.[78] Upon Sir Henry's death in 1904, his place on the company board was taken by his eldest son Ernest, who relinquished it to his younger brother Stanley in 1909 as he did not wish to be continuously resident in Ireland. In consequence, Stanley found himself in control of a large fortune at the age of only thirty-two. An accomplished sportsman, he spent considerable sums of money on creating superb facilities for playing cricket and golf on his estate at Woodbrook, which was situated near the seaside village of Bray in Co. Wicklow, about ten miles south of Dublin. He was also a keen amateur singer and regularly performed as a soloist in Dublin choral concerts, his passion for music being such that he eventually constructed a private opera house and concert hall at Woodbrook. He was a generous patron of musical events, sponsoring amongst other ventures a visiting production of Wagner's Ring cycle, which came to Dublin in May 1913.[79]

It is likely that the two men encountered one another at the RIAM, where Cochrane was a governor. Cochrane was sufficiently impressed by Esposito's work with the DOS to invite him to continue the series of Sunday Orchestral Concerts with the orchestra, not at the Antient Concert Rooms, but at Woodbrook, commencing on 16 February 1913.[80] To enhance the attractiveness of the events for potential audiences, train tickets to Bray were

76 'Orchestral Concert of New Works', The Times, 1 January 1914
77 See 'Incorporated Society of Musicians' Annual Conference', Musical Times 55, 852 (1914), 115; and 'Opinion of the London Critics', Irish Independent, 1 January 1914.
78 Charles Mosley, ed., Burke's Peerage, Baronetage and Knightage: Clan chiefs, Scottish feudal barons (Delaware, 2003), 841
79 See the entry 'Cochrane, Sir Stanley H., Bart.' in Edward Dent, ed., A Dictionary of Modern Music and Musicians (London, 1924), 97; and also Musical Times, 56, 869 (1915), 428–29. I would like to acknowledge the assistance of Alfred Cochrane and Alex Findlater who provided supplementary biographical information.
80 Irish Times, 17 February 1913

offered at a reduced price from two city centre stations in Dublin and a tea room was set up in the cricket pavilion on the estate. These concerts, charged at the same price as the Antient Concert Rooms, were popular in nature and they proved so successful that a second series was run in May. This time the concerts were more diverse in nature, and featured Esposito both in solo recitals and as a partner to the eminent British pianist Fanny Davies in a programme of piano duos. The series came to a close on 1 June with an orchestral concert which featured Esposito's Second Irish Rhapsody with Simonetti playing the solo part.

The success of these ventures prompted Cochrane to attempt a more ambitious undertaking. In August of the same year, he brought over the London Symphony Orchestra (LSO) to give a series of concerts at Woodbrook under the baton of the eminent Irish composer, pianist and conductor, Hamilton Harty.[81] Harty's involvement had come about through a fortunate constellation of circumstances, for he had a long-standing connection with both Esposito and Cochrane that went back many years.[82] Harty, who came from County Down, arrived in Bray in 1896 to take up the post of organist and choirmaster at Christ Church a month before his seventeenth birthday. His first meeting with Esposito, which came about by chance on a train, did not bode well: he asked the Italian if he would take him on as a piano student, but, rather amusingly in view of Harty's later international renown as a pianist and accompanist, the older man refused on the grounds that his hands were the wrong shape.[83] Matters subsequently took a rather surprising turn. When the DOS was formed, Harty applied to join as a viola player — a rather brave step, as he was entirely self-taught and not very proficient on the instrument, although he had some limited experience of playing with a local orchestra in Belfast. He made an appointment to audition for Esposito at his home in Lansdowne Road. Upon arrival, he was asked to wait in an anteroom, where the manuscript score of Esposito's *Irish Symphony* happened to be lying on a table, its pages open at the Scherzo. The young man perused it with curiosity, whiling away the time before being summoned to appear before the maestro. When called, he duly launched into the audition piece he had prepared, but as he later recalled, Esposito 'scarcely waited for me to finish before turning on me in a bristling rage':

> 'But you play the viola *disgusting*', said he. I knew it was true, but felt stung all the same. A vague idea of revenge flashed into my mind. 'I suppose you think this disgusting too', I said, and played a melody from the *scherzo* of the manuscript symphony I had seen in the other room.[84]

81   *Irish Times*, 28 July 1913
82   David Greer, ed., *Hamilton Harty: His Life and Music* (Belfast, 1978), 30n
83   Hamilton Harty, 'Michele Esposito', *The Irish Statesman*, 7 December 1929, 276
84   Hamilton Harty, 'Michele Esposito', 276

With his remarkable facility for memorizing music, Harty managed to reproduce the theme flawlessly from memory. Esposito was astonished and demanded to know how the young man could have known the score. Harty duly explained, whereupon Esposito roared with laughter, put his arms round the young man and kissed him on both cheeks. From that point, Harty recalled that he became 'not indeed a regular pupil of the *Maestro*, but a close friend who could look with complete confidence to him for help and advice. Indeed with the exception of my own father his was the ruling influence in my musical life.'[85]

With Esposito's encouragement, Harty began to devote himself seriously to composition and won an impressive series of prizes at Feis Ceoil for various chamber works. In 1900, he left Dublin to settle in London, where he rapidly began to make a name for himself as an accompanist, but continued to return to Dublin at regular intervals. In 1904, he was awarded first prize at the Feis for his *Irish Symphony*, which owed much to the example of Esposito's work of the same name, composed two years previously.[86] He conducted its premiere with the DOS on 18 May of the same year — the first time he had ever conducted an orchestra in public. The event was a resounding success and he was gratified to receive an enthusiastic ovation from the audience. The following year he returned to Dublin to give the symphony a second time on 18 April 1905, on which occasion he also accompanied Esposito in a performance of Beethoven's *Emperor* Concerto.[87] The two men remained in close contact for the rest of Esposito's life. Harty continued to rely on the older man for advice, and even at the height of his illustrious career, he would sometimes come to Dublin for the weekend to discuss his most recent scores with him.[88] For his part, Esposito remained continuously supportive of his protégé, whom he referred to by the affectionate soubriquet of 'Hay'.[89] He was extremely supportive of the young man in the early stages of his career, helping to organize performances of his chamber works and subsequently programming his orchestral compositions in DOS concerts.

Not long before Esposito gave his first series of programmes at Woodbrook in 1913 with the DOS, Harty had been engaged to conduct the London Symphony Orchestra (LSO) for several concerts during its season at Queen's Hall in 1912–13. In the event, the series made a financial loss and it did not prove possible to re-engage him for the following season.[90] He had managed to achieve such an excellent rapport with the orchestra, however, that

85 This account of this first encounter between Harty and Esposito is based on David Greer, ed., *Hamilton Harty: Early Memories* (Belfast, 1979), 26–27; and Hamilton Harty, 'Michele Esposito', *The Irish Statesman*, 7 December, 1929, 276–77.

86 Greer, ed., *Hamilton Harty: Early Memories*, 28, note 9

87 *Musical Times*, 46, 748 (1905), 405

88 van Hoek, 'Michele Esposito', 226

89 The origin of 'Hay' as a nickname was explained by Lady Harty (née Agnes Nicholls) in a BBC broadcast in 1951. As an affectionate joke, Harty was often referred to as 'Hale and Harty' which later acquired the diminutive of 'Hayland'. Lady Harty then began to call him 'Hay' which soon became the favoured nickname among his intimate friends. See Greer, ed., *Hamilton Harty: His Life and Music*, 88 note 5.

90 Greer, ed., *Hamilton Harty: His Life and Music*, 30

when Cochrane suggested that it might appear at Woodbrook, Harty was able to muster an ensemble of fifty-two players who were willing to come over to Ireland for a series of daily concerts held at Woodbrook between 11 and 16 August. The orchestra gave six concerts in all, assisted by a distinguished array of soloists. Two of the concerts were devoted exclusively to the music of Wagner and Tchaikovsky, respectively,[91] while the others featured a variety of interesting modern repertoire, including Strauss's *Don Juan*, Debussy's *L'Après-midi d'un faune* and Harty's own *Irish Symphony*.[92] Esposito's student Victor Love appeared as soloist in Rachmaninov's Second Piano Concerto. The eminent English violinist (and close associate of Elgar's) W. H. Reed performed Saint-Saëns's Third Violin Concerto and the nineteen-year-old Isolde Menges played the Tchaikovsky and Mendelssohn violin concertos, while Agnes Nicholls and Joseph O'Mara featured as vocalists. The concerts were very well attended and the press wrote in glowing terms about the rare chance to hear what the *Irish Times* declared to be 'the best orchestra in the world'.[93] Harty's conducting won lavish praise: as one critic wrote, 'one felt immediately that one was in the presence of a master mind, full of grand conceptions and unflinching aims. Conductor, orchestra and audience alike gave themselves up to the spell, and treated the music with what amounted to reverence'.[94]

Cochrane continued to host an impressive roster of events at Woodbrook. During the winter season of 1913–14, Esposito appeared with the Dublin Trio in a number of chamber concerts, the first of which took place on 25 October 1913.[95] He gave the first of several piano recitals on 29 November, one of a number planned by Cochrane to feature great European pianists. A recital by Rachmaninov was announced for 7 February, but he was at the last moment indisposed through serious illness.[96] However, Cochrane was able to secure Alfred Cortot on 21 February who, as part of his programme, performed Saint-Saëns's Fourth Piano Concerto with Esposito playing the orchestral reduction on a second piano. The DOS gave a series of concerts that commenced on 10 May 1914, each of which featured a Beethoven symphony.[97] Harty visited in his capacity as piano accompanist, a role in which he had become renowned. On 10 January 1914, he accompanied the tenor, John Coates, in a recital,[98] and returned at the end of the month with the mezzo-soprano, Kirkby Lunn;[99] in March he appeared in concert with his wife Agnes Nicholls[100] as well as

---

91 *Irish Times*, 13 August 1913
92 *Irish Times*, 15 August 1913
93 *Irish Times*, 12 August 1913
94 *Irish Times*, 14 August 1913
95 *Irish Times*, 21 October 1913. Further concerts by the Dublin Trio took place at Woodbrook on 8 and 22 November and 6 and 13 December. In 1914, the ensemble gave three concerts there between January and March.
96 *Musical Times*, 55, 853 (1914), 192
97 *Irish Times*, 30 May 1914
98 *Irish Times*, 12 January 1914
99 *Irish Times*, 2 February 1914
100 *Irish Times*, 2 March 1914

giving a further concert with Coates.[101] The LSO returned between 3 and 8 August — an event which aroused keen anticipation not least because Esposito had been invited to share the podium with Harty.[102] This time, within the series of six concerts planned by the orchestra, the programmes included works by both men. In the first concert on 3 August, Esposito conducted his *Irish Suite*,[103] and was soloist in his Second Piano Concerto on 4 August,[104] while Harty performed his tone poem *With the Wild Geese* (8 August) and his vocal and orchestral work *The Mystic Trumpeter* with the baritone Robert Radford on 6 August. Esposito must have found this experience of working with a world-class orchestra to be deeply rewarding. The enthusiastic public response to the Woodbrook concerts had also seemed a gratifying sign that, after many years of arduous efforts by himself and other pioneers, the prospects for Irish musical life seemed more promising than ever before.

101 *Irish Times*, 30 March 1914
102 *Irish Times*, 12 May 1914
103 *Irish Times*, 4 August 1914
104 *Irish Independent*, 5 August 1914

6 Final Years, 1914–29

Esposito's appearances with the LSO at Woodbrook marked a high point of his career. During the fifteen years of life that remained to him, he wrote comparatively little music and the turbulent events of the First World War, the War of Independence and the ensuing Civil War in Ireland caused the scope of his performing activities to be curtailed considerably. He can have had little inkling of this at the start of 1914, however, when it seemed as if he might at last be on the threshold of wider international recognition. In that year he received an invitation to come to Russia where plans were afoot to perform some of his work — a surprising development which had come about through the good offices of his brother Eugenio (1863–1950), who was eight years Michele's junior. Eugenio also pursued a musical career, but he remains a rather shadowy figure about whom comparatively little is known.[1] Like his brother, he studied piano with Cesi and composition with Serrao at the Real Collegio, and after graduating in 1883 he spent some years in Paris, where he was employed as house pianist by the Rothschild family. After a spell conducting in smaller opera houses in Italy, he came to Moscow in the spring of 1892 at the invitation of the wealthy industrialist and notable patron of the arts Savva Mamontov, who had founded his own private opera company seven years previously. He appeared as a conductor at the Italian Opera there, and later that year began to work for a company founded by the impresario Aleksei Kartavov, which was based in Kharkov. In 1897, he became principal conductor with Mamontov's celebrated Moscow Private Russian Opera

1   This account of Eugenio Esposito's career is based on the entries 'Esposito, Michele' in *Dizionario biografico degli italiani*, 43 (Rome, 1993), 285–86, and the entry 'Esposito, Eugenio' in Yurii V. Keldish, ed., *Muzykal'naia entsiklopediia* [Musical Encyclopaedia], vol. 6 (Moscow, 1982), 552. There are some minor discrepancies between the facts given in these reference works. I would like to thank Patrick Zuk for drawing my attention to the entry in the *Muzykal'naia entsiklopediia* and the Russian-language sources detailed in footnotes 2, 3 and 4, and for translating relevant passages.

(*Moskovskaya chastnaya russkaya opera*). He performed a considerable quantity of Russian repertoire with this troupe, most notably the premiere of Rimsky-Korsakov's opera *Sadko* on 26 December 1897 (7 January 1898 new style). Sergei Rachmaninov, who joined Mamontov's company as an assistant conductor in 1897, found Eugenio to be a rather dour and unhelpful individual, who regarded him as a potential rival and treated him with suspicion. In Rachmaninov's estimation he was a competent, but uninspiring musician, whose performances tended to be rather routine and lacking in attention to detail.[2] He seems to have manifested his brother's volcanic temper in an even more extreme form: Rachmaninov recounted to a correspondent that the Italian's habit of swearing vilely at the orchestra provoked one of the players into assaulting him, causing them both to end up in court.[3] Whatever his personal or musical shortcomings may have been, they do not seem to have hindered his career: he continued to conduct in major centres throughout the Russian empire, working with opera companies in St Petersburg and Moscow, as well as in Odessa, Tbilisi, Kazan, Kiev and Nizhny-Novgorod. Eugenio was also a fairly prolific composer, who composed four operas to Russian libretti, the first of which, *Camorra*, enjoyed considerable popularity in his country of adoption.[4]

By 1914, he had presumably built up a considerable network of professional contacts and was in a position to make use of them on his brother's behalf. According to Aiello, who, as usual, is frustratingly vague about details, the eminent conductors Serge Koussevitzky and Aleksandr Orlov (an exact contemporary of Rachmaninov's who was later appointed principal conductor of the Moscow Radio Symphony Orchestra when it was founded in 1930) expressed interest in performing Michele's orchestral works in July 1914, seemingly as a result of Eugenio's initiatives. Both Michele and Natalia were anxious to go to Russia for the performances, not least because it would afford them an opportunity to see Eugenio and Natalia's father (who had since returned to Russia) for the first time in

2   See S. A. Satina, 'Zapiska o S. V. Rakhmaninove' [Memoir of S. V. Rachmaninov] in Zarui A. Apetian, ed., *Vospominaniia o Rakhmaninove* [Reminiscences of Rachmaninov], 5th edn., vol. 1 (Moscow, 1988), 12–115, 30ff.; and the reminiscences in the same volume of E. Yu. Zhukovskaya, 'Vospominaniia o moiom uchitele i druge S. V. Rakhmaninove' [Reminiscences of my teacher and friend S. V. Rachmaninov], 251–342, 271ff.

3   See Rachmaninov to N. D. Skalon, 22 November 1897 in Z. A. Apetian, ed., *S. Rakhmaninov: Literaturnoe Naslediie* [S. Rachmaninov: Literary Legacy], vol. 1 (Moscow, 1978), 273

4   The *Muzykal'naia entsiklopediia* entry states that *Camorra* was composed in 1903 to a libretto by Mamontov. Eugenio's second opera, *Meshchanin vo dvoryanstve* [A Bourgeois Amongst the Nobility], was based on Molière's *Le bourgeois gentilhomme* and produced in Moscow in 1905. This was followed by *Chyorniy Tyurban* [The Black Turban], which was staged in Kiev in 1912, and *U morya* [By the Sea], which appeared to have been put on some time in the mid-1920s, but no location is given. The other works listed are *Carmen*, a ballet produced in the early 1920s, a cantata *To the Memory of A. S. Pushkin* (n.d.) and some songs. The entry in the *Dizionario biografico degli italiani* records that he also composed cantatas and small-scale religious works. Yury Yelagin recounts in his memoirs that Eugenio was commissioned by Russian director Yevgeny Vakhtangov (1883–1922) to compose incidental music for his celebrated production of Carlo Gozzi's *Turandot* in 1922, but, in the event, his score was not used: see Yuriy Yelagin, *Ukroshcheniye iskusstv* (Moscow, 2002), 31.

many years. In the event, the rapidly deteriorating political situation in Europe after the assassination of the Archduke Franz Ferdinand in Sarajevo on 28 June 1914 rendered it inadvisable for the couple to embark on a lengthy journey and they cancelled their travel plans, hoping to go at a later date. Orlov nonetheless gave a concert in Moscow at the end of July with the Rostov-on-Don Symphony Orchestra, which was devoted entirely to Esposito's compositions. The programme included a representative selection of his major orchestral works, including the Irish Symphony, Othello, Poem, the Oriental Suite and the Second Piano Concerto. If the reliability of Aiello's account can be trusted, it would appear that the concert was a great success: he quotes the remarks of an unidentified Russian musician (he does not specify whether his source was a newspaper review or a letter) who described the 'stunning impression' that the music made on those present, singling out the Poem for especially favourable mention.[5] Esposito would no doubt have been deeply gratified to learn of this report, in spite of his disappointment at not being able to attend. In the event, another opportunity to have his work performed in Russia never arose and it would be another fifteen years before he was eventually reunited with his brother.

Unfortunately, the years between 1914 and 1922 are amongst the most sparsely documented of Esposito's career. We know nothing about his attitudes to the First World War as it unfolded, but to judge from newspapers reports, he and his family became involved in various fundraising activities — as one might have expected, given his lifelong support of charitable causes. He is known to have given concerts in aid of the Red Cross[6] and it seems safe to assume that other organizations would also have drawn on his services.[7] Natalia joined a committee to organize a flag day in aid of Italian soldiers, sailors and their families in the United Kingdom, as well as the Italian branch of the Red Cross;[8] while their daughter Vera became involved in the Strength of Britain Movement, a prominent organization which strove to promote temperance in the interest of the war effort.[9]

The war inevitably exercised a disruptive effect on musical life. Not least, the restrictions on travel forced foreign performers and ensembles to cancel their Irish engagements. In consequence, the RDS relied heavily on Esposito and his colleagues at the RIAM to sustain its concert series and to supplement the appearances of such foreign artists as the Society was still able to engage. As one of several pianists to give solo recitals (alongside others such as Annie Lord, Harold Bauer, Emile Sauer and Arthur de Greef),[10] Esposito performed at least once every season during the war at the RDS with Simonetti and

5   Aiello, Al musicista, 56
6   Pine and Acton, To Talent Alone, 249
7   See, for example, 'The Royal Irish Academy of Music', Irish Times, 17 December 1917
8   'Pro Italia: Flag Day in Dublin District', Irish Times, 8 November 1915
9   See 'Strength of Britain Movement', Irish Times, 17 March 1917. For an account of the Strength of Britain Movement, see Kenneth L. Roberts, Why Europe Leaves Home (New York, 1922), 285ff.
10 Irish Times, 24 October 1914

Twelvetrees as the Dublin Trio. The difficulty of travelling did not, however, prevent the Wessely and Brodsky Quartets from returning to Dublin, albeit on a more restricted basis. Esposito gave a recital for the RDS with the Wessely Quartet on 22 February 1915 and appeared again with the same quartet on 20 November 1916.[11] In addition to his work for the RDS, Esposito, along with his colleagues from the Dublin Trio, appeared in charity concerts, the most conspicuous of which was a 'Grand Concert' given in aid of the Royal Dublin Fusiliers on 4 March 1916.[12] He also appeared with Annie Lord in a concert for two pianos at Aberdeen Hall on 27 October 1916.

As the war started to drag on, it proved more and more difficult to keep the DOS going. For one thing, one assumes that Esposito probably lost the services of some of his wind players, who were recruited predominantly from regimental and police bands. It would also appear that attendance at DOS concerts began to fall off considerably. The orchestra ceased to perform on weekdays, although the Sunday concerts at the Antient Concert Rooms continued for a time. Some of these were in aid of charity, the proceeds going to the Prince of Wales Fund for the relief of war distress.[13] According to Aloys Fleischmann, the lack of consistent support for the events held at Woodbrook caused them to be discontinued.[14] On 14 February 1915, Esposito conducted what proved to be the orchestra's last concert, after which it effectively ceased to function: an *Irish Times* feature on musical life in Dublin which appeared in October of that year noted that the DOS was 'unable to carry on its work for the present'.[15] Esposito must surely have found it difficult to accept the demise of the ensemble, after so many years of struggling to keep it in existence. Since its foundation in 1899, the orchestra had given a remarkable total of eighty-one concerts featuring an impressively broad range of repertoire and was widely regarded as having immeasurably enriched musical life in the city.[16] Nonetheless, under wartime circumstances, the orchestra had little choice but to disband. The same *Irish Times* article expressed concern that wartime conditions might bring all concert activity to a halt — at least as far as classical music was concerned. The writer's prediction was soon fulfilled, but for reasons he can hardly have suspected. The Easter Rising of 1916 and the subsequent imposition of martial law led to the abandonment of most fixtures until concert life was resumed to some extent in the autumn.[17]

Although he was now nearly sixty, an age when many men would start to reduce the range of their commitments, Esposito was clearly determined to ensure that orchestral activity of some kind would continue in Dublin. The most practical solution in wartime

11   *Irish Times*, 22 February 1915 and 20 November 1916
12   *Irish Times*, 3 March 1916
13   *Irish Times*, 31 October 1914
14   Aloys Fleischmann, 'Music and Society: 1850–1921' in W. E. Vaughan, ed., *A New History of Ireland*, vol. 6, *Ireland under the Union II 1870-1921* (Oxford, 1996), 517
15   'Musical Topics: Opera and Artistes', *Irish Times*, 17 October 1915
16   Dublin Orchestral Society', *Irish Times*, 20 September 1927
17   Fleischmann, 'Music and Society: 1850–1921', 518. See also, Larchet, 'Michele Esposito', 430.

conditions was to create a small string orchestra consisting of local players.[18] This new ensemble gave its first concert at the Aberdeen Hall under the auspices of the ISM on 21 December 1915. On this occasion, the programme included Corelli's *Christmas* Concerto, Op. 6, No. 8, Elgar's *Serenade* for strings and an arrangement of two movements (probably the Scherzo and *Adagio espressivo*) from Esposito's own Second String Quartet[19] In October 1916, the RDS announced that its forthcoming series would include two concerts by this ensemble under Esposito's direction, which were scheduled for 4 December 1916 and 12 February 1917.[20] The programme for the first concert included the Bach Violin Concerto in A minor (with Simonetti as soloist), the Corelli *Christmas* Concerto, the Grieg *Two Elegiac Melodies*, Op. 34, and an unspecified Mozart Serenade.[21] Subsequent programmes featured a broad range of repertoire ranging from early music to works of a more contemporary date, as well as a considerable quantity of arrangements that Esposito made especially for the ensemble. The orchestra eventually gave a total of nine concerts at the RDS until it ceased functioning in 1923.[22]

In addition to his performing activities, Esposito continued to be actively involved in Dublin's musical institutions: he adjudicated annually at Feis Ceoil (which functioned, with some disruption, throughout the war)[23] and continued to serve on its committee.[24] Unlike its counterparts in Britain, the RIAM was not affected by wartime conditions to any significant extent, apart from the loss of its government grant for a brief period.[25] Esposito's commitments there seem to have grown even more time-consuming, for he not only continued to teach his regular piano classes, but also assumed a growing burden of responsibility for the institution's rapidly burgeoning system of local examinations. By 1916, the number of entrants for these had risen to over 300, due to the establishment of further regional centres in Kilkenny, Monaghan and other Irish towns, and, as Esposito carried out a considerable proportion of the examining himself, he was increasingly obliged to travel greater distances around the country.[26] Despite being so busy, he did not neglect his piano students and seems to have remained as exigent a teacher as ever, to

18 *Irish Times*, 5 December 1916. To judge from press reports, the personnel of this string orchestra initially included RIAM professors such as Simonetti, Griffith, Twelvetrees (see *Irish Times*, 5 December 1916) and probably also included RIAM students. Somewhat confusingly, there was also an ensemble known as the 'Academy' or 'RIAM' string orchestra, which operated around this time. This comprised thirty-six players and performed under the direction of Esposito and his colleague Jozé: see *Musical Times*, 58, 891 (1917), 229 and 58, 893, 328; and *Irish Times*, 27 October 1916. It is not clear whether the two bodies are identical or whether the RIAM orchestra was a student orchestra.
19 *Musical Times*, 57, 876 (1916), 108
20 'Royal Dublin Society Musical Recitals', *Irish Times*, 24 October 1916
21 'Classical Music Recital', *Irish Times*, 5 December 1916
22 Hughes, 'The Society and Music', 270
23 *Irish Times*, 18 July 1916
24 *Irish Times*, 4 December 1915
25 Pine and Acton, *To Talent Alone*, 279
26 Pine and Acton, *To Talent Alone*, 304ff

judge from comments by the eminent British pianist Frederick Dawson (1868–1940), who acted as external examiner in 1916. Dawson had high praise not only for the excellence of the students' playing, but also for Esposito's pedagogical approach:

> The examinations I had the pleasure of conducting during the week commencing December 4th, were a matter of complete satisfaction to me, and I am still full of admiration for Dr Esposito's thorough and well-planned scheme which covers the whole course of musical education; a gradual and complete system which, commencing at the lowest classes, works up to the highest classes where one finds the pupil fully equipped as a Teacher and Soloist — a most gratifying and convincing showing of the value of correct grounding.

> The scales and arpeggios throughout were quite excellent. They were played equally, rhythmically, with correct fingering and most note-worthy — without any hesitation. In all the playing there was great clearness, due care in the use of the pedal and many pupils had memorized their pieces; further there were many evidences of a feeling for harmonic value as well as melodic principles, things moving with much musical perception.[27]

When Dawson returned to act as external examiner in 1924, his admiration for the standard achieved by Esposito's students was undiminished. In his report, he declared:

> the reason for these wonderful results is not far to seek — the other Schools have not the incalculable privilege of having their Piano Classes directed by Commendatore Michele Esposito: — an artist who, in addition to possessing the highest mental powers, has also the personality which creates and draws around itself a staff of exceptional talents.[28]

His heavy workload notwithstanding, Esposito also found time for another major undertaking — the establishment of a new music publishing firm in Dublin, in order to remedy an unexpected practical difficulty engendered by wartime conditions. With the outbreak of hostilities, German publications had become unavailable virtually overnight, since imports were suspended and major German music publishers with London bases, such as Breitkopf and Peters, were prevented from trading. Musicians in the United Kingdom consequently experienced considerable difficulty in purchasing scores of much music from the standard classical and romantic repertoire. Esposito's primary concern was to make available inexpensive editions of works suitable for students at the RIAM

27 Report of Frederick Dawson, *RIAM Annual Report*, 1916, RIAM archive
28 Report of Frederick Dawson, *RIAM Annual Report*, 1924, RIAM archive

and entrants for the institution's local examinations. The enterprise was made possible thanks to the generous financial subvention of Stanley Cochrane, who continued to support it until Esposito's death in 1929.

From 1915 onwards, Esposito devoted a considerable proportion of his time to preparing editions of a wide range of music which appeared under the imprint of 'C. E. Music Publishers Co.' — the initials standing for the first letters of his and Cochrane's surnames. These ranged from short pieces by composers as diverse as Arne, Schubert, Weber, Chopin, Schumann and Rubinstein to more extended works by Bach and Mozart, his most substantial production being a three-volume edition of the Beethoven piano sonatas (with the omission of the three smaller scale sonatas of Opp. 49 and 79). As one might expect, these were not scholarly editions in our modern understanding of the term, but were designed primarily for the needs of student performers: Esposito's interventions are generally restricted to indications of fingering, pedalling and phrasing. The firm's publications were brought out in a simple format, with a pale blue cover adorned by a rectangular frame featuring Celtic motifs inspired by medieval Irish illuminated manuscripts. Most of the typesetting appears to have been done by the publishing house of Ricordi in Milan,[29] and the Dublin firm of Pigott acted as distributor. In addition to publishing Esposito's editions of piano music, C. E. Music Publishers also brought out several of his own compositions, including the vocal score of The Tinker and the Fairy, the Irish Suite, the Two Shelley Songs, the Second String Quartet and all his remaining works (with the exception of the Novi preludi) until his death in 1929. The firm also published the full scores of three works by Hamilton Harty — the Fantasy Scenes (From an Eastern Romance) of 1919, the Violin Concerto (1920) and Piano Concerto (1922).

One is intrigued to know how Esposito might have responded to the Easter Rising and the dramatic events that followed in its wake. According to the critic H. R. White (who also composed music under the penname of Dermot MacMurrough),[30] Esposito entertained very strong political convictions which he did not hesitate to express in a forceful and pungent manner, but unfortunately no information has come to light about his views on Irish affairs.[31] Interestingly, his children seem to have had pronounced nationalist and republican sympathies, which led them to take an active, if peripheral role, in the struggle for Irish independence. Vera, who had a modest career as an actress in her youth, came into contact with some of the most prominent figures of the Irish literary revival. She appeared as Nora in the 1904 production of Synge's Riders to the Sea mounted by the

29 This is confirmed by correspondence between Esposito and the Italian publishing firm Ricordi dating
    from the years 1919–24, which has been preserved in the Archivio Casa Ricordi, Biblioteca Nazionale
    Braidense, Milan.

30 This was a somewhat bizarre choice of penname, being the anglicized form of Diarmaid Mac Murchadha,
    a twelfth-century King of Leinster who is generally considered the most notorious traitor in Irish history.
    He is credited with bringing about the first English intervention in Irish affairs when he called on Henry
    II to assist him in regaining his throne.

31 Aiello, Al musicista, 65. Aiello does not indicate a source for White's remarks.

Irish National Theatre, the precursor of the Abbey Theatre which had been founded by the Fay brothers; and she subsequently played the roles of Mrs Tully in the Abbey production of Lady Gregory's *Spreading the News* in the same year,[32] and of Mary Doul in Synge's *The Well of the Saints* in 1905.[33] In 1906, she joined a rival company, the Theatre of Ireland, but her brief career seems to have come to an end not long afterwards.[34] She was personally acquainted with several notable writers of the period including the poet and playwright Padraic Colum, who seems to have had more than a passing infatuation with her.[35] Her sister Bianca, who supported herself by teaching Italian at the Berlitz School and various other institutions in Dublin,[36] evidently shared her sister's political orientation. Many years later, when the two women met de Valera at a reception in Dublin, Vera described to him how they had hidden guns up a chimney shaft (presumably in their family home) for members of the IRA during the Anglo-Irish War.[37]

Esposito's son Mario also seems to have sought some form of active political involvement during these years — a somewhat unexpected development in view of his rather retiring nature. A rather enigmatic figure about whom very little is known, he evidently developed into someone of remarkable intellectual gifts.[38] Having become interested in medieval Irish literature in Latin during his late teens, he decided to make this his specialism. He was apparently offered a place at Harvard, but turned it down, preferring to attend Trinity

32 Hogan et al., *The Abbey Theatre: Laying the Foundations, 1902–1904*, 129–30

33 Hogan et al., *The Modern Irish Drama: A Documentary History*, vol. 3, *The Abbey Theatre: The Years of Synge, 1905–1909* (Dublin, 1978), 22

34 Her last recorded appearance was with the Queen's Royal Theatre in Trinity College Dublin's Amateur Dramatic Club's production of Sheridan's *The Rivals* in 1906: see Hogan et al., *The Abbey Theatre: The Years of Synge*, 27.

35 See Bell, 'Waiting for Mario', 22. Richard Ellman interviewed Vera and her sister Bianca while researching his biography of James Joyce, for both had known him slightly. The sisters first met Joyce in the company of their parents on the evening before Bloomsday, 16 June 1904, at the house of James and Gretta Cousins. On that occasion, Joyce, who had a tenor voice of fine quality, sang for the assembled company. Esposito was deeply impressed by his performance and invited the young man to call on them. Unfortunately, a closer association between Joyce and the Esposito family never had a chance to develop. Four days later, Vera found herself stumbling over his prostrate form in a dark passageway as she was leaving a National Theatre Society rehearsal held at its premises in Camden St: Joyce had evidently wished to attend but turned up in such an intoxicated state that he had collapsed and passed out. An embarrassing scene ensued, and unsurprisingly, Vera did not pursue his acquaintance after this incident. The episode was later evoked in *Ulysses*, when Buck Mulligan tells Stephen: 'O, the night in Camden Hall when the daughters of Erin had to lift up their skirts to step over you as you lay in your mulberrycoloured, multicoloured, multitudinous vomit!' See Richard Ellman, *James Joyce* (New York, 1959), 161–62, 167, 771, 773.

36 Pine and Acton, *To Talent Alone*, 196. Amongst her students was the young Samuel Beckett, who later depicted her as the teacher Adriana Ottolenghi in the first story of *More Kicks than Pricks*: Beckett acknowledged her influence in arousing his interest in Dante. See Bell, 'Waiting for Mario', 22; and Roger Little, 'Beckett's Mentor, Rudmose-Brown: Sketch for a Portrait', *Irish University Review*, 14, 1 (1984), 34–41.

37 Bell, 'Waiting for Mario', 20

38 The account of Mario's career that follows is based on Bell, 'Waiting for Mario', and Gorman, 'Mario Esposito'.

College, Dublin.[39] He enrolled there in 1905, but seems to have pursued his formal studies in a rather desultory fashion, as he did not graduate until 1912.[40] Such was his precocity that he was elected to the Royal Irish Academy, Ireland's foremost learned society, in March 1910, a few months short of his twenty-third birthday. Curiously, he never seems to have held an academic post, but chose to work as a freelance scholar, devoting much of his energies to tracking down Hiberno-Latin manuscripts located in European archives and publishing commentaries on them. During his twenties, he was steadily productive of books and articles on various topics relating to medieval literature and history, which laid the foundations for his later reputation.

When Sinn Féin won a decisive victory in the Irish general election of 1918, this bookish young man apparently decided to offer his services to the revolutionary movement. The evidence concerning the precise nature of his involvement is rather confused and there are two separate accounts of his activities which may not be incompatible. The first of these issued from Mario himself, in a letter to his brother-in-law's nephew Maurice Dockrell written near the end of his life in 1969. In the course of this, he refers to having read Ulick O'Connor's recent biography of the Irish writer Oliver St John Gogarty, with whom he had been acquainted. O'Connor stated that Gogarty, a doctor by profession, forged a medical certificate for Mario to help him avoid being conscripted, as he was a Sinn Féin agent and was required to go on a mission to France.[41] Mario commented:

> [The] statement by Gogarty that he had given me a medical certificate to avoid conscription ... is true in part, but the document was given to enable me to procure a permit from the police in London. De Valera was then in hiding and wished to send messages to Collins [i.e. the revolutionary activist Michael Collins] and others in England. As I was not in any way suspected of being a rebel, the permit was immediately granted by Dublin Castle and I was able to carry the messages to Collins and other Sinn Féiners in London and Manchester. Gogarty was a friend of our family and studied Italian with my sister Bianca who found him an excellent student. I am surprised that he should have recorded the fact that he had given a false certificate! Another doctor, himself a Sinn Féiner, had refused to do this. I was never liable for conscription in any country![42]

The second account of Mario's adventures is more colourful, though perhaps of uncertain reliability. According to J. Bowyer Bell, this is to be found in the autobiography of Robert Brennan, a veteran of the Easter Rising who went on to become a prominent Sinn Féin

39 Watton, *Michele Esposito*, 10
40 Gorman, 'Michele Esposito', 304
41 Ulick O'Connor, *Oliver St John Gogarty* (London, 1973), 173
42 Letter from Mario Esposito to Maurice Dockrell, 26 February 1969, quoted in Pine and Acton, *To Talent Alone*, 198–99

leader,[43] which was published in 1950 under the title of *Allegiance* and presents a firsthand account of the author's involvement in Irish revolutionary politics at this period. Brennan relates that after the Sinn Féin electoral victory, the idea was mooted of sending an agent to the continent who would lobby representatives at the forthcoming Versailles Peace Conference to support the cause of Irish independence. An associate, Frank Gallagher, introduced Brennan to a young man who seemed ideal for this purpose, whom he refers to in his narrative as 'Jean Christophe' and whom Bell, on the basis of his researches, identifies as Mario. This conjecture is certainly plausible: 'Jean Christophe' is described as a young scholar interested in ancient manuscripts, whose father 'had come from the continent to Ireland at an early age, and had spent his life in Dublin in a professional capacity'.[44] Furthermore, the *nom de guerre* that Brennan bestows on the young man was almost certainly suggested by name of the composer-hero of Romain Rolland's celebrated novel *Jean-Christophe* — and thus a covert allusion to the fact that Mario's father was a composer.

Brennan found 'Jean Christophe' to be 'extremely shy, sensitive and serious minded' and 'wholly on the side of Sinn Féin'.[45] His suitability was enhanced by the fact that he not only spoke several European languages, but had plausible reasons to go abroad which would not arouse official suspicion: he was known to Arthur Balfour as a scholar, and could seek the latter's help in obtaining a passport on the pretext that he wished to consult materials in foreign archives. Bell's researches reveal that this plan apparently met with the approval of Count George Noble Plunkett — a Sinn Féin MP who was, incidentally, a Governor of the RIAM. It was consequently decided to send the young man to Switzerland in the company of another agent, the sum of £500 being made available from organizational funds for this purpose.[46] Brennan relates that the young man was instructed 'to find out where the Peace Conference is to be, [and] to try and influence by letters and interviews representatives of the other nations at the Peace Conference with a view to having Ireland admitted'.[47]

At this point, matters became somewhat complicated. According to Brennan, the plan also aroused the interest of the revolutionary leader Michael Collins, who by this time was a central figure in the Irish Republican Brotherhood, a secret society dedicated to the

---

43 Brennan (1881–1964) was leader of the Easter Rising in Wexford in 1916 and director of publicity for the revolutionary movement during the Irish Civil War. He subsequently held important political and diplomatic posts in the Free State: he was director of the *Irish Press* 1930–34 before returning to the diplomatic service as Secretary to the Irish Legation in Washington, becoming Envoy in 1938 and Minister Plenipotentiary in 1947. On his return to Ireland, he became Director of Radio Éireann. He was also a minor writer of some distinction. See the entry 'Brennan, Robert' in Brian Cleeve, *Dictionary of Irish Writers*, Volume 1 (Cork, 1967).

44 Robert Brennan, *Allegiance* (Dublin, 1950), 178

45 Brennan, *Allegiance*, 178

46 Bell, 'Waiting for Mario', 16

47 Brennan, *Allegiance*, 179

cause of national independence. Collins sought out 'Jean Christophe' and issued him with supplementary instructions: if he made no headway through his diplomatic initiatives, he was to send Collins a letter stating that the position was hopeless and advocating 'a rising in Ireland as a demonstration to impress the Peace Conference'.[48] Clearly, Collins was hatching some scheme of his own, unbeknownst to his colleagues. When 'Jean Christophe' alerted Brennan and Gallagher to this development, they impressed on him that the undertaking for which he had initially been recruited must take priority, and that 'as to the second ... he was to use his own judgement'.[49]

'Jean Christophe' duly went abroad, and Brennan, who spent some of the intervening period in prison, did not see him until the spring of the following year, 1919, when he happened to catch a glimpse of him emerging from Sinn Féin's Harcourt St premises seemingly 'in a daze'. He discovered that the young man had just received a tongue-lashing from Cathal Brugha, then Chief of Staff of the Irish Republican Army, for having had what the latter viewed as the temerity to send a letter from Paris urging Sinn Féin to organize a rising. Clearly, his covert diplomatic initiatives had met with no success and he had accordingly followed Collins's instructions. Brugha evidently knew nothing of these, however, and finding his explanations implausible, had accused 'Jean Christophe' to his face of being a British agent. Brennan's attempts to persuade him otherwise were unavailing, largely because of Brugha's intense antipathy to Collins. He learnt the next day from Gallagher that 'Jean Christophe' was 'in the depths of despair' because he believed that Brugha might want to have him shot. Brennan asked Collins to intervene, but he adamantly refused, claiming that 'Jean Christophe' had bungled his mission — a statement on which he refused to expand — and that his life was not in any danger in any case. As a result, Brennan reports, 'Jean Christophe left Ireland and so far as I know he never came back.'[50]

Although one is unsure what to make of this story, it might explain a curious change in the Esposito family's circumstances that came about not long afterwards. In his monograph, Aiello cites what appears to be a letter from Mario, in which he states that his mother moved back to Italy to take up permanent residence in Florence in 1920 and that he joined her there shortly afterwards. No explanation for their departure is offered, or of the fact that Esposito remained in Ireland. On the face of it, it seems not a little peculiar that Natalia should choose to live so far apart from her husband after they had been married for over forty years and that the family should suddenly break up in this fashion. An article in the Irish Times, published eight years later in 1928 when Esposito himself was about to retire to Italy, explained that Natalia had been obliged to move abroad as she was 'unable to live in our climate' — a formulation which suggests that she was not in good health.[51] This

48 Brennan, Allegiance, 179
49 Brennan, Allegiance, 179
50 Brennan, Allegiance, 181
51 'An Irishman's Diary', Irish Times, 15 May 1928

explanation may have been perfectly genuine (although as it transpired, Natalia would live for another twenty-four years), but one is inclined to wonder nonetheless whether her departure had something to do with Mario's revolutionary activities: perhaps he decided that it was safest to leave Ireland for good and she felt unwilling to be separated from her son.

In Natalia's absence, Esposito was cared for by Bianca, who kept house for him.[52] Esposito's youngest daughter Nina also emigrated around 1920: her obituary in the *Irish Times* states that by the time of her death in 1970 she had lived for fifty years in Milan, where she taught English and Anglo-Irish literature and worked as a translator, and interestingly, that she assisted the distinguished writer Carlo Linati to prepare Italian translations of works by Lady Gregory and W. B. Yeats, including some of the latter's poetry and plays.[53] From Bell, we learn that she married a man by the name of Luigi Porcelli by whom she had eight children.[54] According to Aiello, who again gives Mario as his source, Vera followed her brother to Florence in 1924.[55] By this stage, she had married Dr. Maurice Dockrell, although it is not known when the wedding took place.[56] Her choice of suitor was curious, to say the least, given her political views: Dockrell was a veteran of both the Boer War and the First World War and scion of a prominent Dublin Protestant family with staunch unionist sympathies.[57]

One can only speculate as to what Esposito must have felt about the dispersion of his family. By 1920, he had reached the age of sixty-five. Aiello, once again citing Mario as his source, indicates that although his general state of health was good (some intermittent attacks of gout notwithstanding), the cumulative effect of years of overwork inevitably started to take their toll. The deterioration of Esposito's physical state became increasingly evident, but he stubbornly refused to countenance any suggestions that he should retire. He continued to immerse himself in work, despite the fact that conditions in the fledgling Free State were not very propitious for artistic initiatives. For one thing, the Easter Rising and the subsequent Anglo-Irish and Irish Civil Wars had inflicted considerable damage on the centre of Dublin, leaving many of its finest buildings in ruins. Efforts were made to revitalize musical life in the capital after the lean years of 1914 to 1922, but unsurprisingly, these largely seem to have come to nothing for lack of adequate financial support. In 1920, two new organizations were set up in which Esposito became involved. The Society of Irish

---

52 'An Irishman's Diary', *Irish Times*, 15 May 1928

53 'Obituary: Mrs N. E. Porcelly [sic]', *Irish Times*, 30 January 1970. Nina is not credited with joint authorship of Linati's translations, however, as this article might lead one to think.

54 Bell, 'Waiting for Mario', 13

55 Aiello, *Al musicista*, 61

56 One surmises that it must have taken place by April 1923. When Esposito received a decoration from the Italian Crown at a reception in Dublin on the fifteenth of that month, the *Irish Times* reported that the guests included 'Signorina Esposito' and 'Mrs. Dockrell' — presumably Bianca and Vera, respectively. See 'Italians in Dublin: Presentation to Signor Esposito', *Irish Times*, 16 April 1923.

57 Bell, 'Waiting for Mario', 13–14

Composers was established in March, which sought to promote native composers and for a time organized private concerts of their work,[58]and the Irish Musical League, which was set up two months later, aimed to found an Irish Symphony Orchestra and to build suitable concert halls in Dublin, as well as organize regular monthly concerts. These were causes close to Esposito's heart and, unsurprisingly, he lent the organization his support. He participated in the first concert given under its auspices in the Abbey Theatre on 17 October that year, conducting his string orchestra in a programme of works by Bach (the D minor keyboard concerto, which he conducted from the piano), Mozart, Tchaikovsky and a contemporary Italian composer, Leone Sinigaglia, as well as an arrangement of the *Adagio espressivo* from his own Second String Quartet.[59] Unfortunately, the time was not propitious for the accomplishment of the League's ambitious aims and it seems to have effectively ceased operation by 1922.

Esposito's activities as a pianist and conductor seem to have diminished considerably as the 1920s progressed. His solo appearances became noticeably infrequent, but he continued to perform regularly at the RDS with the Dublin Trio. The personnel of this ensemble underwent several changes after the First World War. When both Simonetti and Twelvetrees returned to England in 1919, their places were initially taken by Ferruccio Grossi, a new appointee at the RIAM who also took over as leader of Esposito's string orchestra, and the cellist John Mundy, who had previously worked with the Beecham Symphony Orchestra, the Philharmonic Society and Landon Ronald's New Symphony Orchestra.[60] The reconstituted ensemble gave its first concert at the Abbey Theatre on 4 January 1920, but in the event Mundy did not stay in Ireland long. Fortunately, Twelvetrees agreed to resume his former role, and he travelled over from Manchester fairly regularly to play in duo recitals with Esposito at the RDS.[61] In the short term at least, there seemed no possibility of reviving the DOS, but the string orchestra Esposito had founded continued to give concerts until 1923, including latterly such ambitious works in its programmes as Elgar's *Introduction and Allegro* and Debussy's *Danse sacrée et danse profane*, in addition to a new work of his own, the *Neapolitan Suite*, Op. 69, which was premiered at the RDS on 26 February 1923 at the Theatre Royal, in the presence of the Italian Consul, Signor Nadamlenski.[62]

As its title might suggest, the *Neapolitan Suite* is a nostalgic evocation of the familiar sights and sounds of his native Naples. It is a deftly written work of considerable charm which amply merits revival. The suite comprises five movements. The first of these, marked *Allegro con brio*, is a lively sonata movement in the sunny key of A major,

58 See Letter from M. Kavanagh [Hon. Sec. Society of Irish Composers] to *Freeman's Journal*, 5 March 1920, and *Irish Times*, 20 December 1920.
59 *Irish Times*, 23 October 1920
60 *Musical Times*, 60, 920 (1919), 563
61 Though Twelvetrees had resigned from the RIAM in 1919 for a position in the Hallé Orchestra, he began to give recitals again with Esposito in Dublin at the RDS on 5 December 1921, much to the delight of the audience (see *Irish Times*, 6 December 1921).
62 *Freeman's Journal*, 27 February 1923

with material that is decidedly reminiscent of Neapolitan popular song in its abundant employment of parallel thirds and sixths. The subsequent *Notturno* is in the composer's favourite key of D flat major and has a tripartite structure. It presents a soaring violin solo against an accompaniment pattern that opens with a rather striking progression (Ex. 65). The chromatic rising bass of the central section establishes a contrasting and somewhat more agitated mood. This culminates in the opening chord of Ex. 65, which is skilfully used to effect a return to D flat for a reprise of the A section. The *Intermezzo* features some highly imaginative textures and unusual sonorities. The principal idea, which is announced by a trio of second violins playing *senza sordini*, is constructed from a colourful succession of chromatic triads. It is heard against an elaborate contrapuntal accompaniment on the rest of the strings, playing with mutes, featuring prominent extended pedal points (Ex. 66). From the opening key of F major, the tonality shifts to A flat, whereupon the triadic motion transfers to the violas and cellos and contrapuntal lines are redistributed amongst the other voices. At the close, the same material reappears on muted first violins, bringing the movement to a tranquil close. The fourth movement, entitled *Serenata*, also features an elaborate Neapolitan-style melody, this time given to the 'male' voice of a solo cello to counterbalance the 'female' violin soloist of the *Notturno*. (These solos were almost certainly written with Grossi and Twelvetrees in mind.)[63] This theme has a *pizzicato* accompaniment suggestive of the sound of a strummed guitar (Ex. 67). After a contrasting middle section, it returns in a forceful guise with quasi-operatic embellishments, complete with cadenza. The work concludes with a furious *Tarantella* in A minor. This has an arch-like structure (ABCBA), in which the slower, hymn-like C section is effectively contrasted with the drive of the A and B sections. The reprise of the A section features a brief allusion to the main theme of the *Serenata* on solo cello (heard as part of an intricate nine-part texture) before the rousing final pages bring the movement to a boisterous close.

---

63 Esposito made an arrangement of this movement for cello and piano, which he dedicated to Twelvetrees.

Ex. 65: Notturno, from *Neapolitan Suite*, Op. 69

Ex. 66: *Intermezzo, from Neapolitan Suite, Op. 69*

Ex. 67: *Serenata, from Neapolitan Suite, Op. 69*

The *Neapolitan Suite* proved to be one of Esposito's last works. Aiello records that in 1923 he also completed a Third String Quartet in B flat major, but this does not appear to have even been performed or published, and the manuscript is now lost.[64] Apart from a few preludes for piano written in the last year of his life, the only other work that he completed subsequently was *My Irish Sketch Book*, Op. 71, a set of twelve simple folksong arrangements intended for young pianists, which were brought out posthumously by C. E. Music Publishers in four sets, each consisting of three pieces.

In the same year, Esposito received a welcome, if somewhat belated, token of recognition from his native country when the Italian monarch bestowed on him the title of *Commendatore dell'Ordine della Corona d'Italia* [Commander of the Order of the Italian

64 Aiello, *Al musicista*, 75

Crown]. He was presented with the White Cross of the Order by the Italian consul Signor Nadamlenski at a reception in Dublin on 15 April 1923, at which the Papal Nuncio and other dignitaries were present. In his speech, Nadamlenski extolled Esposito's contribution to Irish cultural life and, in the words of the Irish Times report, averred that 'Italy's recognition of one of her brilliant sons reflected glory on the Italian colony in Dublin'.[65] In November of the following year, he was unanimously elected a vice-president of the RIAM by the institution's Board of Governors — a tribute that was doubtlessly intended to heal old wounds and dispel any lingering bitterness on Esposito's part about his treatment at the hands of Albert Foot thirteen years before. In his speech at the meeting in question, the presiding chairman James W. Drury paid tribute to the Italian's 'valuable and loyal service' to the RIAM for over four decades and made generous acknowledgement of the extent to which his international professional reputation had enhanced the Academy's standing.[66]

Gratifying though these signs of recognition may have been, Esposito probably derived most pleasure from hearing several of his works performed by the Hallé Orchestra under the baton of Hamilton Harty in the mid-1920s. The friendship between the two men seems, if anything, to have intensified at this period and they kept in constant contact. According to Aiello, Harty spent the summers between 1921 to 1923 in Italy with Esposito and his wife in their villa, which was situated in the hills around Fiesole.[67] In an interview published in the Musical Times in April 1920, Harty made admiring reference to his friend's accomplishments, declaring that 'as an all-round musician he is ... unsurpassed in Europe. I send him for criticism everything I write, and put as implicit faith in him now as when a boy – he has always been right.'[68] He did what he could to promote Esposito's music when the opportunity arose. He accompanied the eminent English cellist Beatrice Harrison in a performance of Esposito's Cello Sonata at a concert at the Wigmore Hall in March 1919,[69] and in the same year performed two of Esposito's arrangements for string orchestra — the Andantino by Rossi and Marcello's Toccata — at a concert given by the Hallé Orchestra in Manchester on 18 December.[70] He subsequently invited Esposito to participate in a Hallé concert on 23 March 1922, the programme for which was devoted almost exclusively to works by Italian composers. On this occasion, Esposito appeared as soloist in a Mozart piano concerto and performed his Three Ballades, Op. 59, as well as conducting the orchestral transcription of the Berceuse from Op. 26 and the concert overture Othello.[71]

65 Irish Times, 16 April 1923
66 Irish Times, 8 November 1924
67 Aiello, Al musicista, 61. The location was evidently conducive to creative work, as Harty completed his Piano Concerto there during the summer of 1922: see Greer, ed., Hamilton Harty: His Life and Music, 37.
68 'Hamilton Harty', Musical Times, 61, 926 (1920), 228
69 The Times, 14 March 1919
70 Concert programme, Hallé Orchestra Archive, Manchester
71 Musical Times, 63, 951 (1922), 359

For his part, Esposito followed Harty's career with great interest. Unfortunately, only one of his letters to Harty has survived, but it offers eloquent testimony to the strength of the bond between them.[72] In 1924, after five years with the Hallé, Harty took the orchestra to London for three concerts, in one of which he performed Brahms's Fourth Symphony and some of Esposito's arrangements. The Hallé had not played in the capital since 1913 and the concerts received ecstatic critical notices.[73] Esposito promptly wrote to Harty to convey his congratulations:

> My dear Hay,
> I am so delighted with your letter which I was waiting for with eagerness. Bravo! and with the Brahms No. 4! I remarked in the leaflet that only one critic dared say the truth that the band is your making and they had never heard that symphony performed in such a way as to understand it. The work is a hard-nut for performers and public and you ought to be thankful to the band and take your rightful share in the success. Whatever Strauss may think if the instrument is not reliable the conductor cannot do full justice to a complicated masterpiece. You have got the instrument and the genius to make use of it. I never doubted. It always amazes me to see how the so-called critics believe in their own superior knowledge: they not only know everything but also what a composer or a performer ought to do. What fun if they were presented with the Score of this Brahms No. 4 and an orchestra and invited to conduct!?[74]

Notwithstanding his evident delight in Harty's success, he chided Harty gently for working too hard, with an endearing show of concern for his well-being: 'I see in your letter a passing remark about "health" — be a good boy and don't overwork yourself. I know the attraction of "doing" everything that comes in one's way but try to get regular meals and sleep in bed and not in railways.'

In April 1924, Harty came to Dublin with the Hallé, giving two concerts at the Theatre Royal, and on 17 January of the following year the orchestra visited again, performing Brahms's First Symphony and Stanford's Irish Rhapsody No. 1.[75] In June of the following year he was conferred with an honorary doctorate from Trinity College Dublin. A rather touching photograph taken at a reception held in the RIAM to mark the occasion shows Harty standing besides Esposito, his arm linked affectionately in that of the older man,

---

72 Much of Harty's correspondence was destroyed in 1940 when his London residence was bombed: see Greer, ed., *Hamilton Harty: His Life and Music*, 75.

73 Michael Kennedy, *The Hallé Tradition: A Century of Music* (Manchester, 1960), 222

74 Letter from Esposito to Harty, 2 November 1924, GB-BEq; in Watton, L., *Michele Esposito: A Neapolitan Musician in Dublin from 1882–1928*, unpublished dissertation, Queen's University Belfast (1986), 140

75 *Irish Times*, 12 January 1925

whose face wears an obvious expression of pride.[76] Also included in the picture is Sir Stanley Cochrane, who had been a stalwart supporter of both men's careers. Harty gave *Othello* again with the Hallé Orchestra in Manchester on 21 January 1926.[77] In March of the same year, when he brought over his Chamber Music Orchestra (an ensemble composed of Hallé instrumentalists) to perform at the RDS, he programmed another work by Esposito, giving what one critic described as a 'brilliant' rendition of the *Neapolitan* Suite in front of a virtually capacity audience.[78] Harty returned to Dublin at the end of October for an event he had helped organize in his mentor's honour, at which he presented him with a specially commissioned portrait by the artist Sarah Harrison that now hangs in the National Gallery. In an emotional tribute, he declared 'it would be impossible to overestimate what [Esposito's] presence in Dublin for so many years had meant to Irish music', and that 'as the founder of a great school of piano playing, and as a steadfast enemy of all that was false and unworthy in music ... they owed him a special debt of gratitude'.[79] He also emphasized how unselfishly Esposito had given of his talents in order to assist others, and acknowledged the older man's far-reaching influence on his own development as a musician.

In the same month, Esposito made what were to be amongst his last appearances as a solo recitalist in a series of three concerts organized in anticipation of the forthcoming Beethoven centenary of 1927. These took place in the Baggotrath Hall on 11, 18 and 28 October and featured sonatas that Esposito had programmed frequently during his forty-four years in Dublin.[80] In the first recital, he performed the *Pathétique*, *Moonlight* and *Pastoral* sonatas; in the second, the *Waldstein* and *Tempest* sonatas, the Sonata in A flat, Op. 26, and the Sonata in E Major, Op. 109; and in the third, the *Appassionata* and *Les Adieux* sonatas, the Sonata in F minor, Op. 2/1, and the Sonata in C minor, Op. 111. These concerts received highly appreciative notices, which were full of praise for Esposito's artistry and manifest sympathy with Beethoven's emotional and imaginative world.[81] According to Aiello, who unfortunately does not record his source, one reviewer considered his performances to surpass even those of the celebrated Scottish pianist Frederic Lamond (1868–1948), a notable pupil of Liszt's who had a considerable reputation as a Beethoven specialist.[82]

During the same year, Esposito received what appear to have been his first invitations to broadcast on the fledgling Irish radio station 2RN. On 27 November 1926, he conducted the 2RN Station Orchestra in a performance of his opera *The Post Bag*, with Kathleen

76 *Irish Times*, 4 July 1925
77 Concert programme, Hallé Orchestra Archive, Manchester
78 '2,000 at Dublin Concert', *Irish Times*, 2 March 1926
79 'Tributes to Dublin Musician', *Irish Times*, 1 November 1926
80 Larchet's statement that Esposito played all thirty-two Beethoven sonatas in this series appears to be erroneous: see Larchet, 'Michele Esposito', 432.
81 See, for example, *Irish Times*, 19 October and 26 October 1926.
82 Aiello, *Al musicista*, 59

McCully, Harry O'Dempsey and T. W. Hall in the principal roles,[83] and a month later, on 17 December, he performed Beethoven's *Appassionata* Sonata during an evening broadcast.[84] A survey of the radio listings for 1927 reveals that he does not appear to have broadcast for the station subsequently, but his compositions were aired from time to time. Singers included his arrangements of Irish melodies in their recitals and some of his larger works were given occasionally. On 5 January 1927, Percy Gillespie sang his cycle *Roseen Dhu*, for example, and in the following year, Maude Gavin and Dorothy Stokes performed his First and Second Violin Sonatas on 18 February and 9 March, respectively.[85]

In spite of the fact that he had reached the age of seventy-one, Esposito's workload remained very heavy and he obdurately ignored the advice he dispensed so freely to Harty about the dangers of overwork. In the course of 1926, he not only taught his usual cohort of students at the RIAM, but examined the lion's share of candidates for the Academy's local centre examinations, which were held in seventeen venues around the country and attracted over a thousand entrants that year.[86] Although he had always tended to work excessively hard, the question naturally arises why he should have continued to take on so many extra commitments. The most likely explanation is that he was obliged to do so for financial reasons, as he was now supporting two households, one in Ireland and one in Italy. His exhausting professional schedule, which would have proved tiring for someone of even half his age, no doubt also explains why he wrote so little music during the 1920s. According to an unsigned tribute in the *Irish Times* which appeared after Esposito's death, his physical deterioration became 'distressingly plain' towards the end of the decade, but he evidently refused to countenance any suggestions that he should reduce the scope of his activities.[87]

His slow decline in health notwithstanding, Esposito now directed his energies to another ambitious project: the revival of the Dublin Orchestral Society. For all its likely shortcomings, this body had been keenly missed in the Irish capital, where orchestral activity had remained more or less moribund since the First World War. In 1920, the composer and conductor Vincent O'Brien established a new ensemble, the Dublin Symphony Orchestra, but this proved to be a short-lived venture and ceased operation in 1922. Four years later, however, there were encouraging signs that a reconstituted DOS might meet with adequate public support. In May 1926 the *Irish Times* reported that plans were afoot to establish a new full-time orchestra.[88] These came to fruition the following year when Colonel Fritz Brase, the Prussian conductor of the Irish Army No. 1 Band, revived the Dublin Symphony Orchestra, which joined forces with the Dublin

83 *Irish Times*, 27 November 1927
84 *Irish Times*, 17 December 1926
85 *Irish Times*, 5 January 1927, and 18 February and 8 March 1928
86 Pine and Acton, *To Talent Alone*, 351
87 'Sudden Death of Comm. Esposito', *Irish Times*, 25 November 1929
88 'Proposed Permanent Orchestra', *Irish Times*, 31 May 1926

Philharmonic Choral Society for a concert to mark the Beethoven Centenary on 26 March 1927. On Brase's initiative, both organizations amalgamated the following July to form the Dublin Philharmonic Society and an ambitious programme of symphony concerts was announced for the following season.[89]

This development may well have spurred Esposito into action. A new DOS committee was set up and a public meeting convened on 28 January 1927, at which it was announced that the Society intended to resume its activities and that arrangements were being finalized for a concert series to be given during the forthcoming year. The conducting was to be divided between Esposito and John F. Larchet, who was to act as his assistant.[90] One of the most pressing practical problems confronting the committee was to find a suitable venue for the concerts, as many of the venues the DOS had used before the war had since been turned into picture-houses or were being used for other purposes. It finally settled on the Gaiety Theatre, and the concerts were held on Sunday evenings, when the theatre was generally dark.[91]

By all accounts, the series got off to a propitious start with the first concert on 13 March 1927, at which Larchet and Esposito shared the podium: it seems to have been reasonably well supported and received generally favourable notices. The programme included the overture to Gluck's *Iphigénie*, Beethoven's Seventh Symphony, Wagner's *Siegfried Idyll*, Esposito's orchestrations of four pieces by Domenico Scarlatti[92] and the Mendelssohn Piano Concerto in G Minor in which the maestro appeared as soloist. The critic for the *Irish Times* averred that 'Dr Esposito's playing of the pianoforte part in the Mendelssohn Concerto showed that age has done nothing to impair the brilliance of his technique or the excellence of his powers of interpretation.'[93] Esposito and Larchet also shared the conducting at the second concert on 3 April, which featured the Bach A minor Violin Concerto (with Grossi as soloist) and Mozart's Symphony No. 40 in G minor, together with shorter works by Mendelssohn, Wagner, Weber, Berlioz and Saint-Saëns. During the festivities for Dublin Civic Week later in the year, the DOS gave two further concerts on 19 and 20 September. The first of these was conducted by Esposito and featured his own *Irish Suite* and Beethoven's Fifth Symphony; the second, which was aimed at an audience of children, was conducted by Larchet.[94] Once again, Esposito's direction of the orchestra drew praise from the critics, although it was acknowledged that the quality of the performance was compromised to some extent by unsatisfactory wind playing.[95]

89 'A New Musical Enterprise', *Irish Times*, 9 July 1927

90 'Dublin Orchestral Society', *Irish Times*, 29 January 1927; and Larchet, 'Michele Esposito', 432

91 'Dublin Orchestral Society', *Irish Times*, 5 and 9 March 1927

92 Esposito arranged two sets of pieces by Domenico Scarlatti for orchestra, both of which were published by Oxford University Press in 1925 (see Catalogue of Works, Section F). It is not clear which set was performed on this occasion.

93 'Revival of Dublin Orchestral Society', *Irish Times*, 14 March 1927

94 *Irish Times*, 25 July, 22 August and 3 September 1927

95 'Dublin Orchestral Society', *Irish Times*, 20 September 1927

To judge from contemporary reports, the orchestra's standard continued to remain rather variable. For the first concert of the Society's winter season on 8 October 1927, at which Esposito and Larchet once again shared the conducting, Frederick Dawson was soloist in Liszt's First Piano Concerto and the programme concluded with Dvořák's *New World* Symphony. On this occasion, the orchestra's playing was deemed to have improved considerably and Dawson's dazzling virtuosity made a tremendous impression on the audience.[96] Its performance at the second concert on 3 December, on the other hand, was deemed frankly poor, the ensemble's deficiencies being particularly noticeable in what seems to have been a rather ragged and under-rehearsed account of Beethoven's *Pastoral* Symphony.[97] Plans were announced for a third concert of Beethoven's *Egmont* Overture, Brahms's Second Symphony and Verdi's *Quattro pezzi sacri* on Saturday 18 February.[98]

According to his son Mario, Esposito complained of feeling unwell in the days leading up to this event, but with habitual obstinacy persisted in going about his business as usual. On 7 February 1928, he conducted a rehearsal of the Brahms Second Symphony, but after returning home suffered a heart attack during the night. His daughter Bianca, who was the only other person present in the house, summoned a doctor who clearly feared his death to be imminent.[99] He administered an injection and advised Bianca to call a priest. Esposito was adamant that he did not want to die: 'It's absurd — I still have a lot of work to do', he is reported as saying, adding that he had a great many ideas for compositions that were as yet unwritten.[100] In the event, he rallied and the crisis passed — but it soon became clear that his health had been permanently impaired. The retirement from professional life that he had postponed for so long was thrust upon him at last. Esposito recognized that he could no longer work and submitted his resignation to the RIAM on 23 April 1928.[101]

The institution's Board of Governors agreed to award him a pension of £300 per annum. To supplement this, a benefit fund was established to which many prominent figures contributed, including Alfred Percival Graves and Robert O'Dwyer, and which, according to van Hoek, eventually raised almost £1,500.[102] Esposito had initially hoped that he might be able to continue working at the RIAM in some capacity and offered his services as head examiner for the local centre examinations, but this did not prove feasible.[103] As his

96 'Music Notes and News', *Irish Times*, 10 October 1927

97 'Large Audience at Theatre Royal Concert', *Irish Times*, 5 December 1927

98 'Dublin Orchestral Society', *Irish Times*, 21 December 1927 and 14 February 1928

99 According to van Hoek, Bianca was joined by Larchet and a priest, Father Doyle, and that all three 'spent a sad night of vigil at his bedside': see van Hoek, 'Michele Esposito', 229. This statement is not corroborated by any other source, however.

100 Aiello, *Al musicista*, 60–61. This account differs in some details from that given by Richard Pine and Charles Acton in *To Talent Alone*, 351, where it is stated that Esposito's heart attack occurred during a DOS rehearsal on the 8 February. Pine and Acton do not indicate a source for this information.

101 Pine and Acton, *To Talent Alone*, 351

102 Pine and Acton, *To Talent Alone*, 351; see also van Hoek, 'Michele Esposito', 230.

103 Minutes of the RIAM Board of Governors, 7 March 1928. See Watton, L., *Michele Esposito: A Neapolitan Musician in Dublin from 1882–1928* unpublished dissertation, Queen's University Belfast (1986), 18.

income was now greatly reduced, he could no longer afford the expense of maintaining two separate establishments in Ireland and Italy. In consequence, he had little choice but to sell his Dublin home and join his wife in Florence. He made no secret of his reluctance to take this step: as the *Irish Times* reported, 'that he would prefer to remain in his Irish home did circumstances permit he does not deny'.[104] Having concluded the necessary formalities, he sailed from Ireland in July. One can only speculate about his feelings as he left the city in which he had lived and worked for forty-six years.

Travelling in the company of Bianca, he proceeded first to England, where he stayed for a time with Hamilton Harty's wife, intending to rest before continuing his journey.[105] Unfortunately things did not work out quite as planned: his health deteriorated and he was admitted to a nursing home.[106] When he eventually reached Florence, Esposito rejoined his family and settled into their recently acquired new home, a small villa in the Via Fra Guittone.[107] One imagines that his new circumstances required considerable readjustment: for one thing, a man of his temperament must surely have experienced difficulty in resigning himself to forced inactivity.[108] 'Life in Dublin must be very exciting now that I am out of it,' he wrote wistfully to his friend Alice Yoakley. 'I am now in a very lazy mood; I cannot make up my mind and body to do anything.'[109] Having been at the centre of musical life in Dublin for over four decades, it must also have been difficult to accustom himself to living somewhere where he had few professional contacts and was virtually unknown. Moreover, the country to which he returned in 1928 was very different to the Italy of his youth, though what his attitude might have been to Mussolini's Fascist regime, which had seized power in 1922, is not known.

Nonetheless, being reunited with his wife and children may have helped to compensate for his comparative isolation. Aiello records that he derived particular joy from being reunited with his brother Eugenio, whom he had apparently not seen for the best part of fifty years.[110] Eugenio, it transpired, had experienced his own share of tribulations during the intervening decades. He had remained in Russia for the duration of the First World War and only managed to return to Europe in 1922, five years after the Bolshevik revolution of 1917. When the new regime nationalized music publishing, he lost the rights to his operas and other works that had been brought out by Russian publishers, and was thus unable

104 'An Irishman's Diary', *Irish Times*, 15 May 1928; and 'Sudden Death of Comm. Esposito', *Irish Times*, 25 November 1929

105 Aiello, *Al musicista*, 61

106 Van Hoek, 'Michele Esposito', 230

107 Gorman, 'Mario Esposito', 306. A photograph of this house is reproduced in Esposito, *Studies in Hiberno-Latin Literature*, xxiv.

108 Hubert Foss, Esposito's editor at OUP (see below), wrote that he 'suffered more than most men when his time for retiring came and forced inaction upon him': see letter from Hubert Foss to *The Times*, 28 November 1929.

109 Letter from Esposito to Alice Yoakley, 13 November 1928, quoted in Pine and Acton, *To Talent Alone*, 352

110 Aiello, *Al musicista*, 62

to have them reprinted subsequently. Not only did he receive no compensation from the new administration, but also he had to endure the confiscation of his life's savings. On his return to Italy, he settled in Milan where he supported himself through composing and teaching.[111]

Aiello also mentions that Esposito soon began to receive visits from his former pupils, in addition to making several new friendships, which were a source of great pleasure. Amongst these were the pianist Paolo Denza, a student of Alessandro Longo, who visited him and performed his Op. 59 set of *Three Ballades*, and the poet Clemens Laura Majocchi, who was a sufficiently capable violinist to play through one of his sonatas and the two Irish Rhapsodies with him.[112] The eminent conductor Vittorio Gui (1885–1975), who, in later years, achieved a notable following in England for his operatic performances at Glyndebourne, also lived nearby and became a regular visitor. The two men held each other's abilities in great regard and found a common bond in their admiration for Martucci, about whom Esposito willingly shared his reminiscences with the younger man. He impressed Gui as being a man of great kindness and sincerity, who radiated an immense love of music and was entirely free of affectation. He suspected that Esposito felt a certain amount of bitterness at being virtually unknown and unrecognized in his native country, but could never be drawn to speak on the subject.[113] Gui thought highly of Esposito's creative talent and considered him to be one of the most important Italian composers of instrumental music, declaring that his achievement was comparable to that of Martucci and Respighi.[114] When he knew his death was imminent, Esposito gave the conductor his score of *Tristan* and an autographed copy of Martucci's Second Symphony as keepsakes, in gratitude for their friendship.[115]

As soon as he had recovered sufficiently, Esposito occupied himself by resuming his editorial work. In addition to producing a steady stream of editions for C. E. Music Publications, in recent years he had also started to prepare orchestral arrangements of various kinds. In 1925, Hubert Foss, the head of the newly established Music Department at Oxford University Press, had accepted three of his orchestral transcriptions of early music for publication. Since these were of modest technical difficulty, they were ideally suited to student or amateur ensembles and were thus eminently saleable, as there was a considerable demand for music of this nature at the period. They appeared in the Press's 'Oxford Orchestral Series' together with similar arrangements by other contributors, including the composers Thomas Dunhill and Peter Warlock. In 1927, Foss elicited further contributions from Esposito, who had material ready to hand, having previously arranged a considerable quantity of music — mostly short pieces from the Baroque period

111 'Esposito, Michele' in *Dizionario biografico degli italiani*, 43 (Rome, 1993), 285–86
112 Aiello, *Al musicista*, 62
113 Aiello, *Al musicista*, 9–12, 62. A variant spelling of Gui's surname, 'Guy', is employed in Aiello's monograph.
114 'Esposito as Composer', *Irish Times*, 10 February 1931
115 Aiello, *Al musicista*, 15

by Bach, Handel, Couperin and various Italian composers — for the DOS and his string orchestra.[116] He also appears to have made new transcriptions, some of them of pieces from his anthology *Early Italian Piano Music*. Between 1927 and 1929 Oxford University Press (OUP) brought out a further fourteen items, and Esposito now set about preparing others: in addition to providing a welcome distraction, they no doubt represented a useful source of additional income.

Foss evidently had a very high regard for Esposito and even took the trouble to call on him when he visited Florence in 1929.[117] As he later remarked apropos of Esposito's contributions to the OUP series:

> He was undoubtedly a superb editor of music. ... [He] edited and arranged works for orchestra in a way that deserved the high praise that it did from one of our great conductors. His skill with the instruments and the accuracy of his editing make his work unique, particularly since his arrangements are practical to the point of simplicity for school bands and yet always effective. When he presented an older work in modern orchestral form or even scored (as he did) some harpsichord pieces by Couperin for small orchestra, he did it in such a masterly manner and with such attention to detail that the purist himself could not object. ... I mention this side of Esposito's work because it is the clearest proof first of his practical and imaginative musicianship, second of his desire to spread music around him on every side. Those two characteristics will always be remembered by those who knew him as an ever-working musician of the front rank.[118]

Although Esposito had virtually stopped composing by this point, his interest in creative work revived briefly in the spring and summer of 1929, during which time he completed six preludes for piano. These were intended to form part of a projected set of twenty-four preludes in all the major and minor keys which he had commenced in 1910, but had never completed. Unfortunately the project remained unrealized at the time of his death, and the preludes he had completed were brought out posthumously in 1936 by Ricordi, together with the three preludes he had written between 1910 and 1912, as *Nove preludi*

116 According to Aiello, during his last years in Italy, Esposito transcribed almost a dozen additional pieces for flute and string orchestra: see Aiello, *Al musicista*, 77. For reasons unknown, OUP did not publish them and the manuscripts have since disappeared.

117 Aiello, *Al musicista*, 62

118 Hubert Foss, letter to the *Times*, 28 November 1929. This letter is quoted in a rather free Italian translation in Aiello, *Al musicista*, 58.

[Nine Preludes], Op. 72.[119] The first prelude, in B flat, has the nature of an octave study, and features some athletic writing for the left hand. The second, a Mazurka in G minor, was composed in Bologna in 1912, as was the fifth, a bucolic Italian song in G sharp minor. The third prelude in A minor features rapid exchanges of material between the hands, while the fourth, in C minor has the character of a fughetta. The sixth prelude in D flat is a barcarolle employing an extended inverted dominant pedal, which tolls in bell-like fashion throughout the piece. A melody resembling a popular Neapolitan song pervades the seventh prelude in A flat, the accompaniment texture of which requires considerable dexterity. The eighth prelude in D major is less technically demanding, most of its material being derived from a quirky arpeggiated figure. The last piece of the set, which is in C sharp minor, dates from 1910 and was thus the first to be composed, although it was subsequently revised in 1929. It bears the title *Pensiero elegiaco alla memoria di Giuseppe Martucci* [Elegiac thought in memory of Giuseppe Martucci], indicating that Esposito intended it as a memorial to his old friend. This mournful lament is a dark, almost disturbing utterance, with its sparse textures and drooping chromatic figures (a characteristic passage is shown in Ex. 68).

Esposito's health remained precarious: his daughter Vera later told Harty that the family had sensed that he could die at any time.[120] Later in the year, Esposito sent some of his unpublished piano pieces to OUP, hoping that they might accept them for their catalogue. Much to his distress, he received notification in November that they had been declined.[121] On Friday 15 November, he was making a fair copy of one of the *Preludes* when he suddenly felt faint and thought he had better lie down. Having remained confined to bed over the weekend, he wished to get up and resume work on Monday, but as the weather was very bad he decided to keep to his room. He spent some of the day writing letters and correcting the proofs of his *Impromptu*, Op. 62. At eleven o'clock that night, he bade his family goodnight, telling them that he planned to get up the following day. Just before midnight, however, he suffered another heart attack. A doctor was summoned, but his ministrations were unavailing. Surrounded by his wife and children, Michele Esposito died at one o'clock in the morning on 19 February 1929.[122]

---

119 Dates of completion were added in an unidentified hand to the published copy of Esposito's *Novi Preludi* in the RIAM, as follows: Prelude No. 1 (24 March 1929, Florence); Prelude No. 2 (28 August 1912, Bologna); Prelude No. 3 (31 March 1929, Florence); Prelude No. 4 (2 April 1929, Florence); Prelude No. 5 (6 September 1912, Bologna); Prelude No. 6 (20 April 1929, Florence); Prelude No. 7 (24 April 1929, Florence); Prelude No. 8 (24 May 1929, Florence); Prelude No. 9 (22 June 1910, Dublin; 16 July 1929, Florence).
120 Letter from Vera Esposito to Harty, 27 November 1929, GB-BEq
121 Letter from Vera Esposito to Harty, 27 November 1929, GB-BEq
122 Aiello, *Al musicista*, 63

Ex. 68: Prelude in C sharp minor from *Nove prelude*, Op. 72

The house quickly filled with visitors wishing to pay their last respects to the deceased. The same day, Vera sent Harty a moving letter:

My dear Hay,

Your Miche is no more, as you will have guessed at once by the envelope. You have lost your best friend, I who know his heart so well can tell you. And I hope you love him as well as he loved you or even half as much as he thinks you did, it will still be a great deal. He measured others by himself, I suppose we all do. As I write he is lying so peacefully and all of us around him. He is to be buried very quietly tomorrow morning at Trespiano out on the hills. I wanted San Miniato, but there is no more space there.

There will be a Requiem Mass sung for him by the Choir of Franciscan Monks at a monastery in Piazza Savonarolo, and another special Mass on Friday morning.

Dear Hay, I can't write any more now. Our friends and neighbours are coming to see him in numbers, and all admire him, many weep, and kiss his cold forehead, making the sign of the Cross.

Love him always as much as you can and remember him, he loved you greatly.[123]

Harty was naturally deeply affected by the news and immediately sent a telegram of condolence followed by a letter in which he offered to arrange for a suitable inscription on Esposito's tombstone. In her reply, Vera recounted that the family had experienced considerable difficulty in finding a suitable grave for her father and had been forced to adopt a makeshift solution on account of their modest means:

> In order to respect a strong sentiment of my mother's (which I personally could not understand), no steps whatever were taken to prepare a resting-place for father beforehand. ... [Only] at the last moment after his death did we learn ... that San Miniato was out of the question and Trespiano our nearest possible place. We also realised for the first time that burying him in Italy and in a Catholic manner as he wished (having asked for a priest a week or so before he died, when he was well and not expecting anything to happen, with the intention of confessing! and receiving Holy Communion), would mean burying him as they do here in modest cases like our own, either in a deep grave with others either below or above him, or in a small compartment, reserved to himself, as it were on a shelf — poetically called a 'colombario'.

> We had to make up our minds there and then on the spot in the Cemetery, and we chose the lesser of two evils, namely the 'colombario'. So the tablet is just the size to cover the width of the coffin and its height, with very little to spare. All the graves are masonry and stone, entirely sealed with stone-work, and the only place where there is any earth, and flowers planted, is in the pauper's section where the remains are changed every ten years.[124]

Vera went on to explain that they hoped to find a more suitable final resting place for him in time. Harty's offer concerning the inscription was accepted by the family with deep gratitude.

The news of Esposito's death quickly reached Dublin. The *Irish Times* published a lengthy tribute that made generous acknowledgement of his extensive contribution to

---

123 Letter from Vera Esposito to Harty, 19 November 1929, GB-BEq; also reproduced in Watton, *Michele Esposito*, 141.
124 Letter from Vera Esposito to Harty, 27 November 1929, GB-BEq; also reproduced in Watton, *Michele Esposito*, 142.

Irish musical life, placing particular stress on his role in fostering an indigenous school of pianism and his work with the DOS.[125] An equally appreciative obituary appeared in the London *Times*.[126] A few days later the same newspaper printed a letter from Hubert Foss which paid warm tribute to his former colleague, describing him as 'a great working musician, one to whom the contemplation of music was insufficient, whose hands must be at it with pen and keyboard; one who therefore brought music as a living thing to everyone in his neighbourhood'.[127] Vittorio Gui wrote an appreciation which was printed in *La nazione* on 20 November, and just over a year later, on 25 January 1931, he performed *in memoriam* the concert overture *Othello* — which he regarded as one of Esposito's finest achievements — with the Orchestra Stabile in Florence.[128]

The most heartfelt and personal of these tributes was written by Hamilton Harty, who commemorated his friend with a performance of the *Poem*, Op. 44 (a work that Esposito had dedicated to him) on 5 December with the Hallé Orchestra in Manchester.[129] In his obituary published in the *Irish Statesman*, he gave eloquent expression to his admiration for Esposito's musical gifts and described his countrymen's profound indebtedness to the Italian's selfless efforts to further the cause of music in Ireland:

> [It] was when he was playing in private for a few friends that he was at his finest both poetically and technically. I can never forget the impression I received on these occasions, not only of the depth and beauty of the music of composers like Beethoven and Chopin, but at the nobility of thought and the passion and romance of sentiment which dwelt in the soul of Esposito himself. He gave the best part of his life to teaching us in Ireland that poetic imagination and superficial facility are not enough in matters of art. It is our national failing in music to think that our Irish ease in conjuring up the vision of something emotional and poetic absolves us from the necessity of learning how to support it on a solid basis of learning and craftsmanship. It was in this way that Esposito served us so faithfully, and of all of his friends and pupils no one owes him more in this way than I do myself, or acknowledges it with more eagerness and gratitude. I shall always think of him as the most perfect musician I have ever met — and a still greater thing as the most beautiful and lovable nature with which I have ever been brought into contact.[130]

125 'Sudden Death of Comm. Esposito', *Irish Times*, 25 November 1929
126 'Commendatore Esposito', *The Times*, 25 November 1925
127 Letter from Hubert Foss to *The Times*, 28 November 1929
128 Aiello, *Al musicista*, 56, 63, and 'Esposito as Composer', *Irish Times*, 10 February 1931
129 Aiello, *Al musicista*, 63
130 Hamilton Harty, 'Michele Esposito', *The Irish Statesman*, 7 December 1929, 277

7   Epilogue

In a letter written shortly after her father's death, Vera Esposito appealed to Hamilton Harty, '[Help] us to keep Father's name alive a little. If you can, every now and again, perform something of his; it will please mother and all of us more than anything else, as it would have pleased him in life — and perhaps even now.'[1] Keeping Esposito's music in the repertoire proved an almost impossible task, however. The fact that a considerable proportion of his large-scale works remained in manuscript at the time of his death (including two piano concertos, a symphony, several other orchestral compositions and some substantial chamber works) meant that they stood little chance of attracting the attention of performers. His children may well have tried to interest publishers in these compositions, but if so their efforts met with limited success: a few piano works were issued posthumously by C. E. Music Publishers between 1930 and 1932, and Ricordi brought out the *Nove preludi* in 1936, but that was all. One can readily understand why publishers might have considered Esposito's orchestral and chamber works to be unsalable, since the idiom in which they were couched became increasingly unfashionable once the modernist reaction against the sound-worlds of late-Romantic music began to set in. Aiello reports that Harty made efforts in the late 1930s to secure the publication of *Othello*, a work which, in his view, was worthy of inclusion 'in the repertoire of every leading orchestra', but that his efforts were unavailing: the publishing house he approached declined to accept it on the grounds that it was stylistically outmoded.[2] Harty, who had little sympathy for most contemporary musical developments,[3] wrote ironically to Mario: 'Don't take the unintelligent criticism of this music as being insufficiently *modern* too seriously. Instead,

1   Letter from Vera Esposito to Harty, 27 November 1929, GB-BEq
2   Aiello, *Al musicista*, 56–57. Harty's remarks are quoted in Italian translation in the original.
3   Greer, ed., *Hamilton Harty: His Life and Music*, 40

you should thank God for this fact. Your father was a Romantic composer, and as soon as people come around again to valuing sincerity and simplicity in art, the work of your father will certainly have the recognition it deserves.[4]

Needless to say, an unenthusiastic response on the part of a publisher cannot be taken to constitute a definitive judgement on the intrinsic value of Esposito's compositions, but the fact remained that they were increasingly less likely to meet with a sympathetic reception in the prevailing critical climate. Perhaps this circumstance explains why Harty and Vittorio Gui do not appear to have conducted any of Esposito's orchestral works again subsequent to the performances they gave shortly after his death. If the Esposito family attempted to arouse the interest of other performers, their efforts were presumably unavailing. By the time of his death, Esposito had few professional contacts in Italy and his name was more or less unknown there since he had lived so long abroad. In Ireland, his music did not fare a great deal better — a fact which is scarcely surprising given the impoverished nature of Irish musical life and the dearth of professional ensembles at the period. Students at the RIAM probably played his piano pieces occasionally and a survey of the radio schedules from the 1930s and 1940s reveals that his folksong arrangements were broadcast from time to time, but none of his more substantial compositions seems to have been performed.[5] Elsewhere at this period, performances of his music were extremely rare, the only one known to the present author being a BBC broadcast of the Cello Sonata by Esposito's former colleague Clyde Twelvetrees on 20 July 1933.

It is consequently not surprising to discover that Esposito's music quickly lapsed into obscurity. His published compositions soon became unavailable, since C. E. Music Publishers ceased operations within a few years of his death. This enterprise had run at a persistent loss during his lifetime and only the generosity of Stanley Cochrane, who kept it going out of loyalty, had enabled it to survive as long as it did.[6] Aiello records that the company was taken over by the British firm of Elkin and Co.[7] which evidently did not regard keeping his scores in print to be a commercially viable proposition. Memories of Esposito in Dublin inevitably faded with the passage of time. In view of his remarkable contribution to national musical life, it is perhaps surprising that no significant effort was made to commemorate his life and work in the city where he had resided for

---

4   Extract from letter of 18 July 1939 from Hamilton Harty to Mario Esposito, quoted in Italian translation in Aiello, *Al musicista*, 57.

5   Esposito's orchestral works do not feature in the lists of works by Irish composers performed by the Radio Éireann Symphony Orchestra between 1938 and 1958 given in Richard Pine's recent book *Music and Broadcasting in Ireland* (Dublin, 2005), 84 and 144–45; or of the lists of works performed by the amateur Dublin Orchestral Players and Dublin String Orchestra 1940–49 given on p. 84 in the same volume. According to Séamas de Barra, there is no record that any of Esposito's music was performed by the Cork Symphony Orchestra, the other amateur orchestra operating in Ireland at the period (personal communication, 10 August 2008).

6   See Vera Esposito's remarks in her letter to Hamilton Harty, 27 November 1929, GB-BEq

7   Aiello, *Al musicista*, 58

forty-six years.[8] In 1941, the RIAM eventually got around to inaugurating an Esposito Memorial Scholarship (for middle grade piano students under sixteen), but otherwise the institution did little to assist the posthumous survival of his reputation.[9] The centenary of Esposito's birth in 1955 seems to have passed more or less unnoticed in Ireland, with only two commemorative events of any significance. In September, John F. Larchet broadcast a brief memorial tribute on the Irish national radio station Radio Éireann in which he recalled his former colleague's career.[10] The same year, the Irish state publishing house An Gúm published a full score of the Irish Symphony,[11] perhaps at Larchet's instigation. Unfortunately this initiative was virtually pointless: bizarrely, the handsomely produced score was issued without any accompanying set of orchestral parts.[12] Not that this would have made much difference in any case: the music division of An Gúm was staggeringly inefficient and made no effort to promote the music in its catalogue, so most of it simply gathered dust in storerooms.[13]

The following year, in 1956, when the RIAM celebrated what was mistakenly believed to be its centenary,[14] a concert of Esposito's music was given on 1 October by members of the institution's staff, with the President of Ireland Seán T. O'Kelly and other prominent dignitaries in attendance. The programme consisted of the A major Violin Sonata, the D major Cello Sonata and an extract from the C minor String Quartet, together with some piano pieces and songs.[15] Some months beforehand, an article in the Irish Times had trumpeted this forthcoming event under the caption 'Two Countries Honour a Master',[16] a headline which conveyed a decidedly exaggerated impression of the commemorative activities that had been planned. Nothing else of any consequence was organized, not even the production of a modest commemorative booklet. In Castellammare di Stabia, the local historian Giuseppe Lauro Aiello, who greatly lamented the total neglect of Esposito in his own country and locality, compiled the small monograph on the composer which has been described in the Preface. Aiello had presumably intended this to appear in print the previous year, but failed to have it ready in time.

8   A street in the Dublin suburb of Walkinstown was named 'Esposito Road' after the Second World War, but the present writer has not been able to establish in which year.

9   Pine and Acton, To Talent Alone, 451

10   The text of this radio talk is reproduced in Pine and Acton, To Talent Alone, 429–32.

11   An Gúm published the score under the Irish and Italian titles Árd-shondid Gaelach/Sinfonia irlandese, as it was policy not to use English anywhere in An Gúm publications.

12   See the Irish music critic Charles Acton's article 'Harty's Symphony', Irish Times, 20 April 1981.

13   For an account of the frustrations typically experienced by Irish composers in dealing with An Gúm, see Séamas de Barra, 'The Music of Aloys Fleischmann: A Survey', in Ruth Fleischmann, ed., Aloys Fleischmann (1910–1992): A Life for Music in Ireland Remembered by Contemporaries (Cork, 2000), 338; and Patrick Zuk, 'A. J. Potter: The career and creative achievement of an Irish composer in social and cultural context' (unpublished dissertation, University of Durham, 2007), 59–60.

14   Pine and Acton, To Talent Alone, 348, 375

15   See the articles 'President Attends Reception at Music Academy' and 'Programme of Esposito to Celebrate Centenary', Irish Times, 2 October 1956.

16   Irish Times, 9 June 1956

In the following decades, Esposito's music seems hardly to have been heard at all, apart from an isolated performance of the *Irish Symphony* by the Irish conductor Eimear Ó Broin with the Radio Telefís Éireann Symphony Orchestra in March 1969. His music virtually unknown, his contribution to Irish musical life only dimly remembered, Esposito's legacy seemed in danger of being forgotten altogether. His family similarly lapsed into obscurity, and although several researchers, including the present writer, have attempted to find out something about them, every line of enquiry has so far ended in a blind alley. What little is known of their later lives is worth recounting in some detail here, on account of its bearing on the subsequent disappearance of Esposito's personal papers and most of his manuscripts.

Natalia Esposito died on 5 January 1944, having survived her husband by fifteen years. Upon her death, her husband's remains were transferred to a cemetery at Antella, a small town about six miles south-east of Florence, so that the two of them could be buried together.[17] Harty had arranged for a few bars of Esposito's music to be inscribed on his former tomb at Trespiano;[18] Aiello records that the marble slab was later transferred to his final resting place. Esposito's brother Eugenio died six years later in 1950, in a home for the elderly in Milan. The historian, artist and critic John Bowyer Bell encountered Mario, Bianca and Vera in the spring of 1957 when he visited a friend in Florence who happened to be renting rooms in the Esposito family home. One day, Mario engaged Bell in conversation on the stairs and the young American was subsequently invited to tea on a number of occasions. Mario and his sisters came to fascinate him, and many years later he wrote the evocative article for the periodical *Éire-Ireland*, already alluded to in the Preface, describing what he had managed to find out about their lives.[19]

By the time he met them, they were evidently in rather reduced circumstances and had retreated to the upper rooms of their villa, still living together after a quarter of a century. None of them appeared ever to have worked and the rent from the downstairs rooms seemed to constitute their sole source of income. At some point, Nina had become estranged from her siblings and they had lost contact with her altogether. Vera had been abandoned by her husband many years before, not long before her father died: Morgan Dockrell found living with the Esposito family to be too great a strain and, having announced to Vera one morning that he was off to the 'chuff chuff', decamped on the Florence-Paris train and was never seen again. Vera never remarried and her brother and sister both remained celibate. As he sat talking to them in their darkened sitting-room, surrounded by numerous cats and Mario's old books, Bell sensed that relations between the trio were deeply uneasy, with smouldering antagonisms not far beneath the surface.

17 Michael Gorman, 'Mario Esposito (1887–1975) and the study of the Latin Literature of Medieval Ireland', in Mario Esposito, *Studies in Hiberno-Latin Literature* (Aldershot, 2006), 309
18 Aiello, *Al musicista*, 63. See also *To Talent Alone*, 352. The quotation, signed 'H. H.', is two-and-a-half bars of music on a single stave.
19 Bell, 'Waiting for Mario', 7–26

Mario seemed to live in a world of his own, wholly absorbed in the medieval researches which had taken him to libraries all over Europe during the preceding decades. Although he held no academic post, he was nonetheless held in the highest regard by scholars in his field. He had continued to publish steadily, mostly in English and French, contributing intimidatingly erudite articles to obscure learned journals. By the time Bell met him he was investigating the legendary personage of St Patrick, having come to believe that he had been two or three people rather than one. There seems to have been no question at any point after 1920 of him going back to Ireland: In a letter of 1959 to the Belgian historian Hubert Silvestre, he made no secret of his antipathy to the repressive intellectual climate that prevailed in the Free State:

> As far as religion is concerned, I am, for my part, completely agnostic, anticlerical, but not at all anti-religious. In Ireland under English domination a certain freedom of thought prevailed; today with the advent of the Republic and 'liberty' all intellectual activity has been crushed by the priests, who are as domineering and arrogant as they are ignorant and narrow-minded. De Valera, like the opposition, is completely dominated by the hierarchy of Maynooth and by the Jesuits. Liberalism and Socialism are almost unknown there. The Irish index of prohibited books is an absurd, incredible manifestation of obscurantism. In the north, in Ulster, the Presbyterians in power are almost more bigoted again.[20]

A man holding views of this nature would scarcely have found the Free State a very congenial place in which to live. All his life, Mario seems to have remained a loner who made few friends. He lived very simply, austerely even. By his own account, he was a lifelong vegetarian.[21] Many years later, one of his nieces remembered him as being a deeply strange man, given to going off on long walks in the mountains with only a piece of bread and a lemon in his pocket. The Irish artist, David Hone, who also knew the family in Florence, recalled that Vera regarded Mario with open contempt, remarking one day, 'Look at the old man, tramping off without a penny to his name.'[22] Apart from medieval manuscripts, mountains were the other great passion of his life: he had taken Samuel Beckett on a walking tour of the Dolomites in 1927, but the inexperienced Beckett had met with an accident which had forced Mario to leave him behind. When the Second World War broke out, he may have become involved with the Italian Resistance — drawn to this activity, perhaps, by an impulse similar to that which had drawn him to Sinn Féin. Hone told Bell that he believed Vera to have been a Nazi sympathizer and stories circulated that she befriended a prominent German officer — perhaps the Nazi commander of Florence

---

20   Letter from Mario Esposito to Hubert Silvestre, 10 April 1959, quoted in Silvestre, 'Mario Esposito', 9–10
21   See Michael M. Gorman's 'Preface' to Mario Esposito, *Studies in Hiberno-Latin Literature*, ed., M. M. Gorman (Aldershot, 2006), ix.
22   Bell, 'Waiting for Mario', 12

— when the city was occupied by the Germans between 1943 and 1944. Gossip from the neighbours in Florence confirmed that she was supposed to have been a collaborator, adding the colourful details that she had been Ezra Pound's secretary during the period when he was broadcasting from Rome and was reputed to have had a liaison with a Waffen-SS gym instructor. The story continued that she was spared punishment at the hands of the Italian Resistance because Mario had risked his life taking down German tank directional signs in the evenings, using them to build a bookcase to house his collection of incunabula. In later years, he resorted to selling these rare books and manuscripts one by one whenever he found himself running short of money.

It is difficult to know how much credence to lend these stories, if any at all. Michael Gorman found no evidence that Mario was involved with the Italian resistance when he investigated the matter in the late 1990s and many of the 'facts' presented by Bell might come to seem equally questionable if subjected to thorough critical scrutiny.[23] Nonetheless, we are in possession of some shreds of what is perhaps more reliable information, gleaned from the few letters of Mario's which have survived. In so far as he engaged in correspondence at all, most of it seems to have been with other scholars. From a letter to Hubert Silvestre, we learn that he wrote a small volume of autobiography entitled *Montagne, amore e libertà: Saggi e ricordi di Mario Esposito* [Mountains, love and liberty: Essays and reminiscences by Mario Esposito], which had been published in Florence in 1944. The head of the printing firm, a partisan with strong anarchist and communist leanings, was arrested shortly afterwards when the authorities discovered that he was issuing anti-Fascist and anti-Nazi propaganda. His workshop was completely destroyed and of the 300 copies of Mario's book that had come off the press, barely 20 were saved. Mario remarked tantalizingly to Silvestre:

> I only possess two of these and I consider the volume to be <u>unpublished</u>. I should tell you that my intimate memoirs made various things public in a rather indiscreet way which caused great offence to certain people and caused an outcry in some of the newspapers. I consequently prefer to suppress the volume. Perhaps in time — if there is an 'in time' for a man born in 1891 [*recte* 1887!] — I will prepare a new edition without the offending chapters.[24]

No copy of the book has so far come to light, however, and the efforts of the present author to track down a copy were unavailing.

As Mario led a fairly reclusive existence, little else is known about his life. Two further letters to Silvestre, dating from 1960 and 1964, respectively, allude to serious problems

---

23 Gorman, 'Mario Esposito', 308, note 35
24 Letter from Mario Esposito to Hubert Silvestre, 24 October 1958, reproduced in Silvestre, 'Mario Esposito', 5–6. Original in French.

with his eyesight caused by glaucoma and cataracts.[25] One by one, his sisters died: Bianca in 1961, followed by Vera in 1967 and Nina in 1970. Mario lived on until 1975, dying at the age of 87. Vera was buried at Antella with her parents, while Bianca and Mario were cremated and their ashes placed in a simple urn in the cemetery at Trespiano. In his will, Mario bequeathed his property and possessions to Assunta Mecacci, a woman who had cared for him and his sisters for many decades. At his express request, she destroyed his personal effects and papers after his death, and his books were sold to various bookshops in Florence.[26]

The fate of his father's personal papers is unknown. At least some of them are known to have survived until 1955 or so, when Aiello consulted them: he seems to have been shown various documents including letters and newspapers reviews that had apparently remained in the family's possession. One of the manuscripts of Esposito's unpublished works — that of the First Piano Quartet — was evidently made available to Otello Calbi, so that he could discuss it in his essay on Esposito's music. Curiously, he does not refer to any other work in manuscript and seems to have confined himself to examining only the scores that had been published. Nor does he provide any information on the whereabouts of the scores of the unpublished works at the time of writing. What happened to these materials thereafter is unknown and all attempts to locate them have so far drawn a blank. As a medievalist who had spent much of his life tracking down rare manuscripts, Mario knew full well that their survival in archives depended to an alarming extent on the vagaries of chance circumstances. It would consequently seem inconceivable that he gave no thought to preserving his father's effects or would have wished them to be destroyed along with his own papers. Vera told Hamilton Harty that Mario had been greatly affected by his father's death, a remark which suggests that his relationship with him had been a close one and makes such a posthumous act of filial impiety seem very unlikely. Nonetheless, if he did deposit his father's scores and papers somewhere, he left no record of the fact. Searches in libraries and archives in both Ireland and Italy have so far proved fruitless, but the possibility remains that they will come to light one day. Until such time as they do, any assessment of Esposito's output and his significance as a composer must be regarded as essentially partial and provisional.

---

25 These are reproduced in Gorman, 'Preface', Esposito, *Studies in Hiberno-Latin Literature*, xi–xii.
26 Gorman, 'Mario Esposito', 308–09

Appendix: Catalogue of Works

Some manuscripts of Esposito's juvenilia have been preserved in the Conservatorio S. Pietro a Majella in Naples (I-Nc), along with the autograph of the *Lento*, Op. 16, published in the album *Alla Memoria di Vincenzo Bellini* (1884). The autograph of the String Quartet No. 2 in C minor, Op. 60, is housed in the Library of the Accademia Filarmonica, Bologna (I-Baf). Apart from these, all of the original manuscripts of Esposito's works have been lost. No surviving copies of the unpublished music, apart from the juvenilia alluded to above, have so far come to light. Although the vocal scores of the operas and the cantata *Deirdre* were published, the full scores remained in manuscript and are consequently also missing.

The following work-list is based on the catalogue of works supplied in Giuseppe Lauro Aiello's monograph *Al musicista Michele Esposito nel primo centenario della sua nascita* (Castellammare di Stabia, 1956), 71–79. This is not entirely reliable, however, and the information given in it has been verified independently whenever possible. It has also been also supplemented by data obtained through research in the libraries of the following institutions: the Royal Irish Academy of Music, Dublin, the British Library, the Conservatorio Giuseppe Verdi, Milan and the Conservatorio S. Pietro a Majella, Naples.

Details of first performances of works and important subsequent performances have been supplied insofar as they are known. In the case of the piano music, it can reasonably be assumed that Esposito gave the first performances in most cases. Where this is definitely known, it is indicated.

A: WORKS FOR THE STAGE

The Post Bag, Op. 52, opera in one act, 1901
Libretto by Alfred Perceval Graves. First performed under the auspices of the Irish Literary Society on 27 January 1902 at St George's Hall in London, Denis O'Sullivan *bar* (Seaghan), Joseph O'Mara *ten.* (Phelim), Evangeline Florence *sop.* (Kitty O'Hea), the accompaniment provided on two pianos played by Edith Ladd and Esposito. Dublin premiere, Gaiety Theatre, 14 March 1902, same cast, theatre orchestra, Esposito *cond.* Pub: Boosey & Co., London, vocal score only, 1902. Full score missing.

The Tinker and the Fairy, Op. 53, opera in one act, 1904
English libretto prepared by Belinda Butler from the original Irish play by Douglas Hyde, *An Tincéar agus an tSidheóg*. First performed by the Dublin Amateur Opera Company at the Gaiety Theatre, 29 March 1910, Nettie Edwards *sop.* (the Fairy), Thomas Collins *ten* (the Youth), John Browner *bar.* (the Tinker), theatre orchestra, Esposito *cond.* Pub: Breitkopf und Härtel, London, vocal score only, 1910. Full score missing. This opera appears to have been developed from incidental music written for Hyde's play, which received its first performance (in English) in the garden of the novelist George Moore on 19 May 1902. An extract (identified as 'Fairy Music') from this score was performed by the Dublin Orchestral Society on 9 April 1906, Esposito *cond.* (see Chapter 5, note 54). The same extract also seems to have been performed by the RIAM Students Musical Union, February 1907.

Peggy Machree, romantic comedy with music, 1904
Script by Patrick Bidwell (pseudonym of Elizabeth Curtis O'Sullivan, wife of Denis O'Sullivan}. Irish songs arranged by Esposito. Additional music composed by Clarence Lucas (with words by F. A. Fahr). First performed at Grimsby, 7 November 1904, Denis O'Sullivan (Barry Trevor), Marie Dainton (Lady Margaret O'Driscoll), theatre orchestra, Clarence Lucas *cond.* First London performance, Wyndham's Theatre, 27 December 1904. Unpub. Following a successful production in New York in 1908, three of the songs contributed by Esposito were published in an arrangement for voice and piano in New York in the same year by the firm of Church: 'The birds fly south', 'Peggy Machree' and 'The idle Colleen'.

B: WORKS FOR ORCHESTRA

Sinfonia in Fa Minore, [one movement, *Allegro*], completed 12 September 1873; slow introduction [*Largo*] added in September 1874. Score bears inscription '*scritta per gli esperimenti pubblici dell'anno '73*' [written for the public performances of [18]73]. Unpub. MS I-Nc.

Fantasia per orchestra su 'La Contessa di Mons' del Maestro Rossi, 20 July 1874
There is no record of a performance. Unpub. MS I-Nc.

Sinfonia [Symphony], Op. 24, completed 1874
The only reference to the existence of this work occurs in Aiello, *Al musicista Michele Esposito*, 72: no details are provided. There is no record of a performance. Unpub.

Omaggio a Bellini, fantasia for orchestra, 1875
There is no record of a performance. Unpub. MS I-Nc.

Piano Concerto [No. 1], Op. 18, 1878
This appears to have been a one-movement work in two sections, *Adagio–Allegro*. First performed in Naples, 1878, Florestano Rossomandi *pf*, Benjamino Cesi *cond*. Unpub.

Scherzo fugoso
Written for the 'Irish Toy Symphony' based on Irish folk tunes and composed for the Incorporated Society of Musicians Conference (ISM) in Dublin, (i) *Adagio patetico* (James Cooksey Culwick), (ii) *Erin Variations* (T. R. G. Jozé), (iii) *Scherzo fugoso* (Esposito), (iv) *Stretta finale* (Joseph Smith). First performed on 3 January 1895; repeated at the ISM Conference, London, 6 January 1898. Unpub.

Poem, Op. 44, for solo harp and orchestra, 1898, revised Florence, 1928
Winning entry in the Charles Oberthür Prize offered by the Feis Ceoil. First performed at the Feis Ceoil, Dublin, 18 May 1899 in the Royal University Hall, Dublin Orchestral Society, Esposito *cond*. First performed in version for enlarged orchestra, 7 June 1899, Royal University, Dublin, DOS, Esposito *cond*. Moscow, July 1914, Orchestra of Rostov-on-Don [?], Aleksandr Orlov *cond*. Unpub.

Othello, Op. 45, overture, 1900
First performed in Royal University Hall, Dublin, 18 April 1902, Dublin Orchestral Society, Esposito *cond*. Also Moscow, July 1914, Orchestra of Rostov-on-Don [?], Aleksandr Orlov *cond*. and Manchester, 23 March 1922 and 21 January 1926, Hallé Orchestra, Hamilton Harty *cond*. Unpub.

Oriental Suite, Op. 47, 1900
First performance, Royal University Hall, Dublin, 1 March 1905, Dublin Orchestral Society, Esposito *cond*. Also Moscow, July 1914, Orchestra of Rostov-on-Don, Aleksandr Orlov *cond*. This appears to have been a suite in four movements 'illustrating an Arab story', *Musical Times* 46, 746 (April 1905), 264. Unpub.

Fantasia, Op. 48, for two pianos and orchestra, 1901 [?]
First performed Royal University Hall, Dublin, 25 February 1904, Annie Lord pf, Edith French pf, Dublin Orchestral Society, Esposito *cond.* Unpub.

The Washer at the Ford, Irish melody, arr. for small orchestra, 1901
The only reference to this existence of this work occurs in Aiello, *Al musicista Michele Esposito*, 76, where it is entitled *Lavandaie [recte 'lavandaia']* al guado. Unpub.

Irish Symphony, Op. 50, 1902
(i) *Allegro con brio*, (ii) *Vivace* (Scherzo), (iii) *Lento*, (iv) *Allegro con energia.* Winner of the Dublin Feis Ceoil Prize [for a symphony based on Irish themes] 1902. First performed at the Feis Ceoil, 7 May 1902, Royal University Hall, Dublin, Dublin Orchestral Society, Esposito *cond.* Also performed in Moscow, July 1914, Orchestra of Rostov-on-Don [?], A. Orlov *cond.* Pub: An Gúm [Irish State Publishing Co.], 1956 as *Árd-shonáid Gaelach bhunuithe ar fhionn Ghaelacha/Sinfonia irlandese.* The newspaper notices after the first performance referred to this work as 'Symphony on Irish Airs': see Chapter 4, *supra.*

Irish Suite, Op. 55, 1903 [?]
(i) *Allegro maestoso ed energico*, (ii) *Allegretto vivace*, (iii) *Lento*, (iv) *Tempo di minuetto*, (v) *Molto vivo.* First performed in Dublin, 9 December 1903, Dublin Orchestral Society, Esposito *cond.* Pub: C. E. Music Publishers, Dublin, 1915

Piano Concerto [No. 2] in F minor, Op. 68, 1912
First performed at the Gaiety Theatre, Dublin, 16 December 1913, Esposito *pf.*, Dublin Orchestral Society, Achille Simonetti *cond.* First performed in London at Queen's Hall, 31 December 1913, New Symphony Orchestra, Esposito *pf*, Sir Frederic Cowen *cond.* Performed at Woodbrook by the London Symphony Orchestra, 4 August 1914, Esposito *pf*, Hamilton Harty *cond.* Also Moscow, July 1914, Orchestra of Rostov-on-Don, [soloist unknown], Aleksandr Orlov *cond.* This work appears to have been in three movements. Unpub.

Pace, Idyll by [Carlo?]Albanesi, arr. for string orchestra, 1912 [?]
First performed by the Dublin Orchestral Society at the Sunday Orchestral Concerts, Dublin, 13 October 1912, Esposito *cond.*, Existence of the work known through reference to the above performance in the *Musical Times*, 53, 837 (1912), 740. Unpub.

Neapolitan Suite, Op. 69, string orchestra, 1923 [?]
(i) *Allegro con brio*, (ii) *Notturno: Lento*, (iii) *Intermezzo: Allegretto*, (iv) *Serenata: Molto moderato*, (v) *Tarantella: Molto vivace.* First performed at the Royal Dublin Society (RDS), 23 February 1923, [Esposito's string orchestra], Esposito *cond.* Also performed at afternoon and evening

concerts at the RDS, 1 March 1926, by members of the Hallé Orchestra, Hamilton Harty cond. Pub: C. E. Music Publishers, Dublin, 1923 [?] The *Serenata* was transcribed for cello and piano and is dedicated to Clyde Twelvetrees. Pub: C. E. Music Publishers, Dublin, 1927 [?]

Toccata, by Benedetto Marcello, and **Andantino**, by [Luigi?] Rossi, arr. for string orchestra
The sole reference to these works occurs in Aiello, *Al musicista Michele Esposito*, 76. They appear to have been published as a set. Apart from stating that the score was published in Dublin, no further details are provided and the original works are not identified. There is no record of a performance.

C: CHAMBER MUSIC

Mazurka e Barcarola for mandolin and piano, 1875 [?]
There is no record of a performance. Unpub. MS I-Nc.

Piano Trio, Op. 9, 1877 [?]
First performed Naples, 1878. Unpub.

Piano Quartet [No. 1], Op. 12, 1877
First performed in Naples and Turin, 1877. Unpub.

Piano Quartet [No. 2], Op. 17, 1878
First performed in Naples, 1878. Esposito *pf*. Unpub.

Two pieces for Viola and Piano, Op. 22, 1881
There is no record of a performance. Unpub.

Movement for String Quartet, Op. 21, 1882
There is no record of a performance. Unpub.

Violin Sonata [No. 1] in G, Op. 32, 1881
(i) *Moderato*, (ii) *Lento*, (iii) *Allegro vivace*. First performed at Prince's Hall, London, July 1891, Guido Papini *vn*, Esposito *pf*. First Irish performance at the Dublin Arts Club, St. Stephen's Green, 21 April 1894, Papini *vn*, Esposito *pf*. Pub: Stanley Lucas, Weber, Pitt & Hatzfeld Ltd, London & Leipzig, 1892, later reissued by Schott.

String Quartet [No. 1] in D, Op. 33, 1886
(i) *Allegretto moderato*, (ii) *Intermezzo: Allegretto*, (iii) *Adagio*, (iv) *Allegro con fuoco*. Winner of the Feis Ceoil String Quartet Prize, Dublin, 1899. First performed at the first concert of the

Feis Ceoil in the Royal University Hall, 16 May 1899, with Guido Papini, Patrick Delaney, Octave Grisard and Henry Bast. Pub: Breitkopf und Härtel, Leipzig, 1899

Piano Quintet, Op. 42, 1898
There is no record of a performance. Unpub. Also arranged for flute, clarinet, bassoon, horn and strings in 1928. There is no record of a performance of this version either. Unpub.

Cello Sonata, Op. 43, 1898
(i) *Allegro moderato*, (ii) *Lento*, (iii) *Allegro moderato*. Winner of the ISM Chamber 'Sonata Prize' 1898. First performed at the Royal Dublin Society on 20 February 1899 by Henry Bast *vc* and Esposito *pf*. First London performance at the Salle Érard with Arthur Trew *vc* and Archie Rosenthal *pf*. Pub: Breitkopf und Härtel, Leipzig, 1899

Violin Sonata [No. 2] in E minor, Op. 46, 1899
(i) *Allegro moderato*, (ii) *Andantino*, (iii) *Allegro con fuoco*, First prize in the Concours International de Musique [International Music Competition], Paris, 1907. First performed by Jacques Thibaud and Alfred Cortot, Paris [?] 1907 [?]. First performed in England in the Great Hall of the Hotel Majestic, Harrogate during ISM Conference), 2 January 1908, Sigmund Beel *vn*, Esposito *pf*. First Dublin performance, Royal Dublin Society, 20 January 1908 with same performers. Pub: G. Astruc, Paris, 1907.

Irish Rhapsody No. 1, Op. 51, for violin and piano, 1901
There is no record of a performance in this version. Pub: Ricordi, Milan, 1909. Also arr. (a) with orchestra; first performed in this version in the Royal University Hall, Dublin, Dublin Orchestral Society, Sigmund Beel *vn*, Esposito *cond.*; Unpub. (b) for cor anglais and piano, 1902. There is no record of a performance of this version. Unpub.

Irish Rhapsody No. 2, Op. 54, for violin and piano 1902
Prizewinning work at Dublin Feis Ceoil, 1903. First performed at the Dublin Chamber Music Union at the Antient Concert Rooms on 20 March 1903, John Dunn *vn*, Esposito *pf*; performed by Dunn and Esposito at the opening concert of Dublin Feis Ceoil, 18 May 1903. Pub: Ricordi, Milan, 1909. Also arr. with orchestra, 1913. First performed in this version at Woodbrook, 1 June 1913, Dublin Orchestral Society, Achille Simonetti *vn*, Esposito *cond.* Unpub.

Five Irish Melodies, Op. 56, for violin and piano
(i) 'Rich and Rare', (ii) 'The Coulin', (iii) 'Silent, O Moyle', (iv) 'Fly not yet' (Jig), (v) 'When through life'. There is no record of a performance. Pub: Pigott & Co, Dublin, 1903

Two Irish Airs, Op. 57, for violin and piano
(i) 'Farewell! but whenever' (cradle song), (ii) 'The silver tip' (Irish reel). There is no record of a performance. Pub: Schott, London, 1903 [?]

[Short piece for cornet and piano], 1905
The only reference to this piece occurs in Aiello, *Al musicista Michele Esposito*, 76, where it is listed as 'Breve pezzo per cornetto e pianoforte'. Unpub.

Two Irish Melodies arr. for cello and piano by Sir Francis Cruise and M. Esposito
(i) 'The Coulin', (ii) 'Carolan's Concerto'. There is no record of a performance. Pub: Schott, London, 1906 [?]

String Quartet [No. 2] in C minor, Op. 60, 1906
(i) *Allegro molto*, (ii) *Adagio espressivo*, (iii) *Molto vivace quasi presto*, (iv) *Allegro con fuoco*
Won first prize for the quartet competition at the Concorso internazionale della Reale Accademia Filarmonica di Bologna, 1906. First performance Bologna 1906 [?]. First Dublin performance at the Royal Dublin Society, 2 February 1914, by the Wessely Quartet. Also performed by the Brodsky Quartet, RDS, 19 February 1923. Pub: C. E. Music Publishers, Dublin, 1914. The *Adagio espressivo* was transcribed (a) for the organ by V. H. Vipond Barry, Pub: C. E. Music Publishers, Dublin, n.d. There is no record of a performance of this version. (b) For string orchestra, performed at the first concert of the Irish Musical League at the Abbey Theatre, 17 October 1923, [Esposito's string orchestra] [?], Esposito *cond.* Unpub.

Violin Sonata [No. 3] in A, Op. 67, 1913
(i) *Affetuosamente*, (ii) *Allegretto moderato*, (iii) *Andante cantabile*, (iv) *Allegretto grazioso*. First performed at the Royal Dublin Society on 11 January 1915 by Achille Simonetti *vn* and Esposito *pf*. Pub: C. E. Music Publishers, Dublin, n.d.

String Quartet [No. 3] in B flat major, Op. 70, 1923
The only reference to this work occurs in Aiello, *Al musicista Michele Esposito*, 75. No further information is supplied. There is no record of a performance. Unpub.

D: MUSIC FOR PIANO

[Piano piece in homage of Vincenzo Bellini], 1873 [?]
The only reference to this work occurs in Aiello, *Al musicista Michele Esposito*, 27. The title of the piece is not supplied, and curiously, it is not listed in the catalogue of works in the same volume. The piece appears to have been printed by the Real Collegio and used as a test piece for piano candidates.

Omaggio al Commendatore Lauro Rossi: Rimembranze della sua Benvenuto Cellini, Op. 1, 1873
Fantasia on themes from Lauro Rossi's opera *Benvenuto Cellini*. Pub: Cattrau, Naples, 1873.

Pensiero malinconico, Op. 2 [Melancholy Thought], n.d.
Pub: Ricordi, Milan, 1877.

Allegretto, Op. 5, n.d.
Pub: Lucca, Milan, 1877.

Scherzo [No. 1], Op. 3, n.d.
Pub: Lucca, Milan, 1879.

Allegro, Op. 4, n.d.
Pub: Lucca, Milan, 1879.

Romanza, Op. 6, n.d.
Pub: Lucca, Milan, 1879.

Album, Op. 7, n.d.
(i) *Augurio* [Greeting], (ii) *Malinconico*, (iii) *Duetto*, (iv) *Visione*, (v) *Allegro appassionato*. Pub: Lucca, Milan, 1879.

Fantasia, Op. 8, n.d.
Pub: Lucca, Milan, 1879.

Momento di Fantasia, Op. 10, n.d.
Pub: Lucca, Milan, 1879.

Capriccio, Op. 11, n.d.
Pub: Lucca, Milan, 1879.

Quattro notturni [Four Nocturnes], Op. 13, n.d.
(i) *Moderato*, (ii) *Andante*, (iii) '*Sorrento*', *Lento*, (iv) *Lento*. Pub: Lucca, Milan, 1879.

Valzer, Op. 14, 1879 [?]
Pub: Lucca, Milan, 1879.

[Lento], Op. 16, n.d.
Contribution (No. 7) to album of piano pieces *Alla memoria di Vincenzo Bellini: Album per pianoforte* (see Chapter 1, *supra*). Prefaced with inscription from poem by Ugo Foscolo (1778–1827), *Dei sepolcri* [Of Graves]. Pub: Ricordi, Milan 1884.

Due pezzi **[Two Pieces], Op. 19**, n.d.
(i) *Andante tranquillo*, (ii) *Lento*. Pub: Lucca, Milan, 1879.

Sei Canzoni **[Six Songs], Op. 23**, n.d.
(i) *Moderato*, (ii) *Lento*, (iii) *Allegro moderato*, (iv) *Andante*, (v) *Moderato*, (vi) *Semplice*. Pub: Lucca, Milan, 1880.

Valzer della polenta, 1881
Pub: Ricordi, Milan, 1881.

Tre pezzi caratteristici [Three Characteristic Pieces], Op. 26, n.d.
(i) *Berceuse*, (ii) *Serenata*, (iii) *Papillon*. Pub: Ricordi, Milan, 1882. Also (i) *Berceuse* arr. for small orchestra. Pub: Ricordi, Milan, 1910.

Scherzo [No. 2], Op. 28, n.d.
Pub: Pohlmann & Co., Dublin, 1882?

Two Pieces, Op. 29, 1883 [?]
(i) *Serenata*, (ii) *Improvviso*. Pub: Pohlmann & Co., Dublin, 1883

Four Sketches, Op. 30, 1883 [?]
(i) *Andantino*, (ii) *Animato*, (iii) *Moderato*, (iv) *Vivace*. Pub: Pohlmann & Co., Dublin, 1883

Progressive Studies, Op. 31, 1883 [?]
(i) Book 1 (10 studies), (ii) Book 2 (10 studies). Pub: Pohlmann & Co., Dublin, 1883

Notturno, arr. of song by Luigi Denza, n.d.
Pub: Ascherberg, London, 1885.

Suite, Op. 34, n.d. [in two volumes]
Vol.1: (i) *Prélude*, (ii) *Agitato-Tranquillo*, (iii) *Badinage*; Vol.2: (iv) *Nocturne*, (v) *Valse* (vi) *Petite Sérénade*, (vii) *Rêverie*. First performance at the Royal Dublin Society, 8 February 1904? Esposito pf. Pub: Breitkopf und Härtel, Leipzig, 1902. Also (vi) *Petite Sérénade* and (vii) *Rêverie* arr. for small orchestra. There is no record of a performance of this version. Unpub.

Two Irish Melodies, Op. 39, arr., n.d.
(i) 'Avenging and bright', (ii) 'Though the last glimpse of Erin'. Pub: Pigott & Co., Dublin 1896

Deux Nocturnes [Two Nocturnes], Op. 36, n.d.
(i) *Lento*, (ii) *Andante*. Pub: Forsyth, London, 1898

Deux Valses [Two Waltzes], Op. 37, n.d.
(i) *Tempo di Valse*, (ii) *Tempo lento di Valse*. Pub: Forsyth, London, 1898

Tarantella, Op. 35, for piano duet, n.d.
Pub: Pigott, Dublin, 1900? Also arr. for orchestra, 1905. There is no record of a performance for either version. Unpub.

Ballades, Op. 59, n.d.
(i) *Appassionato*, (ii) *Lento ed espressivo*, (iii) *Con moto ed energico*.
First performed at the Royal Dublin Society on 2 November 1908, Esposito pf. Pub: Ricordi, Milan, 1907

Three Pieces, Op. 61, 1912 [?]
(i) *Alba* [Dawn]. (ii) *Zenith* [Midday], (iii) *Tramonto* [Sunset]. Pub: C. E. Music Publishers, Dublin, 1930

Impromptu, Op. 62, 1912
Pub: C. E. Music Publishers, Dublin, 1930.

Remembrance, Op. 63, 1912
First performed at the Royal Dublin Society, 16 November 1914, Esposito pf. Pub: C. E. Music Publishers, 1930 [?]

A Village Fête, Op. 64, 1912
First performed at the Royal Dublin Society, 16 November 1914, Esposito pf. Pub: C. E. Music Publishers, 1930 [?]

Three Pieces, Op. 65, 1912
(i) 'Vain regrets', (ii) 'In the garden', (iii) 'At the spinning wheel'. Pub: C. E. Music Publishers, 1930?

Preludi [Preludes], Op. 66, 1910–12
Pub: Ricordi, Milan, 1936 as part of Op. 72 (Nos. 2, 5 and 9).

My Irish Sketch Book, Op. 71 (12 pieces for piano in four sets), n.d.

Set I (i) 'The Bard and the Fairy', (ii) 'The Rose-Tree', (iii) 'Dance and Song'; Set II (i) 'The Exile's Vision', (ii) 'A Song', (iii) 'Night Patrol'; Set III (i) 'The Little Stack of Barley', (ii) 'Lullaby', (iii) 'Jig'; Set IV (i) 'King James', (ii) 'A Lament', (iii) 'Bagpipes'. Pub: C. E. Music Publishers, Dublin, 1932.

Nove Preludi, Op. 72, 1910–29 (incorporating Op. 66, Nos. 2, 5 and 9)

(i) *Allegro vivo e appassionato* in B flat (completed 24 March 1929, Florence), (ii) *Tempo di Mazurka* in G minor [completed 28 August 1912, Bologna], (iii) *Sostenuto* in C (completed 31 March 1929, Florence), (iv) *Allegro moderato* in C minor (completed 2 April 1929, Florence), (v) *Languido* in G sharp minor (completed 6 September 1912, Bologna), (vi) *Andante moderato* in D flat (completed 20 April 1929, Florence), (vii) *Con moto e leggero* in A flat (completed 24 April 1929, Florence), (viii) *Con moto e grazioso* in D (completed 24 May 1929, Florence), (ix) *Lento* ('*Pensiero elegiaco alla memoria di Giuseppe Martucci*') in C sharp minor (completed 22 June 1912, Dublin; rev. 16 July 1929, Florence). These preludes were intended to form part of a set of twenty-four in all the major and minor keys, which remained incomplete at the time of Esposito's death. Pub: Ricordi, Milan, 1936

La danza delle memorie, melody of Luigi Caracciolo, arr., n.d.

The only reference to this work occurs in Aiello, *Al musicista Michele Esposito*, 76. No further information is supplied. Unpub.

Edna Baiss: ninna nanna [sic], n.d.

The only reference to this work occurs in Aiello, *Al musicista Michele Esposito*, 76. The Italian *ninna nanna* means 'lullaby', but it is unclear what the first part of the title refers to: it may have been mistranscribed. Aiello also states that it was published by C. E. Music Publishers, but does not give a date.

E: VOCAL MUSIC

Canzonetta per gli Asili infantile, for voice and piano, n.d.

Words by Raffaele de Novellis, 'Regist: nel lato in Agosto 1871', 'Dedicata al Regio Commissario [del Conservatorio]. The manuscript bears the inscription 'Michele Esposito/Anni 16 Pianista/da due anni alla scuola/d'Armonia e Contrappunto.' There is no record of a performance. Unpub. MS I-Nc.

Canti di Lorenzo Stecchetti [Songs of Lorenzo Stecchetti], Op. 15, for voice and piano, n.d.

(i) *Spes, ultima dea*, (ii) *Scritto sopra un sasso*, (iii) *Fior di siepe*. There is no record of a performance. Pub: Lucca, Milan, 1879:

Trois mélodies [Three Songs], Op. 20, for voice and piano, 1880–81
Words by Thomas Gautier and Victor Hugo. As the manuscript of this work is lost, it is not known what poems were set. There is no record of a performance. Unpub.

Tre Canti di Lorenzo Stecchetti [Three Songs of Lorenzo Stecchetti], Op. 25, for voice and piano, 1881
As the manuscript of this work is lost, it is not known what poems were set. There is no record of a performance. Unpub.

Trois Chansons [Three Songs], Op. 27, for voice and piano, 1881
Words by Émile Blémont. As the manuscript of this work is lost, it is not known what poems were set. There is no record of a performance. Unpub.

Deirdre, Op. 38, cantata for soli, chorus and orchestra, 1897 [?]
Libretto specially written by Thomas William Rolleston for the Feis Ceoil of 1897 (pub. Patrick Geddes, Edinburgh, 1897). First performed in Dublin at the Feis Ceoil, 20 May 1897, chorus and orchestra, Esposito *cond*. First performed in London, Queen's Hall Saturday Symphony Concerts, choir and orchestra, Henry Wood *cond*. 26 February 1898. Pub: Pigott & Co., Dublin, vocal score only, 1897. Full score missing.

Three Irish Melodies, Op. 40, for voice and piano, n.d.
Words by George Sigerson. (i) 'O hush O!', (ii) 'The Heather Glen', (iii) 'Mavourneen Mine'. There is no record of a performance. Pub: Pigott & Co., Dublin, 1898 [?]

Irish Melodies, Op. 41, for voice and piano, n.d.
It has only been possible to trace one of the songs in this set — an arr. of 'The Lark in the Clear Air' (words by Sir Samuel Ferguson). This was published as Op. 41/2. There is no record of a performance. Pub: Pigott & Co., Dublin, 1898 [?]

Roseen Dhu, Op. 49, 'Irish Vocal Suite adapted from old Irish airs', for voice and piano, n.d.
Words by Alfred Percival Graves. (i) 'The Shadow of a Dream', (ii) 'My Rose of Hope', (iii) 'In Reason's Despite', (iv) 'Is it true?', (v) 'Her Answer', (vi) 'The Clarion's Call', (vii) 'She stood at my side'. First performed at St James's Hall, London, 11 November 1901 by Denis O'Sullivan *bar*, Esposito *pf*. Also at Dublin Feis Ceoil with the same performers, 5 May 1902. Pub: Breitkopf und Härtel, London, 1901

'The West's Awake!', arr. of traditional Irish air from Munster, for voice and piano, n.d.
Words by Thomas Davis. There is no record of a performance. Pub: Boosey, London, 1901.

Eleven melodies, for voice and piano, 1905
Words by Robert Louis Stevenson. As the manuscript of this work is lost, it is not known what poems were set. The only reference to this work occurs in Aiello, *Al musicista Michele Esposito*, 76, where it is described as 'Undici melodie con canto e pianoforte. Parole di R. L. Stevenson.' There is no record of a performance. Unpub.

'Siubal na mona' [Over the mountains] for voice and piano, n.d.
Words in Irish by Douglas Hyde, with an English singing translation by Padraic Colum. The Irish title literally means 'Walking the bog' and should be correctly rendered *Siúbhal na móna*. There is no record of a performance. Pub. Ricordi, London, 1911.

Seán Glas [Shane Glas], for SATB chorus, n.d.
Words anon. [?].There is no record of a performance. Pub: Vincent, London, 1913.

Dear Land, arr. of Irish melody, for voice and piano, n.d.
Words by John O'Hagan. There is no record of a performance. Pub: C. E. Music Publishers, Dublin, 1920?.

Rest, thou gentle sea, arr. of Irish melody, for voice and piano, n.d.
Words anon. [?]There is no record of a performance. Pub: C. E. Music Publishers, 1920.

Two Shelley Songs, Op. 58, for voice and piano, 1905
(i) 'Time long past' (completed 20 February 1905), (ii) 'To Night' (completed 19 March 1905). There is no record of a performance. Pub: C. E. Music Publishers, Dublin, 1921

Two Irish melodies, for voice and piano, n.d.
The only reference to these songs occurs in Aiello, *Al musicista Michele Esposito*, 76. Aiello states that it was published by C. E. Music Publishers, but does not give a date. It has not been possible to trace the score. There is no record of a performance.

Irish melodies, for voice and piano, n.d.
The only reference to these songs occurs in Aiello, *Al musicista Michele Esposito*, 76. There is no record of a performance. Unpub.

F: PEDAGOGICAL EDITIONS

a)   *Early Italian Piano Music: A Collection of Pieces written for Harpsichord and Clavichord* (Oliver Ditson: Boston, 1906; reprinted as *Early Italian Keyboard Music: 49 Works by Frescobaldi, Scarlatti, Martini and Others*, Dover Publications: New York, 2005).

b)   Piano music published by C. E. Music Publishers

Arne   Sonata in A major [No. 7 from Eight Sonatas]

J. S. Bach   Fantasia in C minor

Beethoven   29 Piano Sonatas (excluding Op. 49/1, Op. 49/2 and Op. 79) in
                       three volumes.
                       Also individual editions of: Op. 2/1, Op. 2/2, Op. 10/1, Op. 13,
                       Op. 14/1, Op. 14/2, Op. 22, Op. 26, Op. 27/1, Op. 27/2, Op. 28,
                       Op. 31/2, Op. 31/3, Op.53, Op. 54, Op. 57, Op. 78, Op. 81, Op.
                       90, Op. 101, Op. 110

Chopin   (Pianoforte Works): 19 Nocturnes, 3 Waltzes, 2 Polonaises,
                       Impromptu, Op. 29, *Fantasia*, Op. 66
                       Waltz in E minor, Op. posth.

Clementi   25 Easy Preludes (from *Introduction to the Art of Playing on the
                       Pianoforte*, Op. 43)
                       Sonatas (selected movements)

L. Dix   *Impromptu*

C. H. Graun   [*recte* Braun, Ludwig von] *Giga* in B flat minor (from *Menuetto e
                       Trio poi Giga*, Op. 1)

Handel   Two Pieces: (i) *Capriccio* (No.3 from Harpsichord Music, 3rd.
                       Collection), (ii) *Minuetto* (from No.4 of VII Sonatas or Trios)

Henselt   *Berceuse* (Wiegenlied, Op. 13)
                       Repos d'Amour (No.4 from 12 Études, Op. 2)

Liszt   Consolation in D flat No. 3
                       Chant Polonaise (No. 1, 'Mädchens Wunsch', from *16 Chants
                       Polonaises de Chopin*)

Mendelssohn   *Scherzo* in E minor (No. 2 from 3 Fantasies, Op. 16)
                       Song without Words in A major (No. 5 from *Lieder ohne Worte*,
                       Op. 102)
                       Two Musical Sketches, (i) *Andante cantabile* in B flat, (ii) *Presto
                       agitato* in G minor

Mozart	Fantasia in C minor, K. 475
	Sonata in C minor, K. 475 (first movt. only)
	Sonata in D, K 576
	Sonata in F, K. 280
	Sonata in F, K. 332
	Sonata in G, K. 283

Rameau   Rigodon (from *Dardanus*)

'Le rappel des oiseaux' [The call of the birds] (from *Pièces de clavessin avec une méthode pour la mechanique des doigts*; rev. as *Pièces de clavecin avec une table pour les agrémens*)

Rubinstein   Romance in E flat (No. 1 from *Soirées à St Petersburg*, Op. 44)

Sérénade (No. 5 from Op. 93)

D. Scarlatti   *Giga* (K. 477)

Toccata (K. 336)

Sonata in E (K. 135)

Schubert   *Impromptu, Op. 90/2 in E flat*

Impromptu, Op. 90/3 in G flat

Impromptu, Op. 90/4 in A flat

Impromptu, Op. 142/2 in A flat

Impromptu, Op. 142/3 in B flat

Schumann   *Arabeske, Op. 18*

In the Distance (No. 17, *Wie an der Ferne* from *Davidsbündlertänze*, Op. 17)

Intermezzo (No. 5 from Op. 4)

Novellette in E, Op. 21/1

Novellette in D, Op. 21/4

Novellette in E, Op. 21/7

Romance, Op. 28/2

Three Pieces (Nos. 21, 23, and 30 from *Clavierstücke für die Jugend* Op. 48)

Slumber Song, Op. 124 /16

Thalberg   *Soirée de Pausilippe, Op. 75/12*

Soirée de Pausilippe, Op. 75/23

Weber   *Menuetto capriccioso* (from Sonata in A flat, Op. 39)

c)   Piano music published by other firms

Students' Classics [for the Pianoforte] in Four Series,
Pub: Pohlmann & Co, Dublin (Bossetti & Co.), 1897 [?]

The New Students' Pianoforte Classics in Five Series
Pub: Pigott & Co., Dublin, 1900 [?]

Czerny,   Studies in Three Books selected from 101 Exercises, Op. 261,
                         160 Exercises Op. 821 and 30 *Études de mécanisme*, Op. 849. Pub:
                         Pigott & Co., Dublin, *c*. 1900.

D. Scarlatti   Studies for the Pianoforte. Pub: Pigott & Co., Dublin, 1900 [?]

Rachmaninov   *Prelude*, Op. 3/2. Pub: Ricordi, Milan, 1908.

Couperin   Allemande *L'ausonienne*. Pub: Ricordi, Milan, 1910.

Liszt   *Liebesträume* [Nocturnes] No. 3, Pub: Ricordi, Milan, 1912.

Albanesi   Sonata (No. 6) in C major. Pub: Ricordi, Milan, 1913.

d)   A series of pieces for string orchestra (some of which include optional parts for
      other instruments) was published between 1925 and 1929 by the newly founded
      Music Department of Oxford University Press as part of the 'Oxford Orchestral
      Series' (OOS):

      D. Scarlatti, Four Pieces (i) *Prelude*, (ii) *Siciliana*, (iii) *Pastorale*, (iv) *Scherzo* (OOS 12)
      OUP, 1925

      D. Scarlatti, Four Pieces (second set) (i) *Toccata*, (ii) *Aria*, (iii) *Minuetto*, (iv) *Giga*
      (OOS 14) OUP, 1925

      J. S. Bach, *Wachet auf*, No.4 of Church Cantata 140, *Sleepers Wake* (OOS 17) OUP, 1925

      Geminiani, Concerto Grosso in C minor, Op. 2/2 (OOS 30) OUP, 1927

      Handel, *Larghetto* (from Concerto Grosso, Op. 6/12) (OOS 43) OUP, 1927

Galuppi, *Adagio e Giga* (from *Sonata per Cembalo*, Op. 1/4) (OOS 44) OUP, 1927

Pasquini, *Canzona francese* (OOS 45) OUP, 1927

Frescobaldi, *Passacaglia* (from *Toccate e partite d'intavolatura*, Lib.1) (OOS 46) OUP, 1927

Vivaldi, Concerto in B minor, Op. 3/10 (OOS 47) OUP, 1927

Grazioli, *Minuetto* (from 12 *Sonate per Cembalo*, No.11) (OOS 58) OUP, 1928

Couperin, *L'Ausonienne* (from *Ordre III*) (OOS 70) OUP, 1928

Couperin, *La Favourite* (from *Ordre III*), (OOS 71) OUP, 1928

Couperin, *Les Barricades mystérieuses* (from *Ordre VI*) (OOS 72) OUP, 1929

Couperin, *Les Moissonneurs* (from *Ordre VI*), (OOS 73) OUP, 1929

J. S. Bach, Brandenburg Concerto No. 6 in B flat major (OOS 74) OUP, 1929

Handel, Concerto Grosso No. 11 in B flat major (HWV 288, known as the 'Sonata a 5') (OOS 75) OUP, 1929

Mozart, *Gavotta* (from *Idomeneo*), (OOS 76) OUP, 1929

e)   Editions and arrangements known to have been left in manuscript at Esposito's death. The only available information about these is to be found in Aiello, *Al musicista Michele Esposito*, 77–78 whose lists are reproduced below.

(i) The following arrangements for strings and wind (many of which were performed by the Dublin Orchestral Society. Esposito's string orchestra) were, according to Aiello, prepared for publication during the last years of the composer's life.

A. Scarlatti, *Toccata and Fugue* in G minor; Leo, Concerto for Four Violins; Leo, *Canzone* [Song]; Martini, *Aria in sol minore* [Air in G minor]; Tartini, Sonata in G minor; Caldara, *Canzone per voce e orchestra d'archi* [Song for Voice and string orchestra]; Boccherini, Sonata A major for solo cello and orchestra; Rameau, *Le rappel des oiseaux* for flute and strings; Loeilly, *Giga* in G minor; Gernstein, *Elohem* (Hebrew melody); Gluck, Three Pieces (i) *Minuetto*, (ii) *Gavotte*, (iii) *Song* from the ballet music in *Orfeo*; Weber, *Canzone di Fatima* [Fatima's Song]; Schubert, 2 *Canzoni* [2 Songs]; Schumann, Suite, Op. 85; Fauré, *Adagietto*, Op. 84/4.

(ii) Other unpublished arrangements and editions left at Esposito's death:

For orchestra: Handel, *Largo* from Concerto Grosso No. 2; Schumann, *Intermezzo* from Op. 4; Scontrino, *Preludio e Fuga*.
For piano 4 hands: Mendelssohn, Scherzo from *A Midsummer Night's Dream*; Chopin, *Étude*, Op. 25/2.
For 2 pianos, 8 hands: Wagner, *The Ride of the Valkyries*.
Editions: Bach, Chromatic Fantasia and Fugue; D. Scarlatti, various [unidentified] pieces for harpsichord.

G: OTHER WRITINGS AND LECTURES

Corso di Contrappunto, 22 June 1875, 65pp. I-Nc.

Lecture 'Italian Harpsichord Composers' (Royal Dublin Society), 9 March 1906. Repeated at the RDS on 1 March 1922. No copy of the text appears to have survived.

Lecture on 'The Origins of Opera' (Royal Dublin Society), 10 February 1911. No copy of the text appears to have survived.

Bibliography

Aiello, Giuseppe Lauro, ed. *Al Musicista Michele Esposito nel primo centenario della nascita* (Castellammare di Stabia, 1956)

Apetian, Zarui A., ed. *Vospominaniia o Rakhmaninove*, 5th edn., vol. 1 (Moscow, 1988)

————. *S. Rakhmaninov: Literaturnoe Naslediye*, vol. 1 (Moscow, 1978)

Bache, Constance. *Brother Musicians: Reminiscences of Edward and Walter Bache* (London, 1901)

Bashford, Christina and Langley, Leanne, eds. *Music and British Culture, 1785–1914: Essays in honour of Cyril Ehrlich* (Oxford, 2000)

Beckett, Brian. 'Tested Teaching: The Local Centre Examination System, 1894–1994', in Pine and Acton, *To Talent Alone*, 297–321

Bennigsen, Olga. 'The Brothers Rubinstein and Their Circle', *Musical Quarterly*, 25, 4 (1939), 407–19

Bomberger, E. Douglas. 'The Thalberg Effect: Playing the Violin on the Piano', *Musical Quarterly*, 75, 2 (1991), 198–208

Bourgeois, Maurice. *John Millington Synge and the Irish Theatre* (London, 1913)

Bell, J. Bowyer. 'Waiting for Mario — The Espositos, Joyce and Beckett', *Eire-Ireland* 30, 2 (1995), 7–26

Brennan, Robert. *Allegiance* (Dublin, 1950)

Caroccia, Antonio. 'Florimo e L'Album Pianistico Bellini' in Seminara, Graziella and Tedesco, Anna, eds. *Vincenzo Bellini nel secondo centenario della nascita: atti del convegno internazionale, Catania, 8–11 novembre 2001* (Florence, 2004), 57–76

————.'Lettere inedite a Francesco Florimo per il monumento a Bellini' in Miozzi, Dario ed. *Francesco Florimo a Vincenzo Bellini* (Catania, 2001), 33–63

Cleeve, Brian. *Dictionary of Irish Writers*, First Series (Cork, 1967)

Cobbett, Walter Willson. *Cobbett's Cyclopedic Survey of Chamber Music*, rev. Colin M. Mason, 2nd edn. (London, 1963)

[Colles, H. C.] 'Hamilton Harty'. *Musical Times*, 61, 926 (1920), 227-230

Cooper, Martin. 'The Nineteenth-Century Musical Renaissance in France (1870-1895)', *Proceedings of the Royal Musical Association* (1947–8), 11–23.

———. *French Music from the Death of Berlioz to the Death of Fauré* (Oxford, 1951)

Croce, Benedetto. *La letteratura della nuova Italia, Saggi critici*, vol. 2 (Bari, 1942)

Daly, D. *The Young Douglas Hyde: The Dawn of the Irish Revolution and Renaissance, 1874–1893* (Dublin, 1974)

Davis, John, ed. *Italy in the Nineteenth Century: 1796–1900* (Oxford, 2000)

Deane, Seamus. *Strange Country: Modernity and Nationhood in Irish Writing since 1790* (Oxford, 1997)

de Barra, Séamas. *Aloys Fleischmann* (Dublin, 2006)

———. 'The Music of Aloys Fleischmann: A Survey', in Ruth Fleischmann, *Aloys Fleischmann*, 325-348

Dennison, Stanley and MacDonagh, Oliver. *Guinness 1886–1939: From Incorporation to the Second World War* (Cork, 1998)

Dent, Edward, ed. *A Dictionary of Modern Music and Musicians* (London, 1924)

Dibble, Jeremy. 'Edward Dannreuther and the Orme Square Phenomenon', in Bashford, Christina and Langley, Leanne, eds. *Music and British culture, 1785–1914 : Essays in honour of Cyril Ehrlich* (Oxford, 2000), 275–98

———. *Hubert H. Parry: His Life and Music* (Oxford, 1992; 1998)

———. *Charles Villiers Stanford: Man and Musician* (Oxford, 2002)

di Benedetto, R. 'Beethoven a Napoli nell'Ottocento', *Nuova rivista musicale italiana* 5, 1971, 3–21 and 201–41

Dunleavy, Janet Eggleston and Dunleavy, George W. *Douglas Hyde: A Maker of Modern Ireland* (Berkeley, 1991)

Edwards, F. G., 'Michele Esposito', *Musical Times*, 44, 729 (1903), 705–07

Ellmann, Richard. *James Joyce* (New York, 1959)

Esposito, Mario. *Studies in Hiberno-Latin Literature*, ed. Michael M. Gorman (Aldershot, 2006)

Ferber, Michael, ed., *A Companion to European Romanticism* (Oxford, 2005)

Fleischmann, Aloys, 'Music and Society: 1850–1921', in W. E. Vaughan, ed., *A New History of Ireland*, vol. 6, *Ireland under the Union II 1870–1921* (Oxford, 1996), 500–22

———, ed. *Music in Ireland: A Symposium* (Cork and Oxford, 1952).

Fleischmann, Ruth, ed. *Aloys Fleischmann (1910–1992): A Life for Music in Ireland Remembered by Contemporaries* (Cork, 2000)

Florimo, Francesco. *Cenni storici sul Collegio di musica S. Pietro a Majella in Napoli* (Naples, 1873)

Friedland, Bea. 'Italy's Ottocento: Notes from the Musical Underground', *The Musical Quarterly*, 56, 1 (1970), 27–53

Ghisalberti, Alberto Maria, et al., eds. *Dizionario biografico degli italiani*, 68 vols. (Rome,

1990)

Gorman, Michael. M., 'Mario Esposito (1887–1975) and the study of the Latin Literature of Medieval Ireland', *Filologia mediolatina* 5 (1998), 299–322, reprinted in Esposito, *Studies in Hiberno-Latin Literature*, 299–322

Graves, Alfred Perceval. *To Return To All That* (1930)

Graves, Charles Larcom. 'Musical Talent in Ireland', *Musical Times*, 27, 524 (1886), 579–82

———. *Life of Sir George Grove* (London, 1903)

Greer, David, ed. *Hamilton Harty: His Life and Music* (Belfast, 1978)

———, ed. *Hamilton Harty: Early Memories* (Belfast, 1979)

Hadow, Henry. *The Needs of Popular Musical Education* (London, 1918)

Hamilton, John. 'The Revival of the Ode' in Ferber, *Companion to European Romanticism*, 345–59

Harding, James. *Saint-Saëns and His Circle* (London, 1965)

———. *Massenet* (London, 1971)

Harty, Hamilton. 'Michele Esposito', *The Irish Statesman*, 7 December 1929, 276–77

Henderson, B. 'Guido Papini', *The Strad* 27 (1906–07), 234–35

Hinnells, Duncan. *An Extraordinary Performance: Hubert Foss, Music Publishing, and the Oxford University Press* (Oxford, 1998)

Hogan, Robert. *Frank J. Fay: Towards a National Theatre* (Dublin, 1970)

———, et al. *The Modern Irish Drama: A Documentary History*, vol. 2, *The Abbey Theatre: Laying the Foundations, 1902–1904* (Dublin, 1976)

———, et al. *The Modern Irish Drama: A Documentary History*, vol. 3, *The Abbey Theatre: The Years of Synge, 1905–1909* (Dublin, 1978)

Hughes, Anthony. 'The Society and Music', in Meenan and Clarke, eds., *Royal Dublin Society*, 265–77

Hull, Arthur Eaglefield, ed. *A Dictionary of Modern Music and Musicians* (London, 1924)

Hutchinson, John. *The Dynamics of Cultural Nationalism: The Gaelic Revival and the Creation of the Irish Nation State* (London, 1987)

Irvine, Demar. *Massenet: A Chronicle of His Life and Times* (Oregon, 1994)

Keldish, Yurii V., ed. *Muzykal'naia entsiklopediia*, 6 vols. (Moscow, 1982)

Kennedy, Michael. *The Hallé Tradition: A Century of Music* (Manchester, 1960)

———, ed. *The Autobiography of Charles Hallé with correspondence and diaries* (London, 1972)

———. *The Hallé 1858–1983: A History of the Orchestra* (Manchester, 1982)

Klein, Axel. 'Stage Irish, or the National in Irish Opera, 1780-1925', *Opera Quarterly* 21, 1 (2005), 27–67

Knowlson, James. *Damned to Fame: The Life of Samuel Beckett* (London, 1996)

Larchet, John F. 'Michele Esposito', in Pine and Acton, *To Talent Alone*, 429–32

Limoncelli, Mattia. *La musica nei salotti napoletani tra l'800 e il 900* (Naples, 1956)

Little, Roger. 'Beckett's Mentor, Rudmose-Brown: Sketch for a Portrait', *Irish University Review*, 14, 1 (1984), 34–41

Longo, Alessandro. 'Michele Esposito', L'Arte pianistica 1, 2 (1914), 1–2

——. 'Artisti italiani all'estero', L'Arte pianistica, 1,3 (1914), 7

Lott, R. Allen. 'Anton Rubinstein in America (1872–1873)', American Music, 21, 3 (2003), 291–318.

Martinotti, Sergio. Ottocento strumentale italiano (Bologna, 1972)

Meenan, James and Clarke, Desmond, eds. The Royal Dublin Society 1731–1981 (Dublin, 1981)

Miozzi, Dario, ed. Francesco Florimo a Vincenzo Bellini (Catania, 2001)

Moss, Sidney. P. 'The Symbolism of the Italian Background in the Marble Faun', Nineteenth-Century Fiction, 23, 3 (1968), 332–36

Mosley, Charles, ed. Burke's Peerage, Baronetage and Knightage: Clan chiefs, Scottish feudal barons (Delaware, 2003)

Novelli, Mauro. Il verismo in maschera: L'attività poetica di Olindo Guerrini (Forli, 2004)

O'Connor, Ulick. Oliver St John Gogarty (London, 1973)

Ó Gallchobhair, Éamonn. 'The Cultural Value of Festival and Feis' in Fleischmann, Music in Ireland, 210–17

[Music Department, Oxford University Press]. Oxford Music: The first fifty years '23–'73 (London, 1973)

Pagani, Umberto. Olindo Guerrini uomo e poeta: Originalità e debiti (Ravenna, 1996)

Pannain, Guido. Ottocento musicale italiano: saggi e note (Milan, 1952)

Perrino, Folco. Giuseppe Martucci: Gli anni giovanili 1856–1879 (Novara, 1992)

Pierce, David. James Joyce's Ireland (New Haven, 1992)

Pine, Richard and Acton, Charles, eds. To Talent Alone: The Royal Irish Academy of Music 1848–1998 (Dublin, 1998)

Potterton, Richard. 'Joseph O'Mara', North Munster Antiquarian Journal xxxii (1990), 83–95

Roberts, Kenneth L. Why Europe Leaves Home (New York, 1922)

Rogers, Brendan. 'An Irish School of Music', New Ireland Review, 13 (1900), 149–59

Rolleston, Thomas William Hazen, Deirdre: The Feis Ceoil Prize Cantata: Dublin 1897 (Edinburgh & Dublin, 1897)

Rosselli, John. Music and Musicians in Nineteenth-Century Italy (London, 1991)

Ruta, M. Storia critica delle condizioni della musica in Italia (Naples 1860)

Samson, Jim, ed. The Late Romantic Era: From the mid-19th Century to World War 1 (London, 1991)

Sanvitale, Francesco and Manzo, Andreina. The Song of a Life: Paolo Francesco Tosti (1846–1916), trans. Nicola Hawthorne (Aldershot, 2004)

Satina, S. A. 'Zapiska o S. V. Rakhmaninove', in Apetian, Vospominaniia o Rakhmaninove, vol. 1, 12–115

Seminara, Graziella, and Tedesco, Anna, eds. Vincenzo Bellini nel secondo centenario della nascita: atti del convegno internazionale, Catania, 8–11 novembre 2001 (Florence, 2004).

Shaffer, Karen. A. and Greenwood, N. G. Maud Powell: Pioneer American Violinist (Iowa, 1988).

Silvestre, Hubert. 'Mario Esposito: brève evocation de sa vie et de son oeuvre', *Studi medievale*, 30, 1989, 1–13, reproduced in Esposito, *Studies in Hiberno-Latin Literature*, 1–13

Smith, Richard Langham and Potter, Caroline, *French Music Since Berlioz* (Aldershot: 2006)

Sonneck, Oscar. *Suum Cuique: Essays in Music* (New York, 1900).

Stanford, Charles Villiers. *Pages from an Unwritten Diary* (London, 1914)

Starkie, Enid, *A Lady's Child* (London, 1941)

Starkie, Walter, 'What the Royal Dublin Society has Done for Music', *Royal Dublin Society Bi-Centenary Souvenir 1731–1931* (Dublin, 1931), 60–65

Sutcliffe, P. *The Oxford University Press: An Informal History* (Oxford, 1978)

Terenzio, Vincenzo. *La musica italiana nell'Ottocento* (Milan, 1976)

Tunley, David. *Salons, Singers and Songs: A Background to Romantic French Song 1830–1870* (Aldershot, 2002)

Van Hoek, Kees. 'Michele Esposito: Maestro of Dublin', *Irish Monthly*, 71 (1943), 223–30

Vaughan, W. E., ed. *A New History of Ireland*, vol. 6, *Ireland under the Union II 1870–1921* (Oxford, 1996)

Vitale, Vincenzo. 'Sigismondo Thalberg a Posillipo', *Nuova rivista musicale italiani*, 6 (1972), 503–11

———. *Il pianoforte a Napoli nell'Ottocento* (Naples, 1983)

Welch, Robert, ed. *The Way Back: George Moore's 'The Untilled Field' and 'The Lake'* (Dublin, 1982)

White, Harry. *The Keeper's Recital: Music and Cultural History in Ireland, 1770–1970* (Cork, 1998)

Watton, Lorna. *Michele Esposito: A Neapolitan Musician in Dublin from 1882–1928*, unpublished dissertation, Queen's University Belfast (1986)

Young, Percy. *George Grove 1820–1900: A Biography* (London, 1980)

Zhukovskaya, E. Yu. 'Vospominaniia o moiom uchitele i druge S. V. Rakhmaninove', in Apetian, *Vospominaniia o Rakhmaninove*, vol. 1, 251–342

Zuk, Patrick. 'A. J. Potter: The career and creative achievement of an Irish composer in social and cultural context', unpublished dissertation, University of Durham (2007)

———. 'Music and Nationalism', *Journal of Music in Ireland*, 2, 2 (2002), 5–10, and 2, 3 (2002), 25–30

———. 'Music and Nationalism: The Debate Continues', *Journal of Music in Ireland*, 3, 5 (2003), 12–21

———. 'Words for Music Perhaps? Irishness, Criticism and the Art Tradition', *Irish Studies Review*, 12, 1 (2004), 11–27

Index